Smiths

Holstein cattle

Smiths

Holstein cattle

ISBN/EAN: 9783743324060

Manufactured in Europe, USA, Canada, Australia, Japa

Cover: Foto ©ninafisch / pixelio.de

Manufactured and distributed by brebook publishing software (www.brebook.com)

Smiths

Holstein cattle

HOLSTEIN CATTLE.

SMITHS & POWELL

Lakeside Stock Farm,

SYRACUSE, N. Y.

OFFICE, 199 W. GENESEE STREET.

OCTOBER, 1884.

[THIRD EDITION.]

LAKESIDE STOCK FARM

—AND—

SYRACUSE NURSERIES,

SMITHS & POWELL,

PROPRIETORS.

OFFICE, 199 WEST GENESEE STREET,

SYRACUSE, N. Y.

W. BROWN SMITH,
EDWARD A. POWELL.

WING R SMITH.
W JUDSON SMITH.

SMITH & BRUCE, PRINTERS AND BINDERS.

❖Announcement❖

TO PARTIES *interested in Holstein Cattle, we would urge the careful perusal of the Announcement and Introduction of this Catalogue, as the facts herein stated have been carefully prepared in order to more clearly set forth the merits of this famous breed of cattle and particularly of animals of our own importing and breeding.*

Lakeside Stock Farm is situated on the western shore of Onondaga Lake, extending to the line of the New York Central and Hudson River Railroad, and the New York, West Shore and Buffalo Railroad, and is divided by the Oswego Division of the Delaware, Lackawanna and Western Railroad, "Lakeside" being a flag station on this road, about two and one-half miles from our office, 199 *West Genesee Street, in the City of Syracuse.*

SPECIALTIES.

We make a specialty of Holstein Cattle, Hambletonian Horses, Clydesdale Horses and Nursery Stock.

HOLSTEIN CATTLE.

Our herd now numbers over 600 *head (* 168 *head being in quarantine and not catalogued) which is, we believe, by far the largest Holstein herd in the world. They* have all been selected by a member of our firm in person or bred from such.

With such a large herd to select from, and with the advantages which large importers are able to obtain in the way of special freight rates—comparatively low expenses, etc., WE ARE ABLE TO OFFER TO OUR CUSTOMERS RARE AND UNUSUAL INDUCEMENTS ON THE BEST CLASS OF STOCK. A *choice animal costs but little more than a medium and in the end is much cheaper.* TO BREED FROM, THE BEST IS THE CHEAPEST.

We have heifers for sale in calf by such bulls as "Neptune," "Netherland Prince," "Sir Henry 2d. of Aaggie," "Prince Imperial, "Prince of Artis," "Netherland King," and other highly bred bulls. No one designing to breed Holsteins OF FIRST QUALITY can afford to buy even a single animal without first inspecting this herd, or at least corresponding with us. START RIGHT! SEE FOR YOURSELF!

BULLS FOR SERVICE.

A limited number of approved pure bred cows will be accepted to be bred to "Neptune No. 1," and "Netherland Prince No. 2," at $100 each, and "Sir Henry 2d. of Aaggie No. 4," "Prince Imperial No. 5," "Prince of Artis," No. 8 and "Netherland King No. 15," at $50 each.

HAMBLETONIAN HORSES.

We now have on hand four very elegant young Hambletonian Stallions of the highest breeding, one Hambletonian and Daniel Lambert, three Hambletonian on *both sides. Three of these Stallions will breed grand coachers as well as trotters, as they will make horses of 16 to 16½ hands and 1200 to 1300 pounds. They will all be sold very cheap. Send for full pedigrees.*

CLYDESDALE HORSES.

We have spared neither pains nor expense, in obtaining the very best representatives of this noted stock both in Scotland and on this continent, for breeding purposes, and now have on hand a few choice Stallions, about thirty very superior pure-bred mares imported or bred from imported stock, and several rarely bred colts and fillies. Prices low, send for pedigrees.

OUR TERMS *of payment, on acceptable paper, will be made satisfactory to our customers.*

PRICES.

Our facilities for importing, breeding and growing are such that we can offer stock of the best quality and choicest breeding at very reasonable figures—far below those usually paid for stock of equal merit.

Prices will be given on application, and will be based on the merits of the animal at that time.

We purposely omit naming prices in our catalogue, as that can seldom be done with justice to the purchaser.

The actual value of an animal constantly changes by development. No buyer wishes to pay now what an animal SHOULD *be worth six or twelve months hence; nor does he wish to pay to-day for an animal that has* been tested and found a failure, what it was worth in PROSPECT before the trial.

Every buyer should have an equal chance with the seller. To do this all prices must be based on the PRESENT value of the article.

GUARANTEES.

All stock will be found fully up to representation in every particular; and no animal will be sold with any kind of blemish, either from accident or otherwise, until such fact is fully understood by the purchaser.

As an evidence of the class of stock we handle, and of our manner of doing business, we would mention that a large percentage of our sales have been made to parties who were unable to give the matter personal attention, and have left the selection entirely with us. In every instance the most perfect satisfaction has been expressed.

For business character and standing we would refer our customers to any Banker or Banking House, to any business man in this city, or to either of the Mercantile Agencies.

SHIPPING.

Our arrangements and facilities for shipping are of the best. Situated as we are on the Great Trunk Lines running East, West, North and South, (see map) stock can be shipped long distances on short time, at through rates, and generally without transfer.

Much care is exercised in loading, and for the comfort of the stock. In all our shipping not an accident has occurred. Every animal has been received in perfect condition, and in. EVERY INSTANCE the most perfect satisfaction has been expressed, not only with the ANIMALS THEMSELVES, but with the condition in which they were received.

CATALOGUES.

We issue SEPARATELY Catalogues of Holstein Cattle, Hambletonian Horses and Clydesdale Horses. In ordering STATE DISTINCTLY WHICH CATALOGUE YOU WISH, and in asking for prices, give us some definite idea of the BREED and KIND of animal desired.

Visitors always welcomed, and shown our stock with pleasure.

Correspondence solicited and promptly answered.

SYRACUSE NURSERIES.

We call special attention to our extensive nursery—one of the largest and oldest establishments of the kind in this country. Orders for either Fruit or Ornamental Trees, at wholesale or retail, will be promptly executed, and satisfaction guaranteed.

INTRODUCTION.

IN presenting to our patrons this new issue of our catalogue any lengthy history of, or treatise on the Holstein breed of cattle seems unnecessary. An intelligent reading public, through the various able stock and agricultural journals and the public press generally, has become familiar with the history and general characteristics of the breed. By its marvelous achievements it has already become famous.

It is an almost universally admitted fact that no other breed so successfully combines milk, cheese, butter and beef.

MILK AND CHEESE.

As milk producers the Holsteins stand without a parallel and containing, as the milk does, a large per cent. of caseine, it is of the very highest quality for the manufacture of cheese.

BUTTER.

As a butter breed the Holsteins are fast coming to the front. Only for the past three years have they been tested to any extent for butter, and yet to-day many weekly and monthly records compare favorably with, while some surpass the best made by cows of those breeds, which have long been bred exclusively for butter. We think the general average will compare favorably with that of any other breed. The quality and flavor of Holstein butter is very superior. It holds its flavor and carries unusually well, as actual experiments have proven.

At the Iowa State Fair, the Tri-State Fair at Toledo, including the states of Ohio, Michigan and Indiana and at the Onondaga County Fair, at Syracuse, N. Y., Holstein butter was awarded the First Prize over all other, there being fine Jersey butter in competition at each exhibition.

BEEF.

For beef purposes this breed is deservedly attracting much attention. In size the Holsteins compare favorably with the Shorthorn, their form, probably, being hardly equal, but they are more hardy and vigorous and we are confident they will make more beef, on the same feed, at an early age. For veal they far surpass all other breeds. This season we had calves at five months eleven days and five months twenty-three days old, each of which weighed 600 pounds: Another at seven months five days weighed 705 pounds. One of these calves commencing at three months gained 148 pounds in twenty-one days. Some seasons all our calves at five months of age have averaged over 500 pounds each.

FAMILY COWS.

For family use, where quantity and quality of milk are both an object, the Holsteins have no superiors. Their strong, vigorous constitutions and marked freedom from disease are important considerations, as milk conveys disease more readily than any other food.

OUR OWN HERD.

Our object in this catalogue will be to present, in a brief, fair and impartial manner, the merits of our own herd.

"By their works ye shall know them" is a proverb that will apply as well to the bovine as to the human race, and it is by this, the truest of all tests, that of actual performance, that we ask the public to judge our herd. We will not confine ourselves to records of a single cow or family or a few choice animals, but will give yearly averages of the entire herd and of large numbers of cows, which is the only true standard of excellence.

We keep a strict and careful continuous record, by actual weight, of each milking of every cow, whether good or poor, so that our customers can know the actual merits of each animal offered. By these records a very safe and reasonable estimate can be formed of the future capacity and merits of heifers or even calves selected from this herd.

On the universally admitted principle in breeding that "like begets like" far better results can reasonably be expected from young animals selected from the herd or family, where every cow has proven a deep-milker for the entire year, than from herds which are unproven or only estimated by a day's or month's trial. Short tests are very deceptive. An ordinary cow can be forced to a large record for a day or a short period, but will utterly fail on a year's trial.

SUCCESS IN BREEDING.

The last year has added greatly to the size and character of our herd. We have approached near the high ideal which has been our standard from its foundation and have practically demonstrated the fact that superior quality, high finish and beauty of form can be successfully combined with the largest production of milk and that these qualities can be reproduced by judicious breeding with almost unerring certainty.

Within the last year some of our cows have made individual milk records, which, considering the age of the animals, have never been equaled and what is to our mind of vastly greater importance, as an evidence of its superior quality, the yearly averages made in our herd far surpass all others from a similar number of cows.

SIZE OF HERD.

Our herd of this famous breed of cattle is, by far, the largest in this country, numbering, at present, 611 head, (including the importation in quarantine not catalogued) and the pains we have taken in selecting, in person, the finest animals from the best stables and largest milking families in this country and Holland, warrants us in saying it is, as a herd, without a superior. All our cattle are selected with the utmost care by a member of our firm from the most noted herds and best breeding districts of Holland. We see the ancestors of nearly every animal before buying. A large per cent. are prize animals in Holland and their descendants. We buy the best and the best only, regardless of price. We aim to buy and breed only straight, handsome, fine-boned, symmetrical animals, as well as deep milkers, and assure ourselves that these are family characteristics, not accidents. We breed only pure-bred stock, recorded in the Holstein-Herd-Book-of-America.

IMPORTATIONS.

Our importations for the past year are the largest ever made by any firm, consisting of about 400 head, and we have spared neither time, trouble nor expense to make them the *best*, both in point of individual excellence and high breeding. Our aim has been to have every animal a superior specimen of the breed. One of our firm personally inspected every animal before buying, spending three months in Holland in so doing. Nearly all were from families of the highest reputation, not only in Holland, but in America.

PRIZES WON.

Pressure of business has thus far prevented us from exhibiting our herd outside of our own State, but at the New York State Fair (in which State are owned a large share of the most noted herds in America), the Gold Medal for best herd for five years, the First Prize for best bull for six years, the First Prize for best cow for four years, the Sweepstakes Prize for the best cow of any breed for the last three consecutive years, as well as a large number of First Prizes each year, for heifers, young bulls, calves, &c., have been awarded to animals of this herd. At the last New York State Fair at Elmira ninety-six head of

Holsteins were exhibited and the Gold Medal for best herd, all the First Prizes but one and all the Second Prizes but three in the Holstein class and also the First and Second Prizes in the Sweepstakes class for the best cows of any breed were awarded to animals owned by us.

YEARLY AVERAGE MILK RECORDS.

The yearly average records made in our herd are without a parallel in any herd of a similar number of cows, which is the surest indication of the superior general character and breeding of our animals, as well as the high standard which we have continually kept in view in making our selections. We ask the careful attention of our patrons to the following tables of records, especially to the yearly averages. Over thirty yearly records made by cows in our herd have averaged 14,212 lbs. 5 oz. per year at an average age of 4½ years.

In 1881 our entire herd of mature cows averaged 14,164 lbs. 15 oz. In 1882 our entire herd of eight three-year-olds averaged 12,388 lbs. 9 oz. On April 1, 1884, ten cows in this herd had made records from 14,000 to 18,000 lbs. each, the average being 15,608, lbs. 6 3-10 ozs,, which included every mature cow in the herd that we had owned long enough to make a year's record, excepting one kept for family use.

We milked through the year ending in June last five mature cows, the entire lot averaging 15,621 lbs. 1 2-5 oz. Seven heifers of one family (the Netherland family,) five of them two-year-olds and two three-year-olds, averaged 11,556 lbs. 1 2-5 oz.

The last is a family record.

NOT ONE OF THESE RECORDS HAS EVER BEEN EQUALED, WITH AN EQUAL NUMBER OF COWS, BY ANY HERD.

In 1881, our entire herd of two-year-old heifers averaged 9,711 lbs., while the *entire* herd averaged 11,270 lbs. 1 oz., notwithstanding a large majority of them were heifers and seven did not complete the year.

We have just completed an average of the largest day's milkings of our cows and heifers with the following result: forty-five cows, *all we have in the herd*, averaged for the best day's milking 61 lbs. 6½ oz.; twenty-four cows averaged 70 lbs. 15½ oz.; eight cows averaged 80 lbs. 9½ oz. in one day, twenty three-year-old heifers, *all there are in the herd*, averaged 44 lbs. 2 oz.; fifteen three-year-old heifers averaged 47 lbs. 13 4-15 oz.; thirty-five two-year-old heifers, *all there are in the herd*, averaged 38 lbs 13 5-7 oz.; sixteen two-year-old heifers averaged 48 lbs. 5⅞ oz., while the *entire milking herd counting in every milking animal* numbering 100 head, averaged 50 lbs. 1 3-5 oz.

Members of this herd have almost continuously taken the lead in large yearly milk records.

In this herd was made the first two-year-old record of 13,500 lbs.; the first (commencing at twenty-two months of age) of 12,200 lbs.; the first record of 16,800 lbs.; the first of 18,000 lbs; the first three-year-old record of 15,600 lbs.; the *only* four-year-old record of 17,970 lbs. or 18,000 lbs. in 365 days; the only two-year-old heifer to give 76 lbs. in a day, while the only three-year-old record of 16,391 lbs. 6 oz. was made by an animal imported by us, and the only two-year-old record 17,746 was by a heifer out of one of the cows of our herd.

Below we give the records of a number of animals sold by us to other parties, farmers, dairymen and breeders, and records made on their farms which prove that the animals sold by us do quite as well in the hands of others as they do in our stables and under our management; in other words, it is the breed of cattle, not the men who own them, and any farmer with reasonable care and feed, can obtain the same results as ourselves, with the same quality of stock.

Mr. Mitchell, of Orange Co., New York, makes the following report:

Aaggie Louise, three years old, 9156 lbs. in 335 days.

Oriana, four years old, 60 lbs 4 oz. in one day, 1705 in one month.

HOLSTEIN CATTLE.

Amethyst, three years old, 47 lbs. 4 oz. in a day, 1321 in one month.

Mermaid, five years old. 1533 lbs. in one month.

Mr. Eugene Smith, of Tennessee:

Aaggie Laura, two years old, gave 54 lbs. in one day.

Mr. S. J. Roberts, of Tennessee:

Aaggie Clara, two years old, gave 65 lbs. 12 oz. in one day, 1705 lbs. 12 oz. in thirty days, and 5582 lbs. 4 oz. in 107 days.

Aaggie Maud, two years old, 40 lbs. 8 oz. in one day, 1080 lbs. in thirty days, 2550 lbs. in seventy-two days.

Mr. Thos. R. Smith, of Virginia:

Middy Morgan, two years old, 41 lbs. in a day.

Mr. George Geddes, Onondaga Co., New York:

Lola, two years old, 40 lbs. 6 oz. in one day, 996 lbs. 9 oz. in one month.

Mr. W. A. Howard, of Massachusetts:

Susie, four years old, 57 lbs. 12 oz. in one day.

Netty, five years old, 52 lbs. 2 oz. in one day.

Mr. C. H. Warren, of Herkimer Co., New York:

Bountiful Maid, two years old, 40 lbs. in one day, 1123 lbs. in one month.

Lockspur, two years old, 38 lbs. 8 oz. in one day, 956 lbs. in thirty days.

Messrs. Hibbard & Hammond, of Vermont:

Winsome Maid, two years old, 55 lbs. in one day, 1504 lbs. in thirty days.

Aaggie Lula, 39 lbs. in one day, 1017 lbs. 8 oz. in thirty days.

Mr. C. W. Horr, of Ohio:

Nundine, two years old, 63 lbs. 5 oz. in one day, 1802 lbs. 10 oz. in May and 9093 lbs. 11 oz. in six months.

Aaggie Jennie, two years old, 50 lbs. 15 oz. in one day, 5104 lbs. 6 oz. in four months and thirteen days.

Molly Bawn, as a three-year-old gave 70 lbs. 11 oz. in one day, 2012 lbs. 4 oz. in a month and 16391 lbs. 6 oz. in one year ; as a four-year.old, although just recovered from a severe sickness she gave 76 lbs. 7 oz. in one day, 2183 lbs. 11 oz. in thirty-one days.

Marjorie Daw. gave 42 lbs. as a two-year-old, 54 lbs. 14 oz. in one day as a three-year-old, and 65 lbs. 1 oz. in one day as a four year old.

Clementine gave 62 lbs. 7 oz. in one day as a four-year-old.

Lady of Lyons, two years old, 54 lbs. 5½ oz. in one day.

Marjorie Daw II, two years old, 47 lbs. 6 oz. in one day.

Jannek III, three years old, 53 lbs. 6 oz. in one day.

Messrs. Burrell & Whitman, of Herkimer Co., New York :

Octoroon, 79 lbs. 12 oz. in one day, 2178 lbs. in one month, 10212 lbs. 12 oz. in seven months and eight days.

Finesse II, 10633 lbs. in nine months and twenty-five days.

Coral, 10313 lbs. in eight months and two days.

Mr. J. Allis, of Minnesota :

Fatinitza, 61 lbs. 8 oz. in one day, 1687 lbs. in thirty days.

Aaggie Allis, 40 lbs. in one day as a two-year-old.

Lady of Broek II, 45 lbs. in one day as a two-year-old.

Rose of Lakeside, 49 lbs. 3 oz. in one day as a two-year old.

Mr. J. R. Beuchler, of Virginia :

Maid of Purmer, 68 lbs. in one day, 1830 lbs. in one month, 11473 lbs. in nine months.

Mr. Westover, of Michigan, says of his heifers :

Rosa Bonheur, two years old, 58 lbs. 4 oz, in one day, 1646 lbs. 13 oz. in one month, 7259 lbs. 8 oz, in five months, 13411 lbs. 4 oz. in one year.

Coquette, two years old, 49 lbs. 13 oz. in one day, 5446 lbs. 2 ozs. in four months ; as a three-year-old she gave 62 lbs. to 64 lbs. per day for some time.

Mr. H. F. W. Breuer, of South Carolina :

Perfection three years old, gave August 2d 60 lbs. 5 oz., 3d, 61 lbs. 3 oz., 4th, 62 lbs. 9 oz., and as a seven-year-old has *never* been dry, and gave by actual measurement 35 quarts per day for nearly seven months.

Arminda has given 19 quarts as a two-year-old.

Mr Gillett, of Wisconsin, says of his heifer, Duchess of Springvale :

The last thirty days before she was two years old she gave 39 3-10 lbs. per day ; largest daily yield 42½ lbs. on dry feed in January.

Record for four months from January 5th, to May 5th, 4179 lbs.; ten months, 9189½ lbs. ending November 5th.

Mr. Lightner, of Iowa, reports that Etta, two years old, during the month of June averaged 42¼ lbs. per day ; as a five-year-old in a 200 day record she gave the first 50 days an average of 56¼ lbs., for the third, 50 days, 61¼ lbs., for the fourth, 50 days, 58½ lbs., making a total of 11887½ lbs. for the 200 days.

Porceleintje II, three years old, gave between 50 and 60 lbs. per day.

Mr. N. H. Albaugh, of Ohio :

Bianca, six years old, 61 lbs.

Ægis, 3d, five years old, 50 lbs.

Messrs. A. W. Wood & Son, of Otsego Co., New York :

Aaggie Saphira, two years old, 35 lbs 4 oz. in one day, 1006 lbs. 1 oz. in 30 days on grass alone.

Mr. Scatcherd, of Erie Co., New York :

Aaggie Ida, three years old, 47 lbs. in one day, 1294 lbs. in thirty days.

Fadetta, two years old, 41 lbs. in one day, 1143 lbs. in thirty days.

Dr. O. C. Wiggin, Rhode Island :

Aaggie Maria, 48 lbs. in one day as a two-year-old.

Aaggie of Hoorn, 51 lbs. in one day as a two-year-old.

Aaggie of Midwoud, 53 lbs. in one day, as a two-year-old. None of these heifers had any green feed.

We have tested but a few of our cows and young heifers for butter as our conveniences for butter-making are not such as would give us the results we are confident could be reached under favorable circumstances, but considering all the circumstances, the very young age of most of the heifers, the fact that they dropped their calves soon after coming out of quarantine and before they were acclimated, also that these tests were made in winter and on winter feed, excepting Jannek—coarse corn fodder and ensilage, long hay, with grain feed of bran and ground oats with very little corn meal, feed not calculated to produce butter,—we are very much gratified with the result which we give below :

Netherland Queen in Dec. 1882,	20 lbs. in 1 week.	
" " " "	39 lbs. 8 oz. in 2 weeks.	
Jannek, 7 years old,	19 " 15 "	1 week.
" in 10 consecutive days,	28 " 6 "	
Crown Jewel, 6 years old,	19 " 9 "	1 "
Ægis, 9 "	18 " 2 "	1 "
Netherland Baroness, 6 years old,	17 " 5 "	1 "
Netherland Duchess, 5 "	14 " 12 "	1 "
Netherland Princess, 4 "	17 " 11 "	1 "
Ægis 2d, 4 "	15 " 8 "	1 "
Topaz, 4 "	13 " 3½ "	1 "

Netherland Belle,	3 years old,	16 lbs.	7 oz.	in 1 week.
Netherland Princess,	3 "	14 "	11½ "	1 "
Isadora,	3 "	13 "	13 "	1 "
Frolicsome.	3 "	13 "		1 "
Meadow Lily,	3 "	12 "	10 "	1 "
Clothilde,	3 "	12 "	3½ "	1 "
Carlotta.	3 "	12 "	1 "	1 "
Cameo,	3 "	11 "	8 "	1 "
Netherland Princess,	2 "	14 "	4 "	1 "
Oriana,	2 "	13 "	3¼ "	1 "
Lida,	2 "	11 "	13½ "	1 "
Isadora,	22 mos. old,	10 "	13½ "	1 "
Netherland Countess,	2 years "	10 "	4 "	1 "
Daisy Dale,	22 mos. "	9 "	8 "	1 "
Careno,	2 years "	9 "	7 "	1 "
Meadow Maid,	23 mos "	9 "	4½ "	1 "
Amazon,	2 years "	9 "	5½ "	1 "
Catalpa 2d,	2 " "	8 "	14¼ "	1 "
Marjorie Daw.	23 mos. "	8 "	13¼ "	1 "

All the above tests but two were made on winter feed.

A few of these heifers were tested for four or eight days, but for the sake of uniformity we give the exact rate per week.

Aaggie was tested, one churning of four days the first season in this country, four months after calving, and 2 lbs. 8¼ oz. in a day,—(17 lbs. 11½ oz. per week).

The following average butter records more clearly show the quality of Holstein milk and the superiority of our herd than anything we can say in their praise: Nine cows averaged 17 lbs. 5½ oz. per week; eight heifers, three-year-olds, averaged 13 lbs. 4¾ oz. per week; eleven heifers, two-year-olds and younger, averaged 10 lbs. 8 oz. per week. The entire original imported Netherland family or six cows (two being but three years old) averaged 16 lbs. 7 7-12 oz. per week.

The following butter records have been made by animals

sold by us in various sections of the country and under different management, feed, etc., and though not marvellous we think are worthy of note:

Aaggie Clara, two years old, owned by Mr. S. J. Roberts, of Tennessee, made 1½ lbs. of butter in one day.

Maid of Purmer, owned by Mr. J. R. Beuchler, of Virginia, made 3 lbs. 14 oz. of butter in two days.

May Overton, two years old, owned by Mr. R. K. Allerton, of New York, made 1 lb. 5¾ oz. of butter in one day, and Satella, two years old, same owner, made 1 lb. 7½ oz. in one day.

Lola, two years old, owned by Mr. George Geddes, of Onondaga Co., N. Y., made 8 lb. of unsalted butter in one week.

Winsome Maid, two years old, owned by Messrs Hibbard & Hammond, of Vermont, made 13 lbs. 4 oz. of butter in one week.

We would suggest to all those desirous of advancing the interests of Holsteins, that they take the trouble to test their cows and heifers for butter, even if but for a short time, and we honestly believe the result will be gratifying, as well creditable to the breed in almost every instance.

THE AAGGIE FAMILY.

For years this family has stood in advance of all others as great milk producers.

The records made by Aaggie cows have done more to give to the Holstein breed the wonderful reputation which it has attained in this country than those of any other family.

When Lady Clifden made her yearly record of 16,275 lbs. it long stood far in advance of all others.

It had only just been surpassed by the record of our cow Ægis, 16,823 lbs. 10 oz. when Aaggie just after importation and while carrying twins, astonished the dairy world with her hitherto unparalleled record of 18,004 lbs. 15 oz.

This was soon followed by the marvelous two-year-old record of her daughter Aaggie 2d, of 17,746 lbs. 2 oz in a year, which still stands unrivaled, and this year the family has produced the two phenomenal young heifers Aaggie Constance and Aaggie Clara. Commencing when just past two years old the former has given 76 lbs. 6 oz. in one day, and 6,392 lbs. 9 oz. in four months and twelve days to September 26th, and the latter has given 65 lbs. 12 oz. in one day, 1,705 lbs. 4 oz. in thirty consecutive days, and 4,453 lbs. in two months and twenty-three days.

As shown by the following table, these cows are almost universally deep milkers, while a large number have stood in the foremost rank, making for themselves by their marvelous records, a reputation, as extended as the improved dairy interests of our country.

By tracing the pedigrees of this family it will be observed that all are descendants of the wonderful bull Rooker, a large share of them tracing on the sides of both sire and dam to the same great fountain head.

A large number of these animals contain seventy-five per cent. or more of the same blood as Aaggie 2d, and her full brother Neptune.

We know of no family of the same size where all its members contain such a large per cent. of the same blood. In general appearance, form, finish, color markings, &c., the family is strikingly uniform. Nearly all have the same handsome markings, the same well developed milk form, wedge shape, deep hind quarters, light clean necks, prominent milk organs, large crooked milk-veins, large well balanced and well developed udders, with good even teats, in short, all the characteristics of great milkers.

So uniform are the animals of this family, that a good judge, although a stranger can readily select them in a large herd

MILK RECORDS OF THE AAGGIE FAMILY.

All records not specified as made in Holland were made in this country.

No.	ROOKER, Sire of	Age.	Lbs. in 1 day	Lbs. in 1 month.	Lbs. in 1 year, and to Sept. 26, '84.	
1	Aaggie, while carrying twins, dam of No. 17...	6	$84\frac{3}{4}$	$2{,}362\frac{1}{2}$	$18{,}004\frac{15}{16}$	
2	Lady Clifden........................				16,275	
3	Porcelein (N. H. B., 147), dam of No. 28..		$80\frac{1}{6}$			In Holland.
4	Jansje (N. H. B., 88), winner of three First Prizes and Silver Medal, dam of No. 11........................... ...		68			Not imported.
5	Aaggie Cornelia, Imported.....................		$73\frac{1}{5}$			In Holland.
	" "	7	$53\frac{11}{16}$		$8{,}877\frac{5}{8}$	in 6 m., 25 dys.
	" " is dam of A. Cornelia 2d...	5	$51\frac{12}{16}$		$7{,}985\frac{5}{8}$	in 7 m., 6 dys.
	" " " " 3d...	4	$78\frac{3}{4}$		$5{,}616\frac{3}{16}$	in 3 m., 2 dys.
6	Blokker, (N. H. B., 390), dam of No. 26....		$82\frac{1}{3}$			Not imported.
7	Maritje, (N. H. B., 570), dam of No. 20....		$80\frac{1}{6}$			"
8	DeSchot, (N. H. B., 573), dam of No. 47, 52.		76			"
9	Lamberta, (N. H. B., 576)		$68\frac{2}{3}$			In Holland.
10	Jacob 1st, (N. H. B., 20), see below..........					
	" " dam, DeGoede, prize cow at Paris Exposition.......................... ...		$91\frac{1}{2}$			Not imported.

No.	JACOB 1st, Sire of	Age.	Lbs. in 1 day.	Lbs. in 1 month.	Lbs. in 1 year. and to Sept. 26, '84.
11	Aaggie Rosa, dam No. 4	5	91		In Holland.
	" " dam of No. 24,	6	$68\frac{1}{2}$	$1,920\frac{3}{16}$	$16,156\frac{5}{8}$ After imp'r'tion.
12	" Idaline	6	60		$9,360\frac{15}{16}$ in 6 m., 25 dys.
13	" Kathleen	6	$56\frac{1}{2}$		$8,243\frac{3}{4}$ in 6 m.
14	Altje, (N. H. B., 324), dam of No. 25		$82\frac{1}{3}$		Not imported.
15	Trijntje, dam of No. 30		$68\frac{2}{5}$		"
	" is dam of Aaggie Isadora 2d	2	$44\frac{3}{4}$		$4,832\frac{3}{8}$ in 6 m., 14 dys.
16	Jacob 2d, (N. H. B., 56), see below				
	" 2d's dam, Trijntje, (N. H. B., No. 35)		80		Not imported.

No.	JACOB 2d, Sire of	Age.	Lbs. in 1 day.	Lbs. in 1 month.	Lbs. in 1 year. and to Sept. 26, '84.
17	Aaggie 2d, dam No. 1	2	$61\frac{5}{16}$	$1,700\frac{1}{8}$	$17,746\frac{1}{8}$
18	" Sarah	4	$80\frac{1}{2}$		3.009 1 m., 16 dys.
19	" Hannah	4	$71\frac{15}{16}$		$3,338\frac{5}{8}$ 1 m., 25 dys.
20	" Beauty, dam No. 7	4	$51\frac{3}{8}$	$1,461\frac{7}{8}$	$13,573\frac{15}{16}$
21	" Belle, dam, 80 lbs. in a day	4			$9,673\frac{3}{8}$ in 11 m.
22	" Idaline 2d, dam same as No. 12	5	$53\frac{3}{4}$		$8,750\frac{7}{8}$ in 7 m., 17 dys.
23	" " 3d, dam same as No. 12 and 22	4	$55\frac{3}{4}$		$8,315\frac{11}{16}$ in 7 m., 9 dys.

HOLSTEIN CATTLE.

JACOB 2d, Sire of

No.		Age.	Lbs. in 1 day.	Lbs. in 1 month.	Lbs. in 1 year, and to Sept. 26, '84.
24	Aaggie Louise.........	4			9,156 in 335 dys.
25	" Cora, dam No. 14.....	4	65¾		7,994⅞ in 5 m., 12 dys.
26	" Bonnie, dam No. 6.....	4	66		7,425⅝ in 5 m., 12 dys.
27	" Rosa 2d, dam No. 11...	4	65¼		5,367$\frac{5}{16}$ in 3 m., 15 dys.
28	" Anna, dam No. 3........	3	42$\frac{15}{16}$		5,564$\frac{11}{16}$ in 5 m., 21 dys.
29	" Beauty, 2d, dam No. 20.	2	48	1,117	9,684¾ in 11 m., 14 dys.
	" " " "	3	49¾		6,895½ in 6 m.
30	" Isadora, dam No. 15...	4	54¼		7,852$\frac{13}{16}$ in 7 m., 6 dys.
31	" Saphira.................	2	35¾		
32	Neptune, dam No. 1, and full brother to No. 17.		See below.		
33	DeRuiter, (N. H. B., 89) dam No. 3, and full brother to No. 28.				See below. Not imported
34	Lincoln, (N. H. B., No. 120) dam, Marie, (N. H. B., No. 361).				"
35	Jacob 4th, (N. H. B., No. 210) Jacob Wit, (H. H. B., No. 2662).				"
36	Napoleon, (N. H. B., No. 129) dam. Porcelein 2d.				"
	" G-Dam, No. 3. See below.				"
37	Jacob III.				
38	Mr. Wit.				

NEPTUNE is Sire of

| 39 | Aegis 6th............. | 2 | 44$\frac{9}{16}$ | | 8,927¾ in 9 m., 12 dys. |
| 40 | Music 2d .... | 2 | 44 | | |

No.	DE RUITER, Sire of	Age.	Lbs in 1 day.	Lbs. in 1 month.	Lbs in 1 year, and to Sept. 26, '84.	
41	Aaggie Constance	2	$76\frac{3}{8}$		$6,392\frac{9}{16}$	in 4 m., 12 dys.
42	" Clara	2	$65\frac{3}{4}$	$1,705\frac{1}{4}$	4,453	in 2 m., 24 dys.
43	" Jennie	2	$50\frac{15}{16}$		$5,104\frac{3}{8}$	in 4 m., 13 dys.
44	" May, beginning at 23 months	2		$913\frac{11}{16}$	$9,279\frac{3}{8}$	in 11 m.
	" "	3	$57\frac{13}{16}$		7,642	in 5 m., 13 dys.
	" May's dam, Blokker II	2	$45\frac{1}{2}$			Not imported.
	" " grand-dam, No. 6					
45	" Ida	3	47			
46	" Leila	3	44		$6,486\frac{1}{4}$	in 7 m., 16 dys.
48	" Sadie	2	$46\frac{5}{16}$		$5,184\frac{1}{4}$	in 6 m., 20 dys.
49	" Merrel	2	$46\frac{1}{16}$		$5,771\frac{3}{16}$	in 5 m., 15 dys.
50	" Pauline	2	$35\frac{1}{16}$		$3,796\frac{13}{16}$	in 4 m., 17 dys.
51	" Eva	2	$36\frac{11}{16}$		$6,716\frac{3}{4}$	in 7 m., 16 dys.
52	Sir Henry of Aaggie, dam No. 8					
53	Sir Henry 2d of Aaggie, dam No. 11					

No.		Age.	Lbs. in 1 day.	Lbs. in 1 month.	Lbs. in 1 year, and to Sept. 26, '84.
	LINCOLN, Sire of				
54	Aaggie Josie	2	$46\frac{3}{4}$		$3,380\frac{3}{8}$ in 3 m., 2 dys.
55	" Etta	2	$38\frac{3}{4}$		
56	" Lily	2	$41\frac{1}{8}$		
	NAPOLEON, Sire of				
57	Aaggie Maria	2	48		$3,972\frac{15}{16}$ in 4 m., 18 dys.
58	" Lee	2	$38\frac{5}{8}$		
59	" Maud	2	$40\frac{3}{4}$		
60	" Laura	2	54		
	MR. WIT, Sire of				
61	Aaggie of Midwoud	2	53		
62	" Hoorn	2	51		
	JACOB III., Sire of				
63	Aaggie Grace	2	$54\frac{3}{8}$		
64	" Lulu	2	39		

THE NETHERLAND FAMILY.

This is one of the most beautiful, attractive and useful families we have ever known of any breed, combining milk, butter and beef, all in a marked degree, and with these qualities are united unusual beauty of form, very fine quality and high finish in every detail. Marked uniformity is a family characteristic.

The type of this family is our standard, low, lengthy, very straight, carrying well up on the rump, with broad level back and hips, very square, deep quarters, with straight fine limbs, bright clean heads and necks, beautifully curved horns, mellow rich skin and short glossy coats, and with it all unusual vigor and constitution. They milk long and evenly. All are rich deep milkers and superior butter cows.

Netherland Prince No. 2, stands at the head of this family, and Netherland Queen, Netherland Duchess, Netherland Princess, Netherland Belle, Netherland Countess, and Netherland Dowager 2d, are each sisters, or almost equivalent thereto, containing 75 to 100 per cent. of the same blood, and all are of the same beautiful form and finish. All are very deep milkers as the following table will show:

	Age, Yrs.	Lbs.	Oz.	
Netherland Queen............	2	13,574	3	in 345 dys.
" "	4	15,614	9	in 1 yr.
" "	5	83	4	in 1 dy., and
		10,046	8	in 7 m., 18 dys.
Netherland Duchess. (Commencing at 22 months.)		12,200	4	in 1 yr.
Netherland Duchess.	3	11,401	12	"
" "	5	16,520	7	"
" Princess	3	14,101	2	"
" "	4	12,789	13	"
" "	5	4,769	8	2 m., 25 d., to Sept. 26.
" Belle............	3	13,649	6	in 1 yr.
" "	4	5,136	2	2 m., 17 d., to Sept. 26.

Netherland Countess... (Commencing while in quarantine)	2	9,481	12	in 1 yr.
Netherland Baroness	6	11,249	7	in 1 yr.
" " 2d...	2	10,825	9	"
" Consort.........	2	10,238	7	"
" "	4	9,770	11	7 m , 25 d., to Sept. 26.
" Queen 2d......	3	10,471	15	in 1 yr.
" " "	5	3,670	4	in 2 mo , 1 dy. " "
" Dowager........	9	12,734	2	in 1 yr.
" " 2d...	3	6,185	7	5 m., 14 d., to Sept. 26.
" Peeress.........	5	8,328	12	6 " 18 " "

Seven heifers of this family, five two years old and two three years old averaged 11,556 lbs. 1 2-5 oz which has never been equalled by one family of same age and number.

THE NETHERLANDS AS A BUTTER FAMILY.

Netherland Queen in November, 1882, made 20 lbs. of butter in one week, and 39 lbs. 8 oz. in two weeks without any change from her feed in quantity or quality. Butter weighed after working and before salting.

Netherland Princess made before she was three years old 14 lbs. 4 oz. of butter in one week, and when she was three years old she made in one week on winter feed 14 lbs. 11½ oz.; as a four-year-old she made in a four days test at the rate of 18 lbs. 9½ oz. of butter in one week.

Netherland Belle made as a three-year-old 16 lbs. 7 oz. of butter in one week.

Netherland Countess made as a three-year-old in one week 15 lbs. 15 oz. of butter.

Netherland Duchess made when five years old 14 lbs. 12 oz. of butter in one week.

Lady Netherland was injured soon after being imported, before we were able to test her for butter, but while laboring under this disadvantage which reduced her flow of milk at least one third, she made 13 lbs. 2 oz. of butter in one week on winter feed.

These six members of the original Netherland Family all bought of one breeder in Holland, all he had, averaged 16 lbs. 7 7-12 oz., which we believe has never been equaled by any entire family of the same number.

Several other members of this family not so closely related, have proven good butter cows.

Netherland Baroness, a niece of Lady Netherland soon after importation and before she was acclimated, made 17 lbs. 5 oz. in one week.

Netherland Dowager in winter just after importation made 13 lbs. 2 oz. in one week.

This family has won marked honors in the show ring,

Netherland Prince, Netherland Queen, Netherland Baroness, Lady Netherland, Netherland Duchess, Netherland Princess and Netherland Queen 2d, having all been awarded prizes at the New York State Fair.

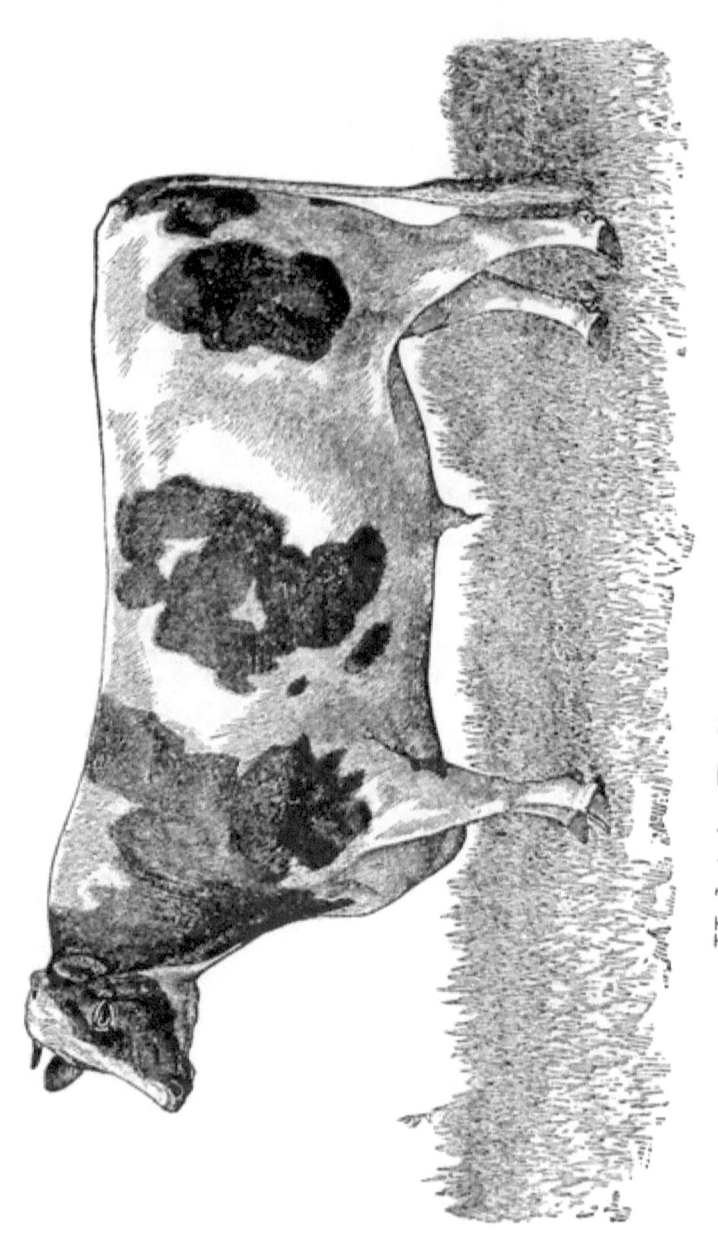

Holstein Bull, "Neptune." (No. 1.)

BULLS.

No. 1.   NEPTUNE.

(See Cut.)

(Not for Sale.)

(H. H. B. Vol. 5, No. 711.) Imported in dam Aaggie (901). Calved March 23d, 1880.

Sire, Jacob 2d, (N. H. B. 56), (See cut), which weighed 2,700 lbs. at three years of age, he by Jacob (N. H. B. 20). he by Rooker.

Jacob 2d's dam, Trintje (N. H. B. 35), gave 80 lbs. of milk in one day.

Jacob's dam, De Goede, had a milk record of 81 lbs. 8 oz. in one day. Prize cow at Paris Exposition.

Dam, Aaggie (901), (See No. 98), imported by us in September, 1879. When six years old, while carrying twins and just after being imported, she made a record of 18,004 lbs. 15 oz. in one year, and the following year without any attempt to make a large record and under unfavorable conditions she gave 15,709 lbs. 10 oz. She made the first year after importation, 2 lbs. 8½ oz. of butter in one day. Her daughter Aaggie 2d, has made the largest two-year-old record known, having given 61 lbs. 5 oz. in one day, and 1,700 lbs. 2 oz. in thirty consecutive days and 17,746 lbs. 2 oz. in one year. She also made 13 lbs. 6 oz. of butter in one week on dry feed, and after milking between ten and eleven months made 11 lbs 3 oz. in one week.

Aaggie's sire, Rooker.

Aaggie's dam, Oude Aaggie, gave 76 lbs. in one day.

Aaggie's sister, Lady Clifden, gave in one year 16,275 lbs. which at the time exceeded any previous record.

Aaggie Rosa, Aaggie Rosa 2d, Aaggie Beauty, Aaggie Beauty 2d, Aaggie Bonnie, Aaggie Cora, &c., are also closely related on both sides, and are all deep milkers, as will be seen by reference to their pedigrees.

Neptune is full brother to Aaggie 2d, and we feel safe in saying, without fear of contradiction, that no living bull, of any breed is so highly bred for *milk* or traces so directly to ancestors with such remarkable records.

He is straight and square, and a fine model, fine coat and skin, and these points, together with his rare breeding (directly descended from the greatest milking family known), make him one of the most desirable bulls of this breed.

He weighed when four years old 2,260 lbs.

We desire to call especial attention to the near relationship of this superior animal to the many wonderful milkers that belong to the Aaggie family whose records and their relation to each other appear in the milk records of the Aaggie family in the introduction of this catologue page 22.

No. 2.   **NETHERLAND PRINCE.**

(Not for Sale.)

(H. H. B. Vol. 5, No. 716.) Calved April 1st, 1880. Imported by us October, 1880.

(See Cut for Color Markings.)

Sire, Schemmel, he by Schreuder.

Schemmel is an elegant bull of superior breeding, and a son of Netherland Dowager, (See No. 97), also sire of Netherland

Princess, Netherland Countess, Netherland Belle, and Netherland Baroness II. See records of Netherland Family in Introduction Page 27.

Netherland Dowager gave in Holland just before importation 91 lbs. of milk in a day. Her first year's record after importation was 12,734 lbs. 2 oz. This season she has given 73 lbs. 11 oz. in one day, and 4,548 lbs. 12 oz. in two months and sixteen days to Sept. 26th. She is a dam of Netherland Dowager II , (2,633) See No. 141.

Netherland Dowager's dam, Oude Schemmel, has a record of over 80 lbs. of milk in a day.

Schreuder is sire of Netherland Queen and Netherland Duchess. See Netherland records.

Dam, Lady Netherland, (1,263), (See No. 99), an elegant cow with a milk record of 73¾ lbs. of milk in a day as a four-year-old on grass alone. She gave in five months and six days, ending with February, 1883. 6,130 lbs 11 oz.

Lady Netherland is dam of Netherland Queen (414), (See No. 104), Netherland Princess (862). See No. 123.

Grandam, Gert Met 2d, a beautiful cow that gave 71 lbs. 8 oz. of milk in a day on grass alone.

G-g-dam, Gert Met, an elegant cow and great milker was kept twenty years for breeding.

Netherland Prince is a beautiful bull, and is our favorite type of the Holstein breed, low, blocky, square, but of good length, well marked, with fine head and shoulders, beautiful fine waxy horns, very straight and broad on the back and hips, with well-developed hind quarters, fine, short, straight limbs, a rich yellow skin, mellow hide, a good coat and a broad, well-defined curveline escutcheon, with distinct thigh ovals. Weight at four years old, 2,050 lbs.

This bull, now four years old, has been exhibited four years in succession at the New York State Fair, and has been awarded three First Prizes and one Second Prize. As a three and four years old he stood at the head of the herd that was awarded the Gold Medal.

This is one of the most uniform beautiful, attractive and desirable families of Holsteins we have ever seen. As the strongest evidence of the wonderful breeding of this bull for both milk and butter we ask the reader to carefully study the milk and butter records of the Netherland Family given on page 27. The calves by this bull are nearly all of the same beautiful form and finish as himself, and command in market the highest prices. We think it is no exaggeration to state that the get of no Holstein bull has commanded such uniformly high figures. Several calves having sold for $1,000 to $1,500 each.

No. 3.   STRATHMORE.   No. 762.

(H. H. B. Vol. 7, No. 2,364.) (Benjamin N. H. B. 268.) Calved March 11th, 1882. Imported by us August, 1883. Three-fourths black, large star, two white spots on shoulder, large white spot over hips to flanks and belly both sides; left fore leg black to knee outside, legs, belly and two-thirds tail white.

Sire, District bull of Ven Huisen, a fine bull, also sire of St. Catharine. See No. 174.

Marked similar to Strathmore and his dam has a record of 80 lbs. 6 oz. of milk in a day.

Dam, Marie with a five-year-old record of 82¼ lbs. in a day, a fine large cow with an extra escutcheon and milk veins

Grandam, a very fine, large cow with record of over 82 lbs. in a day.

Strathmore, is a large, straight, square and stylish bull of elegant breeding.

No. 4.   **SIR HENRY 2d, OF AAGGIE.**   No. 153.

Ruiter 2d, (N. H. B. 189.)

(See Chart.)

(Not for Sale.)

(H. H. B. Vol. 7, No. 1,451.) Calved March 18th, 1882. Imported by us September, 1882. About two-thirds black, strip in the face.

Sire, de Ruiter, (N. H. B. 89). (See cut.) (See milk records of Aaggie family page 22) he by Jacob 2d, (N. H. B. 56) he by Jacob 1st, (N. H. B. 20) he by Rooker, the sire of Aaggie, (901) (N. H. B. 148), (See No. 98), with a milk record of 18,004 lbs 15 oz. in a year, Porcelein, (N. H. B. 147) with a record of 80 lbs. 1 oz. of milk in one day, Lady Clifden, (159) with a record of 16,275 lbs. of milk in one year, Lambertina, (6,889) with a milk record of 68 2-5 lbs. in one day, and Jansje, (N. H. B. 88) with a milk record of 68 lbs. in one day on grass.

Dam of de Ruiter, Porcelein (N. H. B. 147), she by Rooker. See above.

Dam of Jacob 2d is Trintje, (N. H. B. 35) with a milk record of 80 lbs. in one day.

Dam of Jacob 1st is de Goede, a Prize Cow at the Paris Exposition, with a milk record of 91 lbs. 8 oz. in one day.

Jacob 2d is the sire of Neptune (711), and Aaggie 2d, (1360) which has a two-year-old milk record of 17,746 lbs. 2 oz. in one year. She made 13 lbs. 6 oz. of butter in one week on dry feed, and after milking between ten and eleven months, made 11 lbs. 3 oz. of butter in one week. Jacob 2d is also sire of Aaggie Cora, No. 136, Aaggie Bonnie, No. 137, Aaggie Rosa II., No. 139, Aaggie Isadora, No. 131, and many others.

Dam of Sir Henry 2d of Aaggie is Aaggie Rosa, (H. H. B. 2,605) also called Wemeltien, (N. H. B. 323) by Jacob 1st, also sire of Aaggie Idaline No. 105, Aaggie Kathleen, No. 111.

Aaggie Rosa has a milk record in Holland, as a five-year-old of 91 lbs. in one day. She gave her first season in this country in one year 16,156 lbs. 10 oz., and this season has given 4,687 lbs. 8 oz. in two months and 18 days to Sept. 26th.

Dam of Aaggie Rosa is Jansje, (N. H. B. 88) with a milk record of 68 lbs. in one day on grass. She won First Prize at Amsterdam and the Silver Medal at Rotterdam.

Dam of Jansje is Oude Jansje.

de Ruiter is also sire of the following remarkable heifers, all of which are two years old, and the records were made in several stables in various parts of this country.

Aaggie Constance (2,629), See No. 182, gave 76 lbs. 6 oz. in one day, and 6,392 lbs. 9 oz. in four months, twelve days to Sept. 26th.

Aaggie Clara (2,626), 65 lbs. 12 oz. in one day, 1,705 lbs. 4 oz. in one month, and 5,582 lbs. 4 oz. in 107 days, and made 1½ lbs. of butter in one day.

Aaggie Jennie (2,625), 50 lbs. 15 oz. in one day, 5,104 lbs. 6 oz. in four months, thirteen days.

Aaggie Sadie (4,472), 46 lbs. 5 oz. in one day, 5,184 lbs. 4 oz. in six months, twenty days, to Sept. 26th.

Aaggie Merrel (2,628), 46 lbs. 4 oz. in one day, 5,771 lbs. 3 oz. in five months, fifteen days.

Aaggie Eva (4,354), 36 lbs. 11 oz. in one day, 6,716 lbs. 12 oz. in seven months, sixteen days, to Sept. 26th.

Aaggie May (2,601), 9,279 lbs. 6 oz. in eleven months.

Aaggie May, three years old, 57 lbs. 13 oz. in one day, 7,642 lbs. in five months, thirteen days, to Sept. 26th.

Sir Henry 2d of Aaggie, is one of the choicest representatives of the Aaggie Family and is a half brother to the cele-

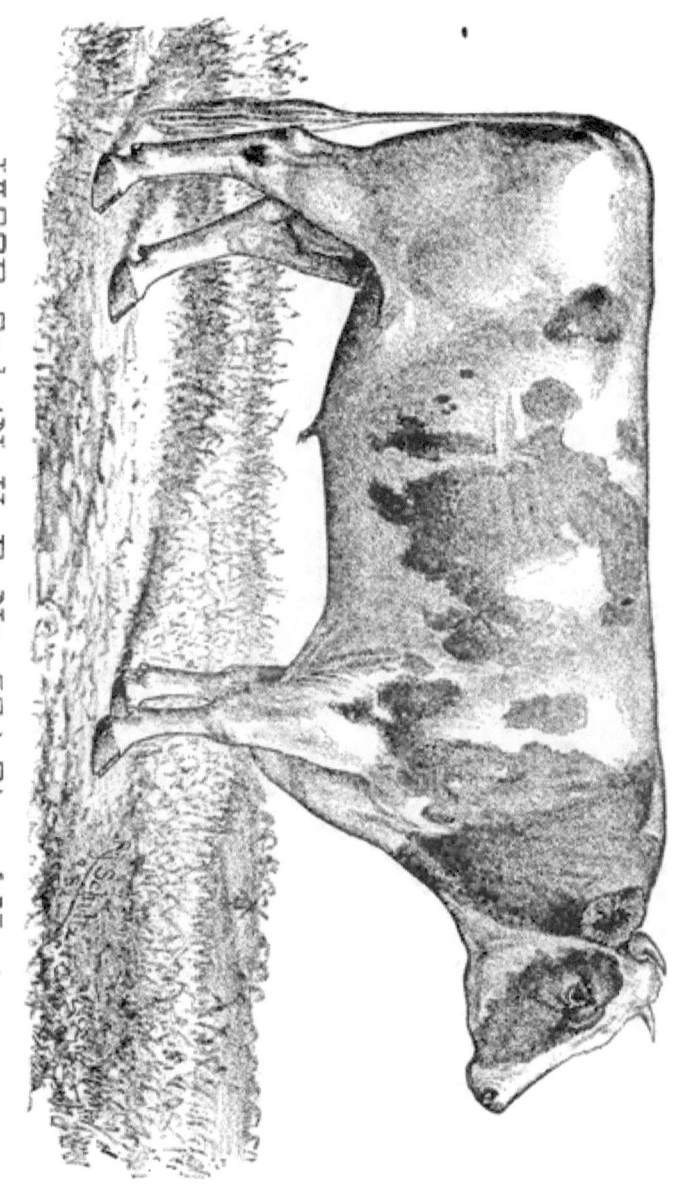

JACOB 2nd, (N. H. B. No. 56,) Sire of Neptune.

(From a photograph.)

brated bull Sir Henry of Aaggie (1,450), which we sold for $1,500. We call especial attention to his remarkable breeding, as given in chart annexed.

No. 5.   PRINCE IMPERIAL.

(Not for Sale.)

(H. H. B. Vol. 6, No. 1164.) Calved April 15, 1882. Long star, snip, white over both shoulders connecting with belly, broad white over hips to flanks, beautifully marked.

Sire, Netherland Prince, (716), (See No. 2), (See cut), he by Schemmel, son of Netherland Dowager, (See No. 97), and sire of Netherland Princess, (See No. 123), Netherland Countess, (See No. 133), Netherland Belle, (No. 138), Netherland Baroness II., (See No. 141), he by Schreuder, sire of Netherland Queen, (See No. 104), Netherland Duchess, (See No. 112).

Dam, Carlotta, (1,266), (See No. 119). (See cut). Carlotta is a very choice, fine animal and deep milker. She has given as a three year old 57 lbs. 8 oz. of milk in one day, 1,637 lbs. 8 oz. in one month, and 11,886 lbs. 4 oz. in one year, and has made 12 lbs. 1 oz. of butter in one week on winter feed. As a four-year-old she has given 1,544 lbs. 6 oz. in one month, 10,509 lbs. 14 oz. in ten months and nineteen days. And as a five-year-old she has given 70 lbs. 3 oz. in a day, and 2,948 lbs. 11 oz. in one month and eighteen days to Sept. 26th.

Grandam gave 64 lbs. in one day.

Carlotta was winner of First Prize at New York State Fair as a two-year-old, and was one of the herd that won the Gold Medal at New York State Fair in 1882 and 1883.

Carlotta's calf of 1883 we sold for $1,000 when a few months old.

Prince Imperial won First Prize at New York State Fair in 1882, and second in 1883 and 1884.

Cousidering the very superior quality and fine size of this bull and the rare breeding and marked beauty of both his sire and dam, with the remarkable milk and butter records of these families, we consider Prince Imperial a very choice specimen of the breed. Prince Imperial weighed when just two years old 1450 lbs. We refused $1,000 for this bull when a calf.

No. 6.   **CHESTERFIELD.**   No. 593.

(H. H. B. Vol. 7, No. 2,483.) Calved January 7th, 1883. Imported by us June, 1883. Three-fourths black, large star, snip, irregular white over shoulders, two small white spots middle of left side, black to left gambrel.

Sire, Lof's District bull of Beemster, a very choice animal.

Dam, P. Kwadijk, with a four-year-old record of 64 lbs. in one day.

Grandam, a fine large cow with a record of 68 2 5 lbs in one day.

Chesterfield is very large, straight, square, handsome animal, and a very desirable bull, weighing now 1,250 lbs.

No. 7.   **SIR DONALD OF AAGGIE.**   No. 510.

(H. H. B. Vol. 7, No. 2,358.) Calved February 19th, 1883. Imported by us, August, 1883. One-half black, small star, large black spot on right shoulder, two large black spots on each side joined at back, white over hips to flanks, large black spot on right side forward of flank.

Sire, Sir Henry of Aaggie (1 450) (Ruiter 2d, N. H. B. 189) sold by us for $1,500, he by de Ruiter (N. H. B. 89), (See milk record of the Aaggie family in introduction) he by Jacob 2d, (N. H. B. 56) he by Jacob 1st, (N. H. B. 20) he by Rooker the sire of Aaggie (901). See No. 98.

Dam of Sir Henry of Aaggie, DeSchot (N. H. B. 573) by Jacob 1st, (N. H. B. 20), he by Rooker.

Grandam, Oude Schot 2d by Rooker.

G-g-dam, Oude Schot.

DeSchot has a milk record of 76 lbs. in one day.

de Ruiter's dam Porcelein, (N. H. B. 147) milk record, 80 lbs. 1 oz. in one day, she by Rooker. Porcelein's dam Oude Porcelein.

Jacob 2d's dam Trintje (N. H. B 35) has a record of 80 lbs. in one day, and is the dam of Aaggie Belle, See No. 121.

Jacob 1st's dam, DeGoede was a prize cow at the Paris Exposition and has a milk record of 91 lbs. 8 oz. in one day.

Dam, Pijper, a large, fine cow, with a record of 73 1-5 lbs. in one day.

No. 8. **PRINCE OF ARTIS.** No. 559.

(Not for Sale.)

(H. H. B. Vol. 7, No. 2479.) Calved March 20th, 1883. Imported by us June, 1883. Four-fifths black, medium star, white strip over shoulders, white over roots of tail to hip, legs, belly and switch white.

Sire, Artis, (N. H. B. 127), whose owner assures us he has refused in Holland 5,000 florins ($2,000) for him; he is large, straight, square, handsomely marked, with good escutcheon and veins, and is in all respects a very superior animal.

Both his sire and dam are in the Zoological Gardens at Amsterdam as specimens of the breed.

Artis won First Prize at Gouda in 1882.

Artis' dam gave as a two-year-old 38 lbs. 14 oz. of milk in a day. His grandam gave 64 lbs. of milk in a day, and his g-g-dam gave 73 1-5 lbs. in one day.

The dam of Artis' grandsire also has a record of 73 1-5 lbs. in one day.

Dam, Lieze 2d, with a two-year-old record of 36 4-7 lbs. in one day.

Grandam, Lieze, with a milk record of 96 lbs. in one day, was a wonderful milker, and was wedged shape, her milk veins extended forward to the arm-pits; she was fine, and a typical milch cow.

Prince of Artis won First Prize as a yearling bull at the New York State Fair in 1884, competing with a large class of meritorious animals, he is very straight and square, hair and hide unusually fine; a grand bull in all respects.

No. 9.   MACKENZIE.   No. 852.

(H. H. B. Vol. 8, No. 3,305.) Calved March 26, 1883. Imported by us May, 1884. Two-thirds black, large star, small white spot on left side and two on right side, white from right shoulder to belly, white over hips to belly both sides, black spot on right hind quarter and above right gambrel, two-thirds of tail white.

Sire, Maximilian 2d, winner of First Prize at Alkmaar in 1883, and Second at Gouda in 1882, the First being won by Artist (127). Grandsire, Maximilian, winner of First Prize at Amsterdam.

Dam, Nannie, a fine old cow, straight and square, good escutcheon, splendid milk veins, good head, and fine horns. A very handsome cow, which has a record of 73 1-5 lbs. in one day.

No. 10.   PIONIS.

(H. H. B. Vol. 7, No. 2,290.) Calved March 29th, 1883. White and black, star, snip, neck black, small black saddle, black spot on each side and black patch at rump.

Sire, Empire (588), he by Billy Boleyn (189) imported.

Empire's dam, Empress (539) imported. She has a record in Holland of 109 5-7 lbs. in one day, and has given in this country 81 lbs. in one day, 19,714 lbs. 4 oz. in one year. A heifer sired by this bull recently sold for $2,000.

Dam, Pink (555), imported in dam, Peternella (540), which won Third Prize at Zaandam, and has a record of 82¼ lbs. of milk in one day.

G-g-dam, Paulina, has a record of 77 4-5 lbs. of milk in one day.

G-g-g-dam, Peternella, has a record of 75½ lbs. of milk in one day.

G-g-g-g-dam, Paulina, has a record of 80 1-6 lbs. of milk in one day

Pink is a fine promising heifer, and has given 40 lbs. of milk in one day.

Empire, the sire of this bull won the First Prize as a calf at the New York State Fair in 1880. This is the only time he was ever exhibited.

Billy Boleyn the grandsire of this bull is celebrated as a prize winner as will be seen by the following list:

Billy Boleyn, with his herd, winner of the *Gold Medal Prize* for best herd at New York State Fair, 1880.

First Prize Ohio State Fair, 1882.

First Prize, Pennsylvania State Fair, 1882.

First Prize, Best Bull any age, Pennsylvania State Fair. 1882.

First Prize, Sweepstakes Herd (1 bull and 4 cows), Pennsylvania State Fair, 1882.

First Prize, Mahoning and Shenango Valley Fair, 1882.

First Prize, Sweepstakes Best Herd, Mahoning and Shenango Valley Fair, 1882.

First Prize, Sweepstakes Herd (1 bull and 4 cows), Ohio State Fair, 1883.

First Prize, Best Bull three years old and over, Tri-State Fair, 1883.

First Prize, Best Herd (1 bull and 4 cows), Sweepstakes, Tri-State Fair, 1883.

First Prize, Best Herd, Sweepstakes, Mahoning and Shenango Valley Fair, 1883.

No. 11.　　　　　ARTIS' TOMAH.　　　　　No. 568.

(H. H. B. Vol. 8, No. 3,307.) Calved March 30th, 1883. Three-fourths black, star, snip, broad white over shoulders to belly on right side, white spot at rump, legs, belly and switch white.

Sire, Artis, (N. H. B. 127). (See No. 8.)

Dam, Geertje, has given 54 6-7 lbs. in a day as a four-year-old.

No. 12.　　　　　DUKE OF ARTIS.　　　　　No. 560.

(H. H. B Vol. 7, No. 2,480.) Calved April 6th, 1883. Imported by us August, 1883. Three-fourths black, long star, snip, white strip over shoulder to belly on left side, large white spot over hips to belly and flank on left side, black to gambrels, right fore leg black to ankle outside, legs, belly and switch white.

Sire, Artis, (N. H. B. 127), a large, straight, square, well marked bull, with good escutcheon. See No. 8.

Dam, Hendrika, a very fine, elegant cow, with a record of 75½ lbs. in a day.

No. 13.　　　　　CLOVIS.　　　　　No. 790.

(H. H. B. Vol. 8, No. 3,303.) Calved April 28th, 1883. Imported by us May, 1884. Four-fifths black, star, irregular white on hips.

Sire, Lincoln, (N. H. B. 120), a very large, handsome, beautifully marked bull of much individual worth. He by Jacob 2d, (N. H. B. 56), the sire of Neptune, (See No. 1), and Aaggie 2d. For extension see Sir Henry 2d of Aaggie, No. 4. See chart of Sir Henry 2d of Aaggie, and milk records of Aaggie family, page 22.

Lincoln's dam, Marie, (N. H. B. 361), has a record of 80 1-6 lbs. of milk in one day.

Marie's dam, Koster, has a record of 68 2-5 lbs. in one day.

Marie is a half-sister to Ethel, (905), imported by us, and which made a record of 45 lbs. in one day, 1,240 lbs. 11 oz. in one month and 10,262 lbs. 8 oz. in one year, as a two-year-old. She is also the dam of Amy Robsart, (1,293), imported by us, and which made a record as a two-year-old just after importation, and before she was acclimated, of 8,340 lbs. 8 oz. in ten months and twenty-eight days

Dam, Emma, a large, straight, square cow, with good escutcheon and milk veins, fine head and horns, gave 75½ lbs. in one day.

No. 14. LAD OF PALMYRA.

(H. H. B. Vol. 7, No. 2,616.) Calved May 5, 1883. White and black, star, snip. Sides of neck, spot on right hip and patch across rump, black.

Sire, Dick Swiveller (504), he by Ike (271), he by Rip Van Winkle (35), imported in dam Fraulein (9).

Dick Swiveller's dam, Arria (86), by Hamilcar (17), imported in dam, Crown Princess (6).

Arria's dam, Fraulein (9), imported.

Ike's dam, Isis (148), by Rip Van Winkle (35), imported in dam Fraulein (9).

Isis' dam, Topsey (61), out of Dowager (7), imported, by Hollander (20), imported.

Rip Van Winkle is the sire of Echo, which has a milk record of 23,775½ lbs. in one year. Ægis, milk record, 16,823 lbs. 10 oz. in one year, (See No. 96). Juniata, milk record 13,880 lbs. 1 oz. in one year, and many other noted milkers.

Fraulein (9) has a record of 70 lbs. in one day, and 1,873 lbs. in one month.

Topsey (61) gave 40 lbs. 8 oz. in one day when less than two years old. In 1879 she gave 70 lbs. in one day, 64 lbs per day for thirty consecutive days, and 6,005 lbs in five months.

Dowager (7) has a record of 12,681 lbs. 8 oz. in one year.

Crown Princess (6), with a milk record of 14,027 lbs. in one year, is the dam of Echo. See record above.

Dam, Welcome (967), imported, she by Zwartbont Kees.

Grandam, Bles, a fine heifer, has a record of 59½ lbs. in one day.

Welcome has a record of 40 lbs. in one day as a two-year-old, milked twice per day and with no extra feed.

No. 15.   NETHERLAND KING.   No. 440.

(Not for Sale.)

(H. H. B. Vol. 7, No. 1,924.) Calved June 13th, 1883. Two-thirds black, left half of face white, two small black spots under left eye, black spot on top of shoulders, three white spots on right side and one on right flank, one near right fore leg, two small white and two small black spots on left side, legs, belly and switch white.

Sire, Netherland Prince, (716), (See No. 2), (See cut), he by Schemmel, son of Netherland Dowager, (See No. 97), and sire of Netherland Princess, (See No. 123), Netherland Countess,

(See No. 133), Netherland Belle, (See No. 138), and Netherland Baroness II, (See No. 141).

Schemmel is by Schreuder, sire of Netherland Queen, (See No. 104), and Netherland Duchess, (See No. 112).

Dam, Netherland Queen 2d, (560), (See No. 126), was awarded First Prize at Onondaga County Fair, 1879. As a two-year-old she gave 40 lbs. 4 oz. in one day, 1,102 lbs. 7 oz. in one month. As a three-year old she gave 49 lbs. 4 oz. in one day, 1,307 lbs. 11 oz. in one month, 6,569 lbs. 7 oz. in six months, and 10,471 lbs. 15 oz. in eleven months. As a five year old she has given 68 lbs. 8 oz. in one day, 3,670 lbs. 4 oz. in two months and one day to Sept. 26th

For form, size and beauty this cow has few equals, and she bids fair to make a large milk record this season.

Netherland Queen 2d, was sired by Uncle Tom (163), he by Rip Van Winkle (35), imported in cow Fraulein (9). She has a record of 70 lbs. in one day, 1,873 lbs. in one month.

Uncle Tom's dam, Topsey (61), by imported Hollander (20), has a record of 40 lbs. in one day, when less than two years old. In the season of 1879, she gave as high as 70 lbs. in a day, 64 lbs. per day for thirty consecutive days, and 6,005 lbs. in five months.

Topsey's dam, Dowager (7), has a record of 12,681 lbs. 8 oz. of milk in one year.

Uncle Tom is half-brother to Aegis (69), (See No. 96), to Echo (121), which has a record of 18,120 lbs. 8 oz. in one year and followed in the succeeding year by a record of 23,775 lbs. 8 oz.

Uncle Tom was awarded the First Prize at the New York State and Onondaga County Fairs four successive years and was never beaten in the show ring.

Grandam, Netherland Queen (414.) See No. 104.

G-g-dam, Lady Netherland (1,263.) See No. 99.

G-g-g-dam, Gert Met 2d. See No. 99.

G-g-g-g-dam, Gert Met. See No. 99.

Netherland King, as will be observed, is of unusually high breeding and in form, general appearance, and color markings, is almost a perfect model of his sire, Netherland Prince, and bears likeness in a strong degree to the noted family to which he is so closely related.

No. 16.   **LEE MORGAN.**   No. 466.

(H. H. B. Vol. 7, No. 2,181.) Calved June 16th, 1883. Four-fifths black, small star, small white spot on left shoulder, hind legs black to below gambrels, white on right fore leg at ankle.

Sire, Duke of Leesburgh (960), he by Ebbo (236), imported in dam Iona (335).

Duke of Leesburgh's dam, Maid of Purmer (382), imported. She gave as a two-year-old, 10,893 lbs. 1 oz. in a year, and after milking eleven months, made 1 lb. of butter per day. As a four-year-old, she has given 68 lbs. in one day, and 11,473 lbs. in nine months, at which time record was discontinued, as she was due to calve within six weeks. She was giving 28 lbs. per day at the close of the nine months. In two days' butter trial she made 3 lbs. 14 oz. This latter record was made in Leesburgh, Virginia, and illustrates the adaptability of Holsteins to the Southern climate.

Ebbo won First Prizes at the New York State and Onondaga County Fairs in 1880, and his dam, Iona, has a record of 12,033 lbs. 8 oz. in 346 days.

Dam, Middy Morgan (1,397), imported, by Kees, (N. H. B. 32), winner of First Prizes at Zaandam, Schiedam, Alkmaar, Haarlem, Rotterdam and Amsterdam, also Second Prizes at Amsterdam and Purmerende.

Kees' dam, Olje, a splendid cow and superior milker.

Italy, son of Kees, is the sire of Molly Bawn (1.288), imported by us and sold when a yearling. She has given as a three-year-old 70 lbs. 11 oz. in one day, 2,012 lbs. 4 oz. in one month, and 16,391 lbs. 6 oz. in one year. This is the highest three-year-old record yet made by any cow of any breed, of which we have knowledge.

Middy Morgan's dam, Lady Beaconsfield, (De Oude Vrouw N. H. B. 480), has a record of 84 lbs. 8 oz. in one day, is now eighteen years old and still breeding.

Middy Morgan gave as a two-year-old, 41 lbs. in a day, and 8,000 lbs. in ten months and twenty days. She made this record in Virginia.

No. 17.   ROBERTUS.   No. 987.

(H. H. B. Vol. 8, No. 3,306.) Calved Jan. 17th, 1883. Two-thirds black star, white on nose, white over shoulder to belly left side and over hips to flanks, both sides. Long black spot on left fore leg. Black spot on right flank. Small white spot back of right shoulder. Black at rump. Two-thirds tail white.

Sire, Lincoln, (N. H. B. 120), a very large, handsome, beautifully marked bull of much individual worth, he by Jacob 2d (N. H. B. 56), the sire of Neptune, (See No. 1), and Aaggie 2d. For extension see Sir Henry 2d of Aaggie No. 4. See chart of Sir Henry 2d of Aaggie, and milk records of Aaggie family, page 22.

Lincoln's dam, Marie, (N. H. B. 361), has a record of 80 1 6 lbs. in one day.

Marie's dam. Koster, has a record of 68 2-5 lbs. in one day.

Marie is a half-sister to Ethel (905), imported by us, and which made a record of 45 lbs. in one day, 1,240 lbs. 11 oz. in one month, and 10,262 lbs. 8 oz. in a year, as a two-year old.

She is also the dam of Amy Robsart (1,293), imported by us, and which made a record as a two-year-old, just after importation and before she was acclimated, of 8,340 lbs 8 oz. in ten months and twenty-eight days.

Dam, Johanna, (N. H. B. 1,421), she by Koning.

G-dam, an extra good milker.

Johanna gave, as a five-year old, 77 4-5 lbs. in one day.

No. 18.   YOUNG APOLLO.   No. 469.

(H. H. B. Vol. 7, No. 2,179.) Calved Oct. 29th, 1883. Two-thirds black, star, very small snip, broad white strip over shoulders to belly, both sides, broad, irregular white over hips to flank on right side, three small white spots on left side, black spot on right side, legs, belly and tail white.

Sire, Neptune (711), (See No. 1), also milk records of the Aaggie family, page 22.

Neptune is the only living son of Aaggie. See No. 98.

Dam, Janet Gray (2,752), imported by us. She by Rooker's bull.

Grandam, Klasina, gave, as a five year old, 59 lbs 8 oz. in one day.

Janet Gray dropped her first calf when only twenty months old, just after she was imported, and before she was acclimated. She gave 5,438 lbs. in eleven months, beginning in November.

No. 19.   NETHERLAND CONQUEROR.   No. 475.

(H. H. B. Vol. 7, No. 2,476.) Calved Dec. 11, 1883. Two-thirds black, large star, broad irregular white over shoulders to belly on left side by fine line, large white spot over hips nearly connected with white on left flank, black on left fore leg to below knee, black to gambrels, **half** tail **white.**

Sire, Netherland Prince (716.) See No. 2.

Dam, Ægis 6th (2,088), (See No. 167.) She by Neptune (711) (See No. 1), out of Aaggie (901.) See No 98.

No. 20. STATESMAN. No. 857.

(H. H. B. Vol. 8, No. 3,295.) Calved Jan. 11, 1884. Three-fourths black, star, white spot over shoulders, and one over hips and rump.

Sire, Pieter (N. H. B 209), he by de Ruiter (N. H. B. 89), (See chart, Sir Henry II. of Aaggie), he by Jacob II. (N. H. B. 56), he by Jacob (N. H. B. 20), he by Rooker, sire of Aaggie. See milk records of Aaggie family, page 22.

Pieter won First Prize at Alkmaar, his dam is Aagje (N. H. B. 691), a very fine cow with a milk record of 64 lbs. in a day, as a four-year old.

Dam, Princess, is a large, handsome cow with prominent milk veins, is straight, square and fine, gave 68 2-5 lbs. of milk in one day.

No. 21. CHILPERIC.

(H. H. B. Vol. 8, No. 2,820.) Calved Jan. 19th, 1884.

Sire, Nabob (719), he by Sentinel (512), imported.

Nabob's dam, Ida May (947), imported, has a milk record of 48 lbs. in one day, 1,257 lbs. in one month, and 10,958 lbs. 2 oz. in one year, as a two-year-old. (Now dead.)

Dam, Onondaga Princess 2d (1,450), by Krelis.

Grandam, Onondaga Princess (1,301), imported by us.

G-g-dam, Katrina, has a record of 65 lbs. in one day.

Onondaga Princess has a milk record of 7,807 lbs. in ten months and twelve days.

Katrina is the dam of **Pride** of Beemster (424), imported by us. She made a record, as a four-year old, of 55 lbs. 4 oz. in one day, 1,537 lbs. 7 oz. in one month, 7,814 lbs. 3 oz. in six months, and 12,759 lbs. 3 oz. in eleven months and twelve days. She weighed, when three years old, 1,440 lbs.

No. 22.   JACOB WIT'S VOLUNTEER.   No. 808.

(H. H. B. Vol. No.   .) Calved February 10th, 1884. One-half black, strip in face, three large black spots on left side, one on right side, black at rump.

Sire, Jacob Wit (2,662), Jacob 4th (N. H. B. 210), he by Jacob II. (N. H. B. 56), he by Jacob (N. H. B. 20), he by Rooker sire of Aaggie (901). See milk records of the Aaggie family, page 22.

Jacob Wit's dam Heiltje (1,006 N. H. B.), a very choice handsome cow.

Dam, Kleine Zwarte, has given as a five-year-old 54 6-7 lbs. of milk in one day. She is large, straight and square, with fine bone, a long milker.

No 23.   AAGGIE IDALINE 2d's ALBERT.   No. 07.

(H. H. B. Vol. 8, No. 3,091.) Calved Feb. 7th, 1884. Three-fourths black, small star, large white spot back of hips, strip of white from right shoulder to belly.

Sire, Stippeltje, a large fine spotted black and white bull, now district bull of Oostwoud.

Dam, Aaggie Idaline 2d (4,363), (See No. 114), has given as a five-year-old the first year after importation, 53 lbs. 12 oz. in one day, 8,750 lbs. 14 oz. in seven months and seventeen days to Sept. 26th. She was sired by Jacob II. (N. H. B. 56), sire of Neptune (711), and Aaggie 2d (1,360), See milk records of Aaggie family, page 22.

Grandam, Naatje has a record of 68 2-5 lbs. in one day, is also dam of Aaggie Idaline (4,362). (See No. 105), which has a record as a six-year old of 60 lbs. in one day, and 9,360 lbs. 15 oz. in six months and twenty five days, to Sept. 26th.

No. 24.   AAGGIE EVA'S RUFUS.   No. 495.

(H. H. B. Vol. 8, No. 3,092.) Calved Feb. 9th, 1884. Three-fourths white, black cheeks, long black spot over neck, eleven black spots on right side, ten on left side.

Sire, Cornelius. a large, fine, light-colored bull. His dam gave 68 2-5 lbs. in one day. She is a fine, handsome cow.

Dam, Aaggie Eva (4,354), (See No. 191.) She has given, as a two-year-old, commencing before she was twenty-three months old, 36 lbs 11 oz. in a day and 6,716 lbs. 12 oz. in seven months, sixteen days, to Sept. 26th, and made 4 lbs. 2 oz. of butter in four days on winter feed. She was sired by de Ruiter (N. H. B. 89.) See milk records of the Aaggie family, page 22.

Dam, Agatha, has a five-year-old record of 68 2-5 lbs. in a day and is unquestionably a descendant of Rooker, sire of Aaggie (901), although the exact relationship has not yet been established.

No. 25. AAGGIE CORNELIA 4th's CLINTON. No. 045.

(H. H. B. Vol. 8, No. 3,093.) Calved Feb. 14, 1884. Three-fourth white, black cheeks and neck, two large and two small black spots on left side, two large black spots on right side and one just back of right flank.

Sire, Jacob Wit (2,662), Jacob 4th, (N. H. B. 210.) For extension, see Jacob Wit's Volunteer, No. 22.

Dam, Aaggie Cornelia 4th, (See No. 173), has given this season, as a two-year-old, the first after importation, 5,506 lbs. 9 oz. in seven months and ten days, to Sept. 26th.

Grandam, Aaggie Cornelia (4,410), (See No. 102), has given this season, the first after importation, 53 lbs. 11 oz. in a day, 8,877 lbs. 10 oz. in six months and twenty-five days, to Sept. 26th.

Aaggie Cornelia 3d (4,342), (See No. 132), is a full sister to Aaggie Cornelia 4th, and has given this season, as a four-year-old, the first after importation, 78 lbs. 12 oz. in a day, and 5,616 lbs. 3 oz. in three months and two days, to Sept. 26th.

Aaggie Cornelia 2d (4,341), (See No. 115), is also a full sister, and has given under the same circumstances as the others, as a five-year-old, 51 lbs. 12 oz. in one day, and 7,985 lbs. 10 oz. in seven months and six days, to Sept. 26th.

Aaggie Cornelia 4th's Sire, Alexander (N. H. B. 83), an unusually fine bull, whose stock in this country are proving superior milkers.

No. 26.   AMBASSADOR.   No. 803.

(H. H. B. Vol. 8, No. 3,296.) Calved Feb. 15th, 1884. Two-thirds white, star, snip, large black spot on each side, three small black spots on right flank, large black below rump.

Sire, Jacob Wit (2,662), Jacob 4th (N. H. B. 210), for extension, see Jacob Wit's Volunteer, No. 22.

Dam, De Zwarte (N. H. B.), is mostly black, star, fine hair, good escutcheon and udder, and has given, as a five-year-old, 80 1-6 lbs. of milk in one day.

No. 27.   JACOB WIT'S DEXTER.   No. 814.

(H. H. B. Vol. , No. .) Calved Feb. 15th, 1884. Two-thirds white, strip in face, large black spot on right side, broad white over hips to flanks on right side, black spot over left forearm, black from belly over back, extending to rump on left side.

Sire, Jacob Wit (2,662), Jacob 4th, (N. H. B. 210), for extension, see Jacob Wit's Volunteer, No. 22.

Dam, Groot Moeder, (Groot Wit), has given 77 4-5 lbs. of milk in one day. She is dam of Aaggie Alice No. 236.

No. 28. AAGGIE IDALINE 4th's ROWLAND. No. 046.

(H. H. B. Vol. 8, No. 3,122.) Calved Feb. 18th, 1884. Imported in dam by us August, 1883. Three-fourths white, black on neck and sides of face Black spot on right side containing three small white spots, two large and several small black spots on left side

Sire, Jan, a large, superior, black and white animal, now district bull of Oostwond.

Dam, Aaggie Idaline 4th (4,365), (See No. 190), has given 3,642 lbs. 8 oz. in seven months and six days, to Sept. 26th.

Grandam, Aaggie Idaline 3d (4,364), (See No. 128), gave 57 1-5 lbs. in one day as a three-year-old in Holland, and has given the first season in this country after importation, 55 lbs. 12 oz. in one day as a four-year-old; 8,315 lbs. 11 oz. in seven months and nine days, to Sept. 26th.

G-g-dam, Naatje, gave 68 2-5 lbs. in one day.

Naatje is also dam of Aaggie Idaline 2d (4,363), (See No. 114), which gave 64 lbs. in one day as a four-year-old in Holland. She has given this season the first after importation as a five-year-old, 53 lbs. 12 oz. in one day, and 8,750 lbs. 14 oz. in seven months and seventeen days, to Sept. 26th, and Aaggie Idaline (4,362), (No. 105), which gave 68 2-5 lbs. in one day in Holland; and has given the first season after importation, 60 lbs. in one day, and 9,360 lbs. 15 oz. in six months and twenty-five days, to Sept. 26th

Aaggie Idaline 4th's Sire, Willem (N. H. B. 84), a very fine bull, and his dam a very choice cow.

Aaggie Idaline 3d's sire, Jacob II. (N. H. B. 56), sire of Neptune and Aaggie II. For extension see milk records of the Aaggie family, page 22.

No. 29.   OGONTZ.   No. 05.

(H. H. B. Vol. 8, No. 2,936.) Calved Feb. 22d, 1884. Imported by us in dam, August, 1883. Three-fourths white, black on right cheek and neck, and around left eye, four black spots on neck left side, large irregular black spot over back, mostly on left side, two small black spots on left side, and one over back.

Sire, Strathmore (2,364), See No. 3.

Dam, St. Catharine (4,488). (See No. 174), she by district bull of Ven Huisen.

Grandam, Jacoba (No. H. H. B. No. 95), a very fine cow which has a record of 77 4·5 lbs. of milk in one day.

St. Catharine is a fine, large, beautiful heifer, and has given as a two-year-old, this season, the first after importation, 35 lbs. 14 oz. in one day, and 4,527 lbs. 13 oz. in six months and twenty-five days to Sept. 26th.

No. 30.   JACOB WIT'S MIRICK.   No. 832.

(H. H. B. Vol. 8, No. ——.) Calved Feb. 23d, 1884. Imported by us May, 1884. Three-fourths black, strip in face, irregular white over shoulders, white over hips to flank and belly left side, two small white spots on right fore leg, two-thirds tail white.

Sire, Jacob Wit (2,662), Jacob 4th (N. H. B. 210), For extension, see Jacob Wit's Volunteer, No. 22.

Dam, Zuster 2d A., by Jacob 2d ((N. H. B. 56), &c. See Neptune No. 1.

G-dam, Zuster 2d (N. H. B. 505).

G-g-dam, a fine cow.

No. 31.   JACOB WIT'S ANTHONY.   No. 871.

(H. H. B. Vol. 8, No. ——.) Calved Feb. 24th, 1884. Imported by us May, 1884. Three-fourths black, star, white over shoulders to belly, right side, white over hips to flank, right side, and nearly to flank, left side.

Sire, Jacob Wit (2,662), Jacob 4th (N. H. B. 210.) For extension, see Jacob Wit's Volunteer, No. 22.

Dam, Smit (N. H. B. 717), has a record of 73 1-5 lbs. in one day as a five-year-old. She is a fine black and white cow, straight and square, has a good escutcheon, elegant veins and crumpled horns. She is the dam of Aaggie of Hoorn (4,481), imported by us and sold while a yearling, and which has given this season, as a two-year-old, 51 lbs. in one day without any green feed.

No. 32.   JACOB WIT'S JUDSON.   No. 804.

(H. H. B, Vol. 8, No. ——.) Calved March 1, 1884. Imported by us May, 1884. Three-fourths white, strip in face, two black spots on left fore leg, six black spots on left side, one large and five smaller spots on right side, black at rump.

Sire, Jacob Wit (2,662), Jacob 4th (N. H. B. 210.) For extension, see Jacob Wit's Volunteer, No. 22.

Dam, Louiza (N. H. B. 445), has given 80 1-6 lbs. of milk in one day.

Grandam, a fine black and white cow and good milker, very large, straight and square, good veins and extra escutcheon.

She is of the same family as Marie, the dam of Lincoln. See Clovis, No. 13.

No. 33.   DeRUITER'S LAD.   No. 1,016.

(H. H. B. Vol. 8, No. 3,299.) Calved March 2d, 1884. One-half white, star, snip, irregular white over shoulders and over hips to flanks both sides, large black spot on right hind quarter.

Sire, de Ruiter, imported by Mr. F. G. Babcock, and sired by de Ruiter (N. H. B. 89), he by Jacob 2d (N. H. B. 56), &c. For extension, see Sir Henry 2d, of Aaggie No. 4.

De Ruiter's dam, de Schot (N. H. B. 573), has a milk record of 76 lbs. in one day. She was sired by Jacob (N. H. B. 20), he by Rooker.

De Schot's dam, Oude Schot 2d, by Rooker.

Oude Schot 2d's dam, Oude Schot.

Dam, Jonge Koningen, gave as a four-year-old 68 2-5 lbs. in one day.

De Ruiter the sire of this calf is a full brother to the bull Sir Henry of Aaggie (1,450), imported by us and which we recently sold to go to Tennessee, the price received for him being $1,500.

No. 34.   RANDALL.   No. 805.

(H. H. B. Vol. 8, No. 3,304.) Calved March 3d, 1884. Imported by us May, 1884. Black predominating, star, white over hips, small white spot on left side near belly and one near left flank, right fore leg black to knee, black on right gambrel.

Sire, Lincoln (N. H. B. 120.) For extension, see Clovis No. 13.

Dam, Langedijk, has a record of 73 1-5 lbs. of milk in one day.

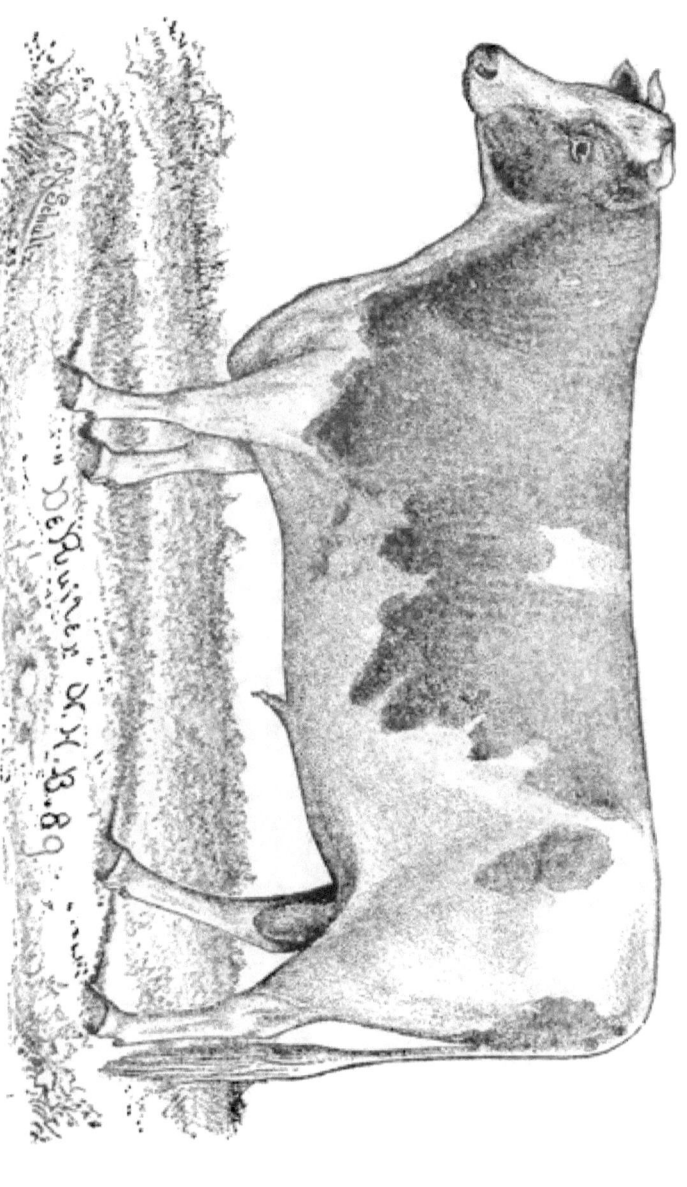

Holstein Bull, "De Ruiter," N. H. B. 89. (See Chart.)

Grandam, a choice cow and fine milker. She was bred by her owner, has fine bone, good hide, fine head, horns and tail, and an extra escutcheon.

No. 35. ROSSMORE. No. 838.

(H. H. B. Vol. 8, No. 3,297.) Calved March 5th, 1884. Imported by us in May, 1884. Three-fourths black, strip in face, white over shoulders to belly both sides, white over hips, black spot above left fore leg and one on left side near belly, little black on fore feet and on left hind foot.

Sire, Jacob Wit (2,662), Jacob 4th (N. H. B. 210.) For extension, see Jacob Wit's Volunteer, No. 22.

Dam, De Zwartkop (N. H. B. 1,089), has a record as a three-year-old of 61 4-5 lbs. in a day. She is a very handsome heifer, straight and square, with good bone.

No. 36. JACOB WIT'S FRANK. No. 870.

(H. H. B. Vol. 8, No. ——.) Calved March 5th, 1884. Imported by us May, 1884. Four-fifths white, irregular black around eyes, long irregular black over neck, three small black spots on left fore-leg and three on right, sides spotted.

Sire, Jacob Wit (2,662), Jacob 4th (N. H. B. 210). For extension see Jacob Wit's Volunteer, No. 22.

Dam, Lady Griswold (6,878), (See No. 127), she by Jacob (N. H. B. 20), he by Rooker, For extension, see Neptune, No. 1.

Grandam, Pleuster, a splendid milker.

Lady Griswold has a record of 77 4-5 lbs. in one day when five years old, and just before importation.

No. 37. TOM ARTIS. No. 858.

(H. H. B. Vol. 8, No. 3,298.) Calved March 6th, 1884. Imported by us May, 1884. Mostly black, star, small white spot above right fore leg, small black spot on right flank, right fore leg black to knee, left fore leg black nearly to knee, hind legs black nearly to gambrels.

Sire, Artis (N. H. B. 127). For extension, see Prince of Artis No. 8.

Dam, Neeltje (N. H. B. 1,764), has a record of 82½ lbs. in one day. She is a grand cow, straight, square and fine, with a mass of milk-veins.

Grandam, a fine cow. The breeder of this calf has for many years kept the same choice strain.

No. 38. JACOB WIT'S CORNELIUS. No. 939.

(H. H. B. Vol. 8, No. ——.) Calved March 7, 1884. Imported by us May, 1884. Two-thirds black, star, snip, large white spot over shoulders, white spot over back, white over hips to roots of tail, two small white spots near left flank, and one near right shoulder, right fore leg black to knee, hind legs black to gambrels.

Sire, Jacob Wit (2,662), Jacob 4th (N. H. B. 210). For extension, see Jacob Wit's Volunteer, No. 22.

Dam, Zijp gave in the spring 77 4-5 lbs. in one day, and in July was still giving 57 1-5 lbs. per day.

No. 39. JACOB WIT'S SAMUEL. No. 934.

(H. H. B. Vol. 8, No. ——), Calved March 9, 1884. Imported by us May, 1884. Three-fourths white, strip in face, white spot back of right ear and two back of left ear, irregular black saddle over back, three small black spots on left side, small white spot near rump, left side.

Sire, Jacob Wit (2,662), Jacob 4th (N. H. B. 210), by Jacob II. (N. H B. 56.) For extension, see Jacob Wit's Volunteer, No. 22,

Dam, Trijntje. gave as a four-year old, 73 1-5 lbs. of milk in a day.

No. 40.   JACOB WIT'S MICHAEL.   No. 837.

(H. H. B Vol. —, No. ——) Calved March 10th. 1884. Two-thirds white, star, snip, white strip over shoulders to belly on left side, broad white over hips and rump to flank on right side, black spot on right flank.

Sire, Jacob Wit (2,662), Jacob 4th (N. H. B. 210), by Jacob II. sire of Neptune and Aaggie II. For extension, see Jacob Wit's Volunteer, No. 22.

Dam, DeZwart Kop (N. H. B. 1,089), which has a three-year-old record of 61 4-5 lbs. of milk in one day. She is a very handsome, straight, square heifer.

No. 41.   JACOB WIT'S PHILIP.   No. 836.

(H. H. B. Vol. —, No. ——.) Calved March 14th, 1884. Three-fourths black, strip in face, four white spots at shoulders, broad white over hips to flank left side.

Sire, Jacob Wit (2,662), Jacob 4th (N. H. B. 210), by Jacob II. sire of Aaggie II. and Neptune. For extension, see Jacob Wit's Volunteer, No. 22.

Dam, Lize, gave as a three-year-old 61 4-5 lbs. of milk in one day. She is large, straight, square and handsome. with superior escutcheon, milk veins, and good hair and hide.

No. 42.   DUKE OF MEDINA.

(H. H. B. Vol. 8, No. 2853.) Calved March 15th, 1884. Two thirds white, strip in face, black saddle extending in large and small spots on both sides to belly, small black spots on flanks, legs, belly and tail white.

Sire, Saladin 7th (807), he by Saladin (336), he by Nestor (127), imported. Saladin's dam, Harriet Ann (696), has a record of 12,840 lbs. in 340 days, she by York (171).

Harriet Ann's dam Betsey Prig (694), has a record of 13,500 lbs. in one year as a four-year-old. She by Opperdoes 4th (29), by Opperdoes 2d (38).

Betsey Prig's dam Electra (286), imported.

Saladin's dam Fausta (125), imported.

York's dam Juno (155), imported.

Opperdoes 4th's dam Zuider Zee 2d (57), imported.

Dam, Caucus Girl (2,071), by Zufrieden (623), he by Dirk Schilp (220), he by Hasselman (106), he by Prince of Orange (137), imported in dam Maid of Zuid (183).

Grandam, Milk Maid (194), has a record of 76 lbs. in one day and 14,700 lbs. in one year.

G-g-dam, Dowager (7), has a record of 12,681 lbs. 8 oz. in one year.

Milk Maid's sire, Hamilcar (17), imported out of Crown Princess (6), which has a record of 76 lbs. in a day, and 14,027 lbs. in one year.

She is dam of Echo (121), which has a record of 18,120 lbs. 8 oz. in one year, and followed in the succeeding year by a record of 23,775 lbs. 8 oz.

Zufrieden's dam, Lady Kurt, (358), has a butter record of 13 lbs. in seven days, she by Kurt (120), imported, and out of Lea (169), imported.

Dirk Schilp's dam, Hillitje (329), imported.

Hasselman's dam, Catrina (106), imported, has a record of 63 lbs. in one day, and 12,063 in one year. The following year she had reached 70 lbs. in one day when she received an injury which stopped her record.

Milk Maid (194), is half-sister to Topsey (61), which has a record of 70 lbs. in one day, 64 lbs. per day for thirty consecutive days, and 6,005 lbs. in five months. And is also half-sister to Agoo (1), the dam of Ægis (69), (See No. 96), which has a record of 16,823 lbs. 10 oz. in one year.

Hamilcar (17), is half-brother to Echo (121). See records given above.

The following named heifers are out of Milk Maid, and half-sisters to Caucus Girl, the dam of Duke of Medina:

Venice (468), gave 67¼ lbs. of milk in one day as a three-year-old, and made 30 lbs. of butter during the month of January, after being eleven months in milk.

Lady Annie (1,083), gave 50 lbs. 8 oz. in one day as a two-year-old.

Clover Top (1,082), gave 46 lbs. in one day as a two-year-old.

Duke of Medina is a straight, square, well-built bull, with very fine curveline escutcheon, and two thigh ovals.

No. 43.   SARATOGA.   No. 813.

(H. H. B. Vol. 8, No. 3,300.) Calved March 23d, 1884. Imported by us May, 1884. Three-fourths white, black cheeks and neck, two small black spots on left fore leg and three on right, black spot on top of neck and one on right side, other black spots scattered over body.

Sire, Jacob Wit (2,662), Jacob 4th (N. H. B. 210.) For extension, see Jacob Wit's Volunteer, No. 22.

Dam, de Ruiter's Bona (6,887). (See No. 200), she by de

Ruiter (N. H. B. 89.) For extension, see Sir Henry 2d of Aaggie (1,451), No. 4.

Grandam, Cornelia, a splendid milker.

No. 44. OTSELIC.

(H. H. B. Vol. 8, No. ——.) Calved March 23d, 1884. Three-fourths black, small star, black hindquarters. saddle over back and neck black.

Sire, Sinclair (1,475), he by Willem (N. H. B. 82), winner of First Prize at Alkmaar and Schagen, and also winner of First Prize as best bull at Gouda, September, 1882, he by Wouter 2d (N. H. B. 30), winner of First Prize at Rotterdam, he by Wouter (N. H. B. 4), prize bull at Zaandam, and also sire of Koningen (N. H. B. 236.)

Sinclair's dam, Witje, a fine cow, with a record of 73 1-5 lbs. in a day.

Sinclair took First Prize at Broome County Fair and First at Marathon, N. Y., in 1883, and also First at the Broome County Fair, in 1884.

Dam, Satella (2,882), imported, she by district bull of Purmer. Satella won Second Prize at Broome County Fair, also at Marathon Fair, 1883, and Second at Broome County Fair in 1884. She gave in one day, when two years old, on grass alone, 32 lbs. and made in one day 1 lb. 7½ oz. of butter.

Grandam, Zuurbier, has a five-year-old record of 68 2-5 lbs.

No. 45. AAGGIE KATHLEEN'S MARQUIS. No. 027.

(H. H. B. Vol. 8, No. 3,094.) Calved March 24th, 1884. White, with tips of ears, spot back of right ear, spots on right side of neck, one on right foreleg, two forward of left shoulder, and two on left fore leg black.

Sire, Jan, district bull of Oostwoud, a large superior spotted black and white bull.

Dam, Aaggie Kathleen (4,492), (See No. 111), she by Jacob (N. H. B. 20) he by Rooker, the sire of Aaggie. For extension, see Neptune No. 1.

Grandam, Bontje Naatje, has a record of 80 1-6 lbs. in one day.

Aaggie Kathleen, has given in six months, ending Sept. 26th, 8,243 lbs.

No. 46.   ALFRIC.   No. 3.

(H. H. B. Vol. 8, No. ——.) Calved March 27th, 1884.

Sire, Lord Bantam (1,011), he by Stentor (346), he by Rip Van Winkle (35), imported in cow Fraulein (9).

Lord Bantam's dam, Valeria (896), imported by us.

Stentor's dam, Dowager (7), imported, has a record of 12,681 lbs. 8 oz in one year.

Fraulein has a record of 70 lbs. in one day, and 1,873 lbs. in one month

Rip Van Winkle is the sire of Ægis (69), (See No. 96), and Echo (121). See records given in Ægis' pedigree.

Dowager (7), is the dam of Milk Maid (194), which has a record of 14,700 lbs. in one year, and is also dam of Topsey (the dam of the famous bull Uncle Tom) (163), which has a record of 70 lbs. in one day, 64 lbs. per day for thirty consecutive days, and 6,005 lbs. in five months.

Dam, Gladiola (1,865), imported by us but sold soon after she commenced her record. She gave as a two-year old 35 lbs. in one day, 973 lbs. 3 oz. in one month, and 2,524 lbs. 11 oz. in two months and twenty-one days.

Grandam, Krampje, a fine, promising heifer, with a record of 52 lbs. in one day.

No. 47. CAPTAIN ARTIS. No. 853.

(H. H. B. Vol. 8, No. 3,301.) Calved March 27th, 1884. Two-thirds black, strip in face, small black spot on lower jaw and one on left fore leg at knee, white over shoulders, two white spots on left side, white over hips to belly, both sides.

Sire, Artis (N. H. B. 127.) For extension, see Prince of Artis, No. 8.

Dam, Sara, a straight, square, fine cow, with fine horns and good milk veins. She has a five-year-old record of 73 1-5 lbs. in one day.

No. 48. POMPINO. No. 5.

(H. H. B. Vol 8, No. ——.) Calved March 26th, 1884.

Sire, Lord Bantam (1,011.) For extension, see Alfric, No. 46.

Dam, Bessie B. (1,195), imported in dam Valeria (896.)

Her owner has kept no record of her milk, but she is a good milker and a choice, handsome cow.

No. 49. CONCORD. No. 4.

(H. H. B. Vol. 8, No. ——.) Calved March 28th, 1884.

Sire, Lord Bantam (1,011.) For extension, see Alfric, No. 46.

Dam, Orelia (1,799), was imported by us and came in soon after importation and before she was fully acclimated, and gave, as a two-year-old, in three month and sixteen days up to the time she was sold, 3,500 lbs. 5 oz.

Grandam, Stolpje, a fine, elegant cow, which gave 68 2-5 lbs. in one day.

AAGGIE MAY'S HORACE.
(H. H. B., Vol. 8, No. 3,096.)
Born April 10, 1884.

- NEPTUNE, (No. 711, H. H. B.)
  - JACOB 2d, (N. H. B
  - AAGGIE, (901.) (N. 148.) Milk record lbs., 15 oz. in a ye

- AAGGIE MAY, (No. 2,601, H. H. B.) 3 years old. Record 57 lbs. 13 oz. in a day. 7,642 lbs. in 5 mos. and 13 days to Sept. 26. 2 year old record 9,279 lbs., 6 oz. in 11 mos. and 11 days. The first season after importation.
  - DE RUITER, (N. 89.)
  - BLOKKER 2d. (B., 391.) 2 yea milk record, 45 oz. in a day.

Neptune is full brother to Aaggie 2d, with milk record of 17,746 lbs. 2 oz. gave as a 2-year old 44 lbs. in a day.
Jacob 2d is the sire of Aaggie 2d, 2-year old, record 17,746 lbs. 2 oz. in a year Beauty 2d. Aaggie Anna, Aaggie Hannah, Aaggie Isadora, Aaggie Idaline 2d, Aa
Jacob 1st is the sire of Aaggie Rosa. Aaggie Idaline and Aaggie Kathleen.
Rooker is the sire of Aaggie, Aaggie Cornelia, Lady Clifden, Lambertina, D
De Ruiter is the sire of Aaggie Constance, Aaggie Clara, Aaggie Jennie, Aa
For records see milk records of Aaggie Family, Page 22.

- JACOB, (N. H. B., 20.)
  - ROOKER.
  - DE GOEDE. A Prize Cow at the Paris Exposition. Milk record, 91 lbs. 8 oz. in a day.
- TRINTJE, (N. H. B., 35.) Milk record, 80 lbs. in a day.
- ROOKER.
- OUDE AAGGIE, milk record, 76 lbs. in a day.

- JACOB 2d, (N. H. B., 56.)
  - JACOB, (N. H. B., 20.)
    - ROOKER.
    - DE GOEDE, a Prize Cow at the Paris Exposition. Milk record, 91 lbs. 8 oz. in a day.
  - TRINTJE, (N. H. B, 35.) Milk rec. 80 lbs. in a day.
- FORCELEIN, (N. H. B., 147.) Milk record, 80 lbs. 1 oz. in a day.
  - ROOKER.
  - OUDE PORCELEIN.
- GERRIT, (N. H. B., 31.)
  - CORNELIUS.
  - DE GOEDE, a Prize Cow at the Paris Exposition Milk record, 91 lbs. 8 oz. in a day.
- BLOKKER. (N. H. B., 390.) Milk record, 82½ lbs. in a day.
  - ROOKER.
  - OUDE BLOKKER.

ar when two years old, and sire of Aegis 6th. See No. 167 and Music 2d, which

tie Sarah, Aaggie Bonnie, Aaggie Rosa 2d, Aaggie Cora, Aaggie Beauty, Aaggie aline 3d.

ot and Porcelein.
errel, Aaggie Leila, Aaggie Sadie and Aaggie Rosa 3d.

No. 50. **RUGBY PRINCE.** No. 043.

(H. H. B. Vol. 8, No. 3,095.) Calved April 1st, 1884. Mostly black, small star, left hind-leg black to below gambrel, right hind-leg black nearly to gambrel, black on right fore-leg outside nearly to knee.

Sire, Prince Imperial (1,164). See No. 5.

Dam, Netherland Queen 3d (1,466), (See No. 166). She has given this season, as a three-year-old, 51 lbs. 6 oz. in one day and 6,514 lbs. 2 oz. in five months and seventeen days, to Sept. 26th.

Grandam, Netherland Queen (414). See No. 104.

G-g-dam, Lady Netherland (1,263). See No. 99.

G-g-g-dam, Gert Met 2d.

G-g-g-g-dam, Gert Met.

Rugby Prince is one of the most perfect specimens of the breed we have ever seen. Unusually straight and square, fine in all respects. He gained 108 lbs. in weight in fourteen consecutive days and 148 lbs. in 21 consecutive days and still retained his almost perfect form and fineness. His breeding, as will be seen, is especially desirable, as it is so strong in the Netherland blood.

No. 51. **TIOGA.** No. 2.

(H. H. B. Vol 8, No. ——.) Calved April 5th, 1884.

Sire, Lord Bantam (1,011) For extension, see Alfric, No. 46.

Dam, Alliky (2,357), by Stentor (346), he by Rip Van Winkle (35), imported in cow Fraulein (9.)

Stentor's dam, Dowager (7), imported, has a record of 12,681 lbs. 8 oz. in one year. For extension, see Alfric, No. 46.

Grandam, Valeria (896), imported by us.

Alliky is a fine cow and good milker, but her owner has kept no record of her milk.

No. 52.   NETHERLAND LEO.   No. 032.

(H. H. B. Vol. 8, No. 2,938.) Calved April 5th, 1884. One-half black, black cheeks, one large and three small black spots on left side, black spot on right side and one near right hip.

Sire, Netherland Prince (716.) See No. 2.

Dam, Aaggie Merrel (2,628). See No. 178

She has given this season, as a two-year-old, 46 lbs. 1 oz. in one day, and 5,771 lbs. 3 oz. in five months and fifteen days, to Sept. 26th.

Grandam, Bregger, gave 64 lbs. in one day, as a three-year old.

Aaggie Merrel's sire, de Ruiter (N. H. B. 89.) See milk records of Aaggie family, page 22.

No. 53.   ROTHESAY.   No. 930.

(H. H. B. Vol. 8, No. 3,302.) Calved April 8th, 1884 Two-thirds black, strip in face, white over shoulders to belly, both sides, broad white over hips to flank left side, small black spot on left leg.

Sire, Jacob Wit (2,662), Jacob 4th (N. H. B. 210.) For extension, see Jacob Wit's Volunteer, No. 22.

Dam, Lambertina (6,889), (See No. 101), has a record of 68 2-5 lbs. in one day, before importation.

Grandam, Lamberta, a very choice cow.

No. 54.   **AAGGIE MAY'S HORACE.**   No. 022.

(See Chart.)

(H. H. B. Vol. 8, No. 3,096.) Calved April 10th, 1884. Three-fourths white, strip in face, three large and three small black spots on right side, four black spots on left side, black spots on rump and tail.

Sire, Neptune (711), (See No. 1), he by Jacob II. (N. H. B. 56), sire of Aaggie II. (1,360). See milk records of the Aaggie family, page 22.

Neptune's dam Aaggie (901), (See No. 98), has given 84 lbs. 12 oz. in one day, and 18,004 lbs. 15 oz. in one year, and is the dam of Aaggie II. (1,360), with a two-year-old record of 17,746 lbs. 2 oz. in one year. For extended records, see records of Aaggie family, page 22.

Dam, Aaggie May (2,601), (See No. 151), gave 9,279 lbs. 6 oz. of milk in eleven months and eleven days, as a two-year-old, the first season after importation, and this season, as a three-year-old, has given 57 lbs. 13 oz. in one day and 7,642 lbs. in five months and thirteen days, to Sept. 26th.

G-dam, Blokker II. (N. H B. 391), has a two-year-old record of 45 lbs. 8 oz. in one day, on grass.

G-g-dam, Blokker (N. H. B. 390), by Rooker the sire of Aaggie (901), has given 82 1-3 lbs. of milk in one day.

G-g-g-dam,, Oude Blokker, a great milker.

Blokker 2d's sire, Gerrit (N. H. B. 31), by Cornelius.

Gerrit's dam, de Goede, the dam of Jacob I. (N. H. B. 20), sire of Aaggie Rosa, etc.

Blokker is dam of Aaggie Bonnie (2,608.)   See No. 137.

No 55.   LYRA'S PRINCE.   No 034.

(H. H. B. Vol. 8, No. 2,939.) Calved April 11th, 1884. Two-thirds black, strip in face, white over shoulder to belly on left and nearly to belly on right side broad white over hips and rump.

Sire, Prince Imperial, (1164), (See No. 5).

Dam, Lyra (2,801), (See No. 157). She made in one week on winter feed, 9 lbs. 3 oz. of butter when only two years old. She has given as a two-year-old 7,476 lbs. 15 oz. in ten months and nineteen days, and as a three-year-old 45 lbs. 10 oz. in one day, 6,117 lbs. 2 oz. in five months nine days to September 24th.

G-dam, Dirkje has a record of 77 4-5 lbs. in a day.

G-g-dam, a great milker.

Her sire Sijmen 2d winner of first prize at Uythoorn, Alkmaar and Mydrecht.

G-sire Prince, (N. H. B. 59), winner of First Prize at London and Second Paris.

G-g-sire, Sijmen, (N. H. B. 23).

G-g-g-sire, Graaf Adolph, winner of First Prize at The Hague.

N.o 56.   AAGGIE CORA'S WILFRED.   No. 050.

(H. H. B. Vol. 8, No. 3,097.) Calved April 12th, 1884. Three-fourths white, strip in face, two large and two small black spots on left side, large black spot on right side, two small black spots above right flank and little black at rump.

Sire, Prince Imperial, (1,164), (See No. 5), he by Netherland Prince, (716), (See No. 2), also records of Netherland family, page 27.

Prince Imperial's dam Carlotta (1,266). (See cut and No. 119.)

Dam, Aaggie Cora (2,609.) (See No. 136), by Jacob II. (N. H. B. 56), See cut, and milk records of the Aaggie family, page 22.

Aaggie Cora gave as a three-year-old the first season after importation 8,451 lbs. 8 oz. in nine months and seven days, and this season as a four-year-old has given 65 lbs. 8 oz. in one day, and 7,994 lbs. 6 oz. in five months and twelve days to September 26th.

G-dam, Aaltje, (N. H. B. 324), has a record of 82½ lbs. of milk in a day.

G-g-dam, Porcelein, (N. H. B. 147), by Rooker.

G-g-g-dam, Oude Porcelein.

Sire of Aaltje was Jacob I. (N. H. B. 20.) See chart of Sir Henry 2d of Aaggie.

It will be observed that the breeding of this bull combines the blood of two of the most famous milk families of this breed. In form he is all that could be desired; straight, square, low, blocky and fine. The form and pedigree make him a valuable animal to place at the head of a herd.

No. 57.   **PHILOSOPHER.**   No. 089.

(H H. B. Vol. 8, No. 3,374.) Calved April 12th, 1884. Three-fourths black, star, white over shoulders and over hips to flank, on right side, small black spot on right side, left fore leg black to below knee, black spot on back side left hind leg above gambrel.

Sire, Kenmore (1,174), imported by us in dam, he by the district bull of Hoogcarspel.

Kenmore's dam, Czarina (1,837), imported, she by the district bull of Westwoud.

Czarina's dam, Klaartje.

Czarina calved when about twenty-two months old and gave in three months and two days 2,683 lbs. 8 oz. of milk when we sold her. She made, when two years old, 8 lbs. of butter in one week, on winter feed.

Kenmore won Second Prize at New York State Fair in 1882, when seven months old.

Dam, Florence Nightingale (2,733), imported by us.

Grandam, Gretje gave, as a two-year-old, 45 4-5 lbs. in a day.

Florence Nightingale is a very fine, promising heifer, which we imported and sold before calving. Her present owner keeps no record, but considers her a superior milker.

No. 58   IBIS.   No 8.

(H. H. B. Vol. 8, No. ——.)   Calved April 12, 1884.

Sire, Lord Bantam (1011). For extension, see Alfric, No. 46.

Dam, Bessie I (1686), she by Stentor (346), by Rip Van Winkle (35), imported in cow Fraulein (9). Stentor's dam Dowager (7). imported, has a record of 12,681 lbs. 8 oz. in one year. Fraulein has a record of 70 lbs. in one day, and 1,873 lbs. in one month. For extension, see Alfric, No. 46.

G-dam, Rosabel (893), imported by us ; she by deHeer's bull.

G-g-dam, a fine cow with a five-year-old year old record of 64 lbs. in a day.

The owner of Bessie I. keeps no record of her milk. She is a choice, handsome cow and good milker.

No. 59.   CZAROWITZ   No. 19.

(H. H. B. Vol. 8, No.   .)   Calved, April 12, 1884.

Sire, Lord Bantam, (1,011). For extension, see Alfric, No. 46.

Dam, Czarina. (1837.) Imported by us, she by the District bull of Westwoud.

G-dam, Klaartje. Czarina calved when about twenty-two months old and gave in three months and two days 2,683 lbs. 8 oz of milk when we sold her. She made when two years old 8 lbs. of butter in one week on winter feed. She is a very choice elegant cow and good milker, but we can give no further records, as her present owner has kept none of this cow.

No. 60.   BONANZA KING.   No. 066.

(H. H. B. Vol. 8, No. 3,123.) Calved April, 25, 1884.

Three-fourths black, large star and snip, white spot over shoulder, white over hips, small white spot on each foreleg, small black spot near belly right side, fore legs black to ankles. Hind legs black to below gambrels.

Sire, Netherland Marquis (2,484), Jacob (N. H. B. 215). imported by us, and he by Tol's Jacob.

Netherland Marquis' dam Tol, a large fine cow by Schreuder the sire of Netherland Queen. (414.) (See No. 104), and Netherland Duchess (2,498), (See No. 112.) She has a record of 68 2-5 lbs. in a day as a five-year-old.

Tol's Jacob's dam, a large fine cow with a record of 68 2-5 lbs. in a day.

Netherland Marquis was selected by a commission appointed by the Netherland Breeder's Association, out of fifty to go to the International Exhibition at Hamburgh as a representative of the breed.

Dam, Bonanza Maid (4,544), imported and she by the District bull of Oosterblokker.

G-dam, Klasina Hengeveld 2d.

G-g-dam, Klasina Hengeveld, (N. H. B. 656), gave 102 lbs. of milk in a day and 956 lbs. 8 oz. in ten consecutive days.

G-g-g-dam, a great milker.

Klasina Hengeveld is the dam of Albino, (See No. 162.)

Bonanza Maid has given this season as a two-year-old and the first year after importation 55 lbs. 14 oz. in one day and 5,557 lbs. 6 oz. in four months and twenty-eight days to September 26.

No. 61. ENSIGN. No. 060.

(H. H. B. Vol. 8, No. 3124.) Calved April 28, 1884. Mostly white. Ears, spots on neck and under throat black. One large and several small black spots on right side; one on right fore leg. Three black spots above left fore leg and four on left side.

Sire, Prince Imperial (1164.) See No. 5.

Dam, Topaz 3d (2106.) See No. 209.

G-dam, Topaz (870), imported. See No. 209.

G-g-dam, Matedor, (N. H. B. 263.) See No. 209.

No. 62. **AAGGIE PAULINE'S PRINCE.** No. 068.

(H. H. B. Vol. 8, No. 3,125.) Calved May 5th, 1884. Three-fourths black. Irregular white in face extending to throat. Black on lower jaw left side, white over hips to flanks and belly both sides. Long white spot on left shoulder. One large and two small black spots on right fore leg. Numerous small white and black spots on both sides.

Sire, Prince Imperial (1,164), (See No. 5.)

Dam, Aaggie Pauline, (2,623.) (See No. 185.) She by de Ruiter (N. H. B. 89.) For extension see Sir Henry 2d of Aaggie. No. 4.

G-dam, De Schot gave 68¼ lbs. of milk in a day.

No. 63.   BASIL.   No. 20.

(H H. B. Vol. 8, No. ——.) Calved May 8, 1884.

Sire, Lord Bantam, (1011.) For extension, see Alfric, No. 46.

Dam, Lady Helen, (No. 1829.) Imported by us; she by the District bull of Hoogcarspel.

G-dam Mina has given 69¼ lbs. in a day.

Lady Helen calved when two years old, soon after importation, and gave 29 lbs. 11 oz. in a day, and 546 lbs. 14 oz. in 18 days, when she was sold. Her present owner keeps no record, but considers her a good milker.

No 64.   NETHERLAND CHANCELLOR.   No. 052.

(H. H. B. Vol. 8, No. 2,940.) Calved May 9th, 1884. Three-fourths black. Right side of face black, spot around and one under left eye black, black spot on right fore leg, black over shoulders to left fore leg, one large and four small black spots on right side, two large black spots on left side.

Sire, Netherland Prince (716), (See No. 2.)

Dam, Aegis 4th, (1,276), (See No. 142), by Beaconsfield, (401), imported, he by Kees, (N. H. B. 32.)

G-dam, Aegis 2d, (235), (See No. 113) by Uncle Tom, (163), he by Rip Van Winkle, (35), imported in cow Fraulein, (9).

G-g-dam, Aegis (69), (See No. 96), by Rip Van Winkle (35), &c.

G-g-g-dam, Agoo (1), imported.

G-g-g-g, Dowager, (7), imported.

For extension and records see Aegis No. 96.

No. 65. AAGGIE CONSTANCE'S SIR HENRY. No 086.

(H. H. B. Vol. 8, No. 3,126.) Calved May 10, 1884. One-half black, strip in face. five large black spots on right side, one large and two small on left side, large one containing long white spot, small black spot on left fore leg.

Sire, Sir Henry of Aaggie (1,450.) Ruiter 2d (N. H. B. 189), he by de Ruiter (N. H. B. 89), he by Jacob 2d (N. H. B. 56), &c. For extension, see Sir Henry 2d of Aaggie No. 4.

Sir Henry of Aaggie's dam de Schot (N. H. B. 573), by Jacob 1st (N. H. B. 20), he by Rooker.

De Schot's dam Oude Schot 2d, by Rooker and grandam Oude Schot. DeSchot has a milk record of 76 lbs. in a day.

Dam Aaggie Constance (2,629.) (See No. 182), she by de-Ruiter (N. H. B. 89.) (See cut.) See chart of Sir Henry 2d of Aaggie.

G-dam, Kappijne gave, as a two-year-old, 41 1-6 lbs. of milk in one day.

Aaggie Constance has made the largest two-year-old record yet published, having given 76 lbs. 6 oz. in one day, and 6,392 lbs. 9 oz. in 4 months and 12 days to Sept. 26.

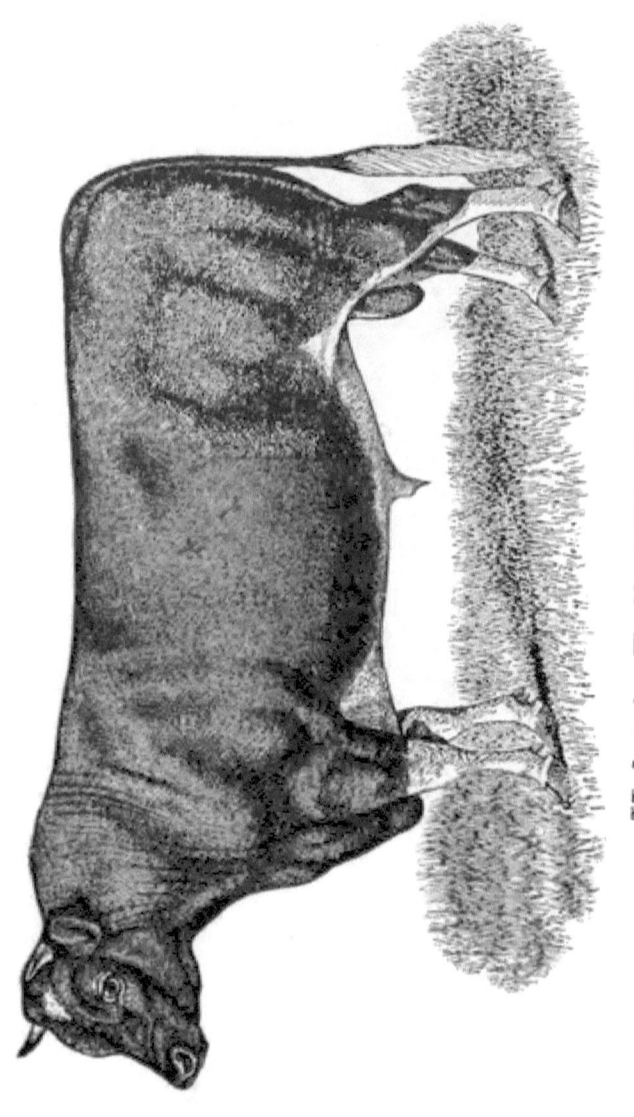

Holstein Bull, "Uncle Tom."

No. 66. NANTASKET. No. 093.

(H. H. B. Vol. 8, No. 3,088.) Calved May 28, 1884. Black with star, spot on shoulders, legs, from knees and gambrels, belly and three-quarters tail white.

Sire, Syracuse (822), he by Ebbo (236), imported in dam Iona (335.)

Syracuse's dam, Netherland Queen, 2d (560.) (See No. 126) by Uncle Tom (163), he by Rip Van Winkle (35), imported in cow Fraulein (9.)

Uncle Tom's dam, Topsey, (61), out of imported Dowager (7), by Hollander (20), imported.

Syracuse's grandam, Netherland Queen (414), by Schreuder. See No. 104.

G-g-dam, Lady Netherland (1,263.) See No. 99.

G-g-g-dam, Gert Met 2d, a beautiful cow that gave 71½ lbs. of milk in a day on grass alone.

G-g-g-g-dam, Gert Met, an elegant cow, that was kept twenty years for breeding.

Ebbo was a large, straight and very stylish bull, and winner of First Prizes as a two-year old at the New York State and Onondaga County Fairs in 1880.

His dam Iona, has a record of 12,033 lbs 8 oz in 346 days.

Netherland Queen 2d gave as a two-year-old 40 lbs. 4 oz. in one day, and 1,102 lbs. 7 oz. in one month. As a three-year-old she gave 49 lbs, 4 oz. in one day, 1,307 lbs. 11 oz. in one month, and 10,471 lbs. 15 oz. in eleven months. She has given this season 3,670 lbs. 4 oz. in two months and one day to Sept. 26th. She was awarded First Prize at Onondaga County Fair in 1879.

Netherland Queen, the Grandam of Syracuse, made the

following remarkable two-year-old record, viz: 58 lbs. 12 oz. in one day, 1,670 lbs. 9 oz. in one month, and 13,574 lbs. 3 oz. in one year. As a four-year-old she gave 76 lbs. in one day, 2,132 lbs. 6 oz. in one month, and 15,614 lbs. 9 oz. in one year.

As a five-year-old she gave 83 lbs. 4 oz. in one day, 2,235 lbs. 4 oz. in one month, and in seven months and eighteen days, 10,046 lbs. 8 oz. of milk. She made in Nov. 20 lbs. of butter in one week.

Netherland Queen took First Premium as yearling heifer at New York State Fair 1878; also First Prize as a two-year-old, in 1879, at both State and Onondaga County Fairs; also Second Prize at New York State Fair, 1880, when three years old, in class with mature cows; gained First Prize at New York State Fair in 1881, also at Onondaga County Fair same year; Second at New York State Fair in 1882 and 1884, and was four different years one of the herd that won the Gold Medal.

Lady Netherland gave with her first calf at two years old 50 lbs. of milk in one day, and at four years old 73¾ lbs. in one day. She has given in five months and five days 6,130 lbs. 11 oz. milk.

She won Second Prize as best milch cow of any breed at New York State Fair in 1882 (Aaggie of same herd winning First Prize), and was one of the herd that won the Gold Medal.

Lady Netherland's dam gave 71 lbs. 8 oz. of milk in one day.

Rip Van Winkle is the sire of Echo (121), which has a record of 18,120 lbs. 8 oz. in one year, and gave in the following year, 23,775 lbs. 8 oz. Of Aegis (69), See No. 96, which has a record for a year, of 16,823 lbs. 10 oz.

Fraulein (9) has a record of 70 lbs. in one day, and 1,873 lbs. in one month.

Topsey gave 40 lbs. 8 oz, of milk in one day when less than two years old. In the season of 1879 she gave as high as 70 lbs. in one day, 64 lbs. per day for 30 consecutive days, and 6,005 lbs. in five months.

Dowager has a record of 12,681 lbs. 8 oz. of milk in one year.

Uncle Tom, the G-grandsire of Nantasket on the sire's side, and grandsire on the dam's side, has been awarded the First Prize at the New York State and Onondaga County Fairs for four consecutive years and has never been beaten in the show ring.

Syracuse weighed when three years old 2,250 lbs.

Dam, Jannek 3d (1,458), by Uncle Tom, (163), he by Rip Van Winkle (35), &c., as given above.

G-dam, Jannek, (871), (N. H. B. 151), imported by us. She made a record in Holland of 78 lbs. in one day, and in August, 1879, nearly six months after calving, and just before importation, one of our firm saw her milk 62 lbs. 12 oz. in a day. Although not fully acclimated, she gave in 1880, 71 lbs. 12 oz. in one day, 2,110 lbs. 8 oz. in one month, 9,250 lbs. in six months, and 13,015 lbs. 15 oz. in one year. In 1881 she gave 75 lbs. in one day, 2,132 lbs. 3 oz. in one month, and 11,980 lbs, 3 oz. in nine months and fourteen days. In the nine months and twenty days, ending Jan 31st, 1882, she gave 12,028 lbs. 4 oz of milk. In 1880, when giving 48 lbs of milk in a day, she made 2 lbs. 2½ oz of butter per day. In 1881, she made 19 lbs. 15 oz. of butter in seven days, and 28 lb. 6½ oz. in ten days.

No. 67.   SEYMOUR.   No. 21.

(H. H. B. Vol. , No.   .) Calved May 28, 1884. Star, body black, left fore leg black to knee, right fore leg black to ankle, hind legs black to hocks.

Sire, Lord Bantam (1,011.) See Alfric, No. 46.

Dam, Daisy Seymour (2,693), imported by us. Her owner has kept no record. She is a fine handsome heifer and will make a good milker.

Daisy Seymour's sire, District bull of Hoogcarspel.

G-dam, Pol has a five-year-old record of 68 2-5 lbs. in one day.

No. 68.   AAGGIE ROSA 2d's EMPEROR.   No. 061.

(H. H. B. Vol. 8, No. 3,127.) Calved June 5th, 1884. Three-quarters white, black cheeks and neck, large black spot on each side, and other black spots on left side.

Sire, Prince Imperial (1,164.) See No. 5.

Dam, Aaggie Rosa 2d (2,610.) (See No. 139), has given, as a three-year-old, the first season after importation, 7,030 lbs. 5 oz. in nine months and nineteen days, and, as a four-year-old, 65 lbs. 4 oz. in one day. 5,367 lbs. 5 oz. in three months and fifteen days to Sept. 26th.

G-dam, Aaggie Rosa (2,605.) (See No. 107.) See chart of Sir Henry 2d of Aaggie, and milk records of the Aaggie family. Page 22. She gave as a five-year-old in Holland 91 lbs. in one day. She gave last season, the first after importation, 68 lbs. 8 oz. in one day, 1,920 lbs. 3 oz. in one month, and 16,156 lbs. 10 oz. in one year, and this season 70 lbs. in one day, and 4,637 lbs. 8 oz in 2 months and 18 days to Sept. 26th.

G-g-dam, Jansje (N. H. B. 88), has a milk record of 68 lbs. in a day on grass, and took First Prize at Zaandam, two First Prizes at Amsterdam, and Silver Medal at Rotterdam. Weight of dressed beef was 1,150 lbs.

G-g-g-dam, Oude Jansje.

Aaggie Rosa 2d's sire, Jacob 2d (N. H. B. 56.)

Aaggie Rosa's sire, Jacob I, (N. H. B. 20.)
Jansje's sire, Rooker.

No. 69.   MEADOW LILY'S PRINCE.   No. 056.

(H. H. B. Vol. 8, No. 3,128.) Calved June 10th, 1884. Three-fourths black, large star, snip, white over shoulders and hips, black on outside fore legs nearly to ankles.

Sire, Netherland Prince (716), (See No. 2,) also records of the Netherland family, page 27, he by Schreuder.

Dam, Meadow Lily came in before she was two years old, and gave 41 lbs. 2 oz. in one day, 1,174 lbs. 14 oz. in one month, and 7,233 lbs. 10 oz. in ten months and eleven days. As a three-year-old she has given 53 lbs. 8 oz. of milk in one day, 1,470 lbs. 8 oz. in one month, 6,705 lbs. in six months, 9,238 lbs. 2 oz. in ten months and eight days. She made in one week on winter feed 12 lbs. 10 oz. of butter. As a five-year-old, and having lost one-half of her udder, she has given 2,549 lbs. 5 oz. in one month, twenty-eight days, to Sept. 26th. But for her misfortune she would doubtless have made one of our deepest milkers.

Grandam, Dirk Jonges.

Meadow Lily's sire Schemmel, is sire of N. Prince, N. Princess, etc.

The unusually high breeding of this calf should be observed, and that, with his fine form will make him very valuable as a sire. He is twin brother to Meadow Lily 4th, No. 431.

No. 70.   AAGGIE JOSIE'S MARQUIS.   No. 042.

(H. H. B. Vol. 8, No. 8,129.) Calved June 20th, 1884. Three-fourths white, strip in face, broad white over shoulders to belly left side, broad white over hips to flanks and belly both sides, black at rump.

Sire, Netherland Marquis (2,484), imported by us, he by Tol's Jacob.

Netherland Marquis' dam Tol, has a five-year-old record of 68 2-5 lbs. of milk in one day. Tol by Schreuder, the sire of Netherland Queen (414), and Netherland Duchess (2,498). See records of the Netherland family, page 27.

Tol's Jacob's dam is a fine large cow with a record of 68 2-5 lbs. of milk in one day.

Dam, Aaggie Josie (4,367), imported by us, and has given this season as a two-year-old 46 lbs. 6 oz. in one day, and 3,380 lbs. 6 oz. in three months and two days, to Sept 26th.

Grandam, Meerhof, gave 68 2-5 lbs. in one day.

Aaggie Josie's sire Lincoln (N. H. B. 120), by Jacob 2d (N. H. B. 56), etc. (For extension, see Clovis No. 13, also milk records of the Aaggie family, page 22.

No. 71.   **CAPTOLA.**   **No. 092.**

(H. H. B. Vol. 8, No. 3,375.) Calved June 23, 1884. Four-fifths black, star, large white spot on right shoulder, small white spot at root of tail, fore legs black to ankles, left gambrel black.

Sire, Kenmore (1,174) imported by us. See Philosopher, No. 57.

Dam, Elsie Wood (2,709), imported by us. She is a fine young cow, but her owner keeps no records.

Elsie Wood's sire, Koster's bull.

G-dam, Mietje, has a five-year-old record of 68 2-5 lbs of milk in a day.

No. 72.   **AAGGIE ROSA'S PRINCE.**   No. 081.

(H. H. B. Vol. 8, No. 3,132.) Calved July 7th, 1884. Three-fourths white, cheeks and sides of neck black, large black spot on each side containing small white spots, smaller black spots on each side.

Sire, Netherland Prince (716), (See No. 2), also records of the Netherland family, page 27, he by Schemmel and he by Schreuder.

Dam, Aaggie Rosa, (2,605.) (See No. 107.) See chart of Sir Henry 2d of Aaggie, also milk records of the Aaggie family, page 22. She has given as a five-year-old in Holland 91 lbs. in a day. She gave, the first season, after importation, 68 lbs. 8 oz. in one day, 1,920 lbs. 3 oz. in one month and 16,156 lbs. 10 oz. in one year, and this season has given 4,637 lbs. 8 oz. in two months and eighteen days to Sept. 26th.

G-dam, Jansje, (N. H. B. 88.) Milk record, 68 lbs. in a day on grass. Jansje took First Prize at Zaandam, Two First Prizes at Amsterdam, and Silver Medal at Rotterdam. Beef weight dressed was 1,150 lbs.

G-g-dam, Oude Jansje.

Aaggie Rosa's sire, Jacob I, (N. H. B. 20), by Rooker.

Jansje's sire, Rooker. This calf, it will be observed, is half brother to Prince Imperial and to Sir Henry 2d of Aaggie, a combination of blood we think that cannot fail to give him a high rank among milk and butter bulls.

No. 73.   **NETHERLAND DEPUTY.**   No. 083.

(H. H. B. Vol. 8, No. 3,133.) Calved July 7th, 1884. Three-quarters white, ears and spots around eyes black, irregular black over neck, large black spot on left side, other small black spots on both sides and at rump.

Sire, Netherland Prince (716). (See No. 2), also records of the Netherland family, Page 27, he by Schemmel, and he by Schreuder.

Dam, Netherland Baroness (2,635), gave 73¼ lbs. in a day as a five-year-old. (See No. 103.) She gave the first season after importation and before she was fully acclimated, 72 lbs. in one day, 1,908 lbs. 4 oz. in one month and 10,249 lbs. 7 oz. in ten months, and made in one week 17 lbs. 5 oz. of butter; and this season has given 72 lbs. 11 oz in one day, 4,134 lbs. 4 oz. in 2 months and 15 days to Sept. 26th.

G-dam, Gert Met 3d, has a record of over 68 lbs. of milk in one day from three teats. She is sister to the dam of Lady Netherland (1,263.) (See No. 99), who is dam of Netherland Prince, Netherland Queen, Netherland Princess, etc.

G-g-dam, Gert Met, a very fine cow and heavy milker. Was kept twenty years for breeding.

Netherland Baroness' sire District bull of Beemster.

This elegant calf, strongly backed by Netherland blood on both sides, cannot fail to impart to his progeny the prominent characteristics of the Netherland family, which are fully set forth on Page 27.

No. 74.   NAUGATUCK.   No. 24.

(H. H. B Vol.   No.   .) Calved July 12th, 1884. Body black except three white spots on shoulders, and one between hips, belly white.

Sire, Lord Bantam (1,011.) For extension see Alfric No. 46.

Dam, Lady Motley, (2,763), imported by us, a fine heifer and good milker, but owner has kept no record.

G-dam, Mina has a record of 73 1-5 lbs, of milk in a day.

Lady Motley's sire, District bull of Beemster.

No. 75.   **AAGGIE HANNAH'S PRINCE.**   No. 067.

(H. H. B. Vol. 8, No. 3,277.) Calved July 30th, 1884. Mostly white, two small black spots over left eye, large black spot on right side of neck, numerous small black spots scattered over body on both sides.

Sire, Netherland Prince (716), (See No. 2), also records of the Netherland family, page 27, he by Schemmel and he by Schreuder, the sire of Netherland Queen, (414.) See No. 104.

Dam, Aaggie Hannah (4,361.) (See No. 130.) She has a record as a four-year-old, made this, the first season after importation, of 71 lbs. 15 oz. in one day, and 3,338 lbs. 10 oz. in one month and twenty-five days to Sept. 26th.

G-dam, Stippeld Naatje has a record of 68 2 5 lbs. in a day.

Aaggie Hannah's sire Jacob 2d, (N. H. B. 56), he by Jacob, (N. H. B. 20), he by Rooker. See chart of Sir Henry 2d of Aaggie, and milk records of the Aaggie family, page 22.

No. 76.   **NETHERLAND CARL.**

(H. H. B. Vol. 8, Vol. 3,279.) Calved August 4th, 1884. Four-fifths white, small black spot in middle of forehead, ears black, three small black spots on right side of face, black around left eye, large black spot on each side, each containing small white spot, black at rump.

Sire, Netherland Prince (716.) (See No. 2), also records of Netherland family, page 27, he by Schemmel, and he by Schreuder, the sire of Netherland Queen (414.) See No. 104.

Dam, Carlotta (1,266.) See No. 119.

This calf is full brother to Prince Imperial (1,164.) See No. 5.

For form, finish and size we think he will equal his brother, who is regarded as one of the finest bulls of this breed, and whose get are remarkable for their fine form, beauty and vigor.

No. 77.   NETHERLAND STATESMAN   No. 095.

(H. H. B. Vol. 8, No. 3,280.) Calved Aug. 15th, 1884. Three-quarters white, black around left eye, black spot under right eye, large irregular black over neck and on each side, numerous black spots scattered over body.

Sire, Netherland Prince (716.) (See No. 2), also records of the Netherland family, (page 27), he by Schemmel and he by Schreuder, the sire of Netherland Queen (414.) See No. 104.

Dam, Lady Fay (4,470), Marie (N. H. B. 1,061), imported, see No. 124.

She is one of the finest specimens of a Holstein milch cow we have ever seen. Her record in Holland was 84½ lbs of milk in a day. She has given this, the first season after importation and before being fully acclimated, 80 lbs. 4 oz. in one day, and 2,326 lbs in one month and eight days to Sept. 26th ; and, had she not been taken to the State Fair at a time when she should have given her greatest flow of milk, she undoubtedly would have made a much larger record.

No. 78.   DERMOT S.   No. 101.

(H. H. B. Vol. , No. ——.) Calved Sept. 18th, 1883. Star, white over shoulders, belly, legs and switch white.

Sire, Crown Prince 3d (625), he by Crown Prince (80), he by Rip Van Winkle (35), imported in cow Fraulein (9).

Crown Prince 3d's dam Ella (122), in 1878, when seven years old, gave 10,850 lbs. during the season.

Crown Prince's dam, Crown Princess (1), imported, gave in one year 14,027 lbs. She is the dam of Echo, with a record of 18,120 lbs. 8 oz. in one year, followed the succeeding year by a record of 23,775 lbs. 8 oz.

Rip Van Winkle's dam Fraulein, gave 70 lbs. in one day, and 1,837 lbs. in one month. Rip Van Winkle is the sire of Echo, (See above), Aegis, with a record of 16,823 lbs. 10 oz. in one year and other noted milkers.

Dam, Katinka 2d (491), has given 53 lbs. in one day, 1,414 lbs. in thirty days.

Grandam, Katinka (350), imported. She gave when five years old 10,843 lbs. in 359 days, when six years old, 11,220 lbs. in 330 days, and the following year 12,116 lbs. in eight months and three days.

Katinka 2d's sire Motley (126), he by Sheridan (153), he by Prince of Orange (137), imported.

Motley's dam Victoria (226), by Vandyke (165), imported.

Sheridan's dam Maid of Zuid (183), imported.

Victoria's dam Roseille (211), imported.

| No. 79. | **DEMETRIUS S.** | No. 102. |

(H. H. B. Vol.   No.   .) Calved Oct. 2d, 1883. Star, white strip on left shoulder, white belly, legs and switch.

Sire, Bobbie (928.) For extension see Donatus S. No. 80.

Dam, Isis 2d. (337), gave as a two-year-old 34 lbs. 7 oz. in one day, 931 lbs. 14 oz. in one month, 9,114 lbs. 12 oz. in one year, under very unfavorable circumstances. The following year she was sold and we have no further records, but she should make a very deep milker.

G-dam, Isis (148), a full sister to Uncle Tom (163.) For extension see pedigree of Netherland King, No 15.

Isis 2d's sire Uncle Tom (163.)

| No. 80. | **DONATUS S.** | No. 103. |

(H. H. B. Vol. 8 No.   .) Calved Oct. 25th, 1883. Black cheeks, black strip down sides of neck, white face, jaws and throat, white strip across the shoulders, white rump, belly, legs and switch.

Sire, Bobbie (928), he by Iagoo (270), he by Oneida Chief (306), he by Kurt (120), imported.

Bobbie's dam, Katinka 2d, (491), by Motley (126), he by Sheridan (153), he by Prince of Orange (137), imported.

Katinka 2d's dam, Katinka (350), imported. She gave when five years old 10,843 lbs. in 359 days, when six years old 11,220 lbs. in 330 days, and the following year 12,116 lbs. in eight months and three days.

Motley's dam, Victoria (226) by Van Dyke (165), imported.

Victoria's dam, Roseile (211), imported.

Sheridan's dam, Maid of Zuid (183), imported.

Iagoo's dam, Opperdoes 16th (44), out of Maid of Opperdoes (22), by Van Tromp (50), both imported.

Oneida Chief's dam, Ella (122), imported.

Dam, Agostina (501), imported.

Opperdoes 16th (44), gave 70 lbs. in one day on grass alone.

Opperdoes 17th (198), daughter of Opperdoes 16th, gave as a four-year-old, 10,254 lbs. of milk in one year. She has given 69 lbs. 8 oz. in one day, and an average of 66 lbs. per day for a whole month.

Ella (122) gave at seven years old 10,850 lbs. in one year.

Agostina has a record of 43 lbs. in one day, and 1,224 lbs. in thirty days.

No. 81.	DUGALD S.	No. 105.

(H. H. B. Vol. 8, No.   ,) Calved Nov. 29th, 1883. Star, white spot on right shoulder and white spot on left hip, white legs, belly and switch.

Sire, Bobbie (928). For extension, see Donatus S., No. 80.

Dam, Abby (586), imported.

G-dam, a fine cow, with a record of 68 2-5 lbs. in a day. Abby gave as a two-year-old 40 lbs. in a day.

No. 82.   DUNSTAN S.   No. 106.

(H. H. B. Vol. 8, No.   .) Calved Dec 26th, 1883. White band across shoulders, white dash on hips, white belly, legs and switch.

Sire, Bobbie (928). For extension, see Donatus S., No. 80.

Dam, Amanda Gwynedd (1,669), has a record of 54 lbs. in one day, and 1,516 lbs. in 30 days as a four-year-old.

No. 83.   DOMINGO S.   No. 107.

(H. H. B. Vol. 8, No.   .) Calved Dec. 30th, 1883. Small star, small white spot on right hip, white belly, legs and switch.

Sire, Crown Prince 3d (625). For extension, see Dermot S., No. 78.

Dam, Pride of Beemster (424), imported by us; she by David, a fine District bull.

G-dam, a large, handsome cow, with a milk record of 65 lbs. in a day.

Pride of Beemster made a record in 1880 as a four-year-old of 55 lbs. 4 oz. in one day, 1,537 lbs. 7 oz. in one month, and 12,759 lbs. 3 oz. in eleven months and twelve days. Since we sold her we have had no record of her milking.

No. 84.   EDGAR S.   No. 108.

(H. H. B. Vol. 8, No.   .) Calved Jan. 7th, 1884. Small star, small white spot on top of right shoulder, white belly, legs and switch.

Sire, Bobbie (928.) For extension, see Donatus S. No. 80.

Dam, Amie (1,075), by Heike (266) imported in dam Hannah (323). Hannah gave when three years old, the first season after importation, 7,891 lbs. in one year.

Amie's dam, Agostina (501), imported, has a record of 43 lbs. in one day, and 1,224 lbs. in thirty days.

No. 85.   EDMUND S.   No. 109.

(H. H. B. Vol. 8, No.   .) Calved Feb. 6th, 1884. Small star, white belly, legs and switch.

Sire, Bobbie (928). For extension, see Donatus S., No. 80.

Dam, Rarity (865), imported by us.

G-dam, Number 43 (N. H. B. 47), has a record of 65 lbs. of milk in a day.

Rarity was awarded First Prize at New York State Fair in 1879.

She has given 49 lbs. of milk in one day, and 1,273 lbs. in thirty days.

No. 86.   EDWARD S.   No. 110.

(H. H. B. Vol. 8, No. ——.) Calved Feb 10, 1884. Star, white band on right hind hip and flank. White belly, legs and switch.

Sire, Bobbie (928). For extension see Donatus S. No. 80.

Dam, Gretje 2d (516), imported, has a record of 58 lbs. in one day, and 1,667 lbs in thirty days.

No. 87.   EDWIN S.   No. 112.

(H. H. B. Vol. 8, No. ——.) Calved March 8, 1884. Star, white spot on right hip, small dash on right shoulder, white belly, legs and switch.

Sire, Bobbie (928). For extension see Donatus S. No. 80.

Dam, Josephine S. (3,053), by Iagoo (270), &c. For extension see pedigree of Donatus No. 80.

G-dam, Jenny (340), by Roland (144), imported.

G-g-dam, Dora (117), by Van Tromp 2d (52), by Van Tromp (50), imported in dam Texelaar (51).

G-g-g-dam, Maid of Opperdoes (22), imported.

Van Tromp 2d's dam Texelaar 3d (52), by 2d Dutchman (37), he by Dutchman (7), imported.

2d Dutchman's dam, Lady Rutten (19), imported

Texelaar 3d's dam, Texelaar (51), imported, has a record of 76 lbs. 5 oz. in one day.

No. 88.   ELDRED S.   No. 114.

(H. H. B. Vol. 8, No. ——.) Calved March 23, 1884. Black head and neck, white shoulders, black saddle, black on left hip.

Sire, Bristol (927), he by Aurora (180), he by Holland Prince (113), imported in dam Holland Queen (144).

Aurora's dam, Gentle Annie (135), by Elswout (94), out of Jufrou (153), both imported.

Gentle Annie averaged for six consecutive years commencing at two years old, 9,366 lbs. 7 oz. and her dam Jufrou averaged for six consecutive years 11,467 lbs. 6 oz. per year.

Dam, Ancie (1,568), by Iagoo (270). For extension see Donatus S. No. 80.

Grandam, Tinaj (512), imported, has a record of 1,220 lbs. in one month.

Ancie has a record of 1,064 lbs. in one month.

No. 89. NETTY'S ARMAND.

(H. H. B. Vol. 8, No. ——.) Calved Feb. 12, 1884. Star, strip over right shoulder, and one over right hip. Left leg black to ankle. Legs and switch white..

Sire, Armand (861), imported in dam Elegans (1,270).

Elegans' sire was Alexander, and dam Siempje (835), imported, which has a two year old record of 45 4-5 lbs. in one day.

She is an unusually fine and handsome cow, and her owner says is a very deep milker.

Dam, Netty (850), imported, has a record of $28\tfrac{1}{2}$ quarts of milk in one day.

Netty's sire, Hendrik.

G-dam, Mooije.

G-g-dam, Pietje, (N. H. B. 192).

G-g-g-dam, Trijntje, (N. H. B. 127).

No. 90. SIR WILLIAM OF AAGGIE'S WARREN.

(H. H. B. Vol. 8, No. ——.) Calved Feb. 12, 1884 Large star, snip, narrow white strip over shoulders, wide strip over hips.

Sire, Sir William of Aaggie (1,455), he by DeRuiter (N. H. B. 89). See cut and chart. For extension, see Sir Henry 2d of Aaggie (1,451) No. 4.

Sir William of Aaggie's dam, Cornelia, a fine, large cow, has a record of 77 4-5 lbs. in one day.

Dam, Sabrina (2,883), imported, she by Koning (N. H. B. 128), he by Willem (N. H. B. 65).

Koning's dam, Koningen (236), she by Wouter (N. H. B. 4).

No. 91.   NAOMI.

(H. H. B. Vol. 8, No. ——.) Calved Feb. 29, 1884. Star. Strip on shoulder down left side. Strip on hip and down right flank. Legs and switch white.

Sire, Armand (861). For extension, see Netty's Armand, No. 89.

Dam, Susie (1,254), imported by us and sold when a yearling.

Susie's sire, deHeer.

Grandam, deZwart, a large fine cow, which has given 57 1-5 lbs. of milk in one day.

Susie has given as a four-year-old 28½ quarts of milk in one day.

No. 92.   ·   VERONA.

(H. H. B. Vol. 5, 1884.) Large star, snip, black spots on right side, left side mostly black, neck and left shoulder black, black spot on left hip.

Sire, Sir Henry 2d of Aaggie (1,451). (See No. 4). See cut and chart.

Dam, Bountiful Maid (4,411), imported by us; she by Feereman's bull.

G-dam, Zwartsnuit, gave as a four-year-old 68 2-5 lbs. of milk in a day.

Bountiful Maid has given as a two-year-old, the first season after importation, 36 lbs. in a day.

No. 93.   BRUYN.

(H. H. B. Vol. 8, No. ——.) Calved March 7, 1884. Star, snip, strip over right shoulder. Two strips down left shoulder, wide strip over hips, small spot on left side.

Sire, Armand (861). For extension, see Netty's Armand, No. 89.

Dam, Brunette (1,251), imported by us.

Brunette's sire was Cornelius.

Cornelius' dam, Trijn, a large, fine cow, which has a record of 82¼ lbs. in a day.

G-dam, Langedijke, a fine two-year old heifer with a record of 36 4-7 lbs. in a day.

Brunette has given as a four-year-old 25 quarts per day.

No. 94.   IRA.

(H. H. B. Vol. 8, No ——.) Calved May 4, 1884. Star, snip, wide strip over hips, narrow strip on right shoulder, wide strip on left shoulder, black spot on belly.

Sire, Armand (861). For extension, see Netty's Armand, No. 89.

Dam, Irene (1,260), imported by us.

Irene's sire, Oostveen.

G-dam, Tiger, has a record of 68 2-5 lbs. of milk in a day.

Irene has given as a four-year-old 24 quarts in a day.

No. 95.   LOLA'S GIFT.

(H. H. B. Vol. 8, No. ——.) Calved April 25th, 1884.

Sire, Prince Imperial (1,162). See No. 5.

Dam, Lola (2,789), imported by us.

Lola's sire deValk (N. H. B. 160). Prize bull at Leyden.

Grandam, Bestegiver has a record of 80 1-6 lbs. of milk in one day.

Lola has given as a two-year-old 40 lbs. 6 oz. in one day, 996 lbs. 9 oz. in one month, and made in one week 8 lbs. of unsalted butter.

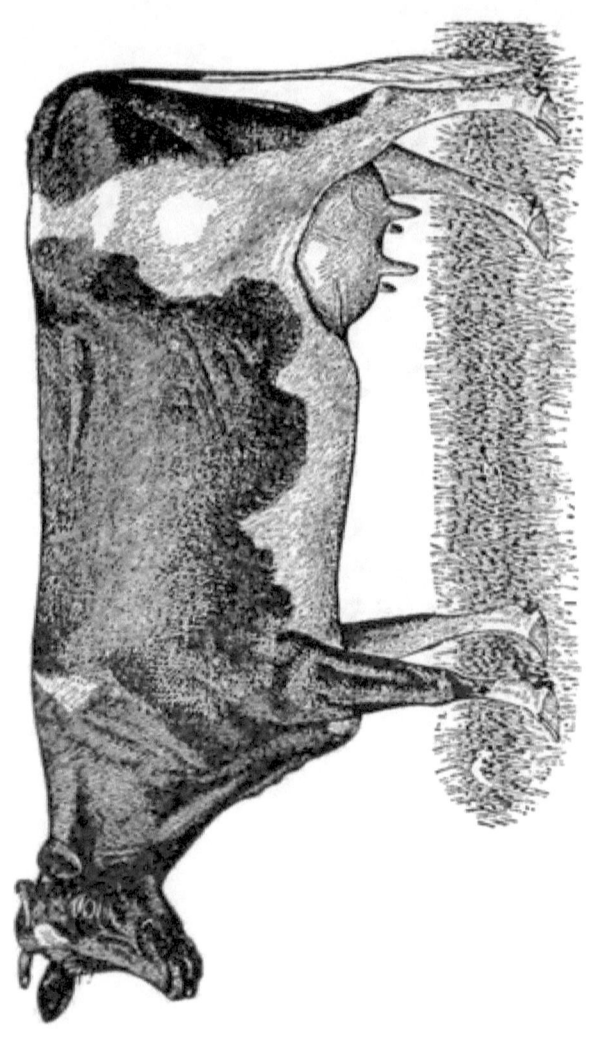

Holstein Cow. "Ægis." (No. 96.)

Cows and Heifers.

In the following pedigrees we give the milk records of our cows for this season from one month to one year as far as we have them, according to the time each has been milked up to date. Most of them are still milking, the year's record not being complete.

No. 96.   Ægis.   No. 5.

(See Cut.)

(H. H. B. Vol. 2, No. 69.) Calved October 2d, 1873.

Sire, Rip Van Winkle (35), imported in cow Fraulein (9). She has a record of 70 lbs. of milk in a day, and 1,873 lbs. in a month.

Dam, Agoo (1), imported in cow Dowager (7). Agoo weighed when three years old 1,530 lbs.

Dowager has a record of 12,681 lbs. 8 oz. in one year, and is dam of Milk Maid (194), which has given 14,700 lbs. in a year; also dam of Topsey (dam of Uncle Tom, 163), who gave 70 lbs. in one day, 64 lbs. for 30 consecutive days and 6,005 lbs. in 5 months.

Ægis gave at six years of age 82 lbs. 12 oz. of milk in one day, 2,289 lbs. 9 oz. in one month, and 10,904 lbs. 5 oz. in six months, and 16,823 lbs. 10 oz. in one year. She gave in eight and one-half months, commencing Nov. 16th, 1881, and milking through the winter, 13,493 lbs. 12 oz. Commencing Nov. 8th, 1882, she gave 77 lbs. 15 oz. in one day, 2,226 lbs. 11 oz.

in thirty days, and 11,486 lbs. 14 oz. in eight months. In Nov., 1882, she made 18 lbs 2 oz. of butter in one week. Commencing in January, she has given in 8 months and 1 day to Sept. 26th, 12,052 lbs. 1 oz.

Ægis is dam of Ægis II. (235). (See No. 113), who gave as a two-year old 9,612 lbs. 5 oz. in one year; as a three-year-old 10,897 lbs. 12 oz. in nine and one-half months; as a four-year old 14,596 lbs. 11 oz. in one year, and this season she has given 10,499 lbs. 9 oz. in eight months and two days, to Sept. 26th, 15 lbs. 8 oz. of butter were made from one week's milk. Ægis is also dam of Ægis 6th, which has given as a two-year-old 8,927 lbs. 12 oz. in 9 months and 12 days, to Sept. 26th.

Echo, a half sister to Ægis, has a record of 18,120 lbs. 8 oz. in one year, and gave in the following year 23,775 lbs. 8 oz.

Ægis was one of the herd that took First Prize at Onondaga County Fair, 1878. She won First Prize at New York State Fair, 1879; was also one of the herd that was awarded the Gold Medal; was also awarded Second Prize (being beaten by Netherland Queen No. 104, one of the same herd) in 1881, and was one of the herd that gained the Gold Medal at New York State Fair in 1881, 1882, 1883 and 1884; also won First Prize at same Fair. Weight 1,811 lbs. Ægis 7th, her calf, dropped in 1881, when six months old, was sold for $1,000.

No. 97. NETHERLAND DOWAGER. No. 343.

(See Cut.)

(H. H. B. Vol. 6, No. 2,632.) Calved March, 1874. Imported by us, September, 1882.

Sire, District bull of Beemster.

Dam, Oude Schemmel, has a record of over 80 lbs. of milk in one day.

Netherland Dowager gave in Holland, just before importation, 91 pounds of milk in one day. She gave the first season

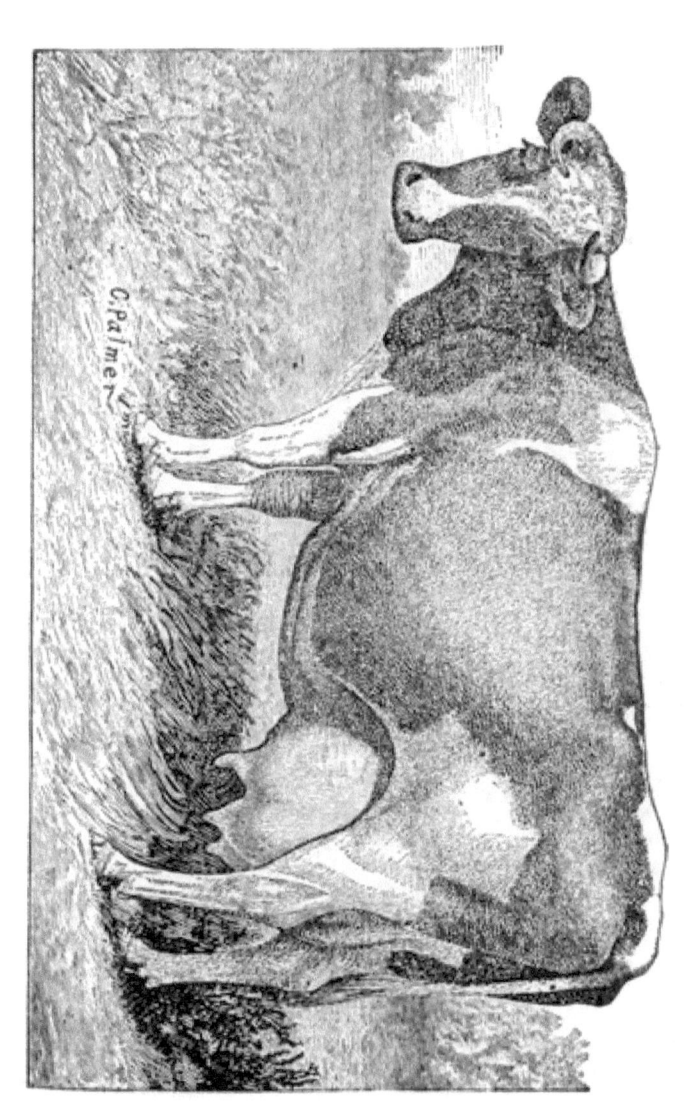

Imported Holstein Cow, "Netherland Dowager," (No. 97.)

after importation, 12,734 lbs. 2 oz. in one year, and this season has given 73 lbs. 11 oz. in one day, and 4,548 lbs. 12 oz. in two months and sixteen days. to Sept. 26th.

Netherland Dowager is dam of Netherland Dowager II (2,633), see No. 153, Netherland Dowager 3d, (3,484), which we sold for $1,000; also Netherland Gem, which gave as a two-year-old 7,695 lbs. 11 oz. in eight months and twenty days, when we sold her for $1,000.

No. 98.   AAGGIE.   No. 60.

(See Cut.)

(H. H. B. Vol. 4, No. 901.) (N. H. B. No. 148.) Calved April 1st, 1874. Imported by us September, 1879.

Sire, Rooker. See chart of Sir Henry 2d of Aaggie, and milk records of Aaggie family, page 22.

Dam, Oude Aaggie, with a record of 76 lbs. of milk in one day.

Aaggie gave in 1880, although not fully acclimated, 84 lbs. 12 oz. in one day, 2,362 lbs. 2 oz. in one month, and 8,231 lbs. 1 oz. in four months, 10,692 lbs. 6 oz. in six months, and 18,004 lbs. 15 oz. in one year. She made, after the best of the season had passed, 2 lbs. 8½ oz. butter per day. After closing above record she dropped a pair of twins in July and made a record of 15,709 lbs. 10 oz. in one year. This we consider, under the circumstances, fully as remarkable as her former record. It is worthy of note that when making her first record she was carrying a pair of twins.

Aaggie won First Prize as best milch cow of any breed, at the New York State Fair in 1882, and was one of the herd that won the Gold Medal.

Aaggie 2d, her calf, gave in the season of 1882 as a two-year-old, 61 lbs. 5 oz. of milk in one day, 1,700 lbs. 2 oz. in thirty consecutive days, and 17,746 lbs. 2 oz. in one year, and made 13 lbs. 6 oz. of butter in one week on dry feed when three and a half months in milk. This is the largest two-year-old record ever made.

Aaggie is the dam of our celebrated bull Neptune (711). See No. 1.

No. 99.   LADY NETHERLAND.

(H. H. B. Vol. 5, No. 1,263.) Calved March 10th, 1875. Imported in 1880. Lady Netherland gave with her first calf at two years old 50 lbs. of milk in a day, and at four years old 73⅔ lbs. in a day. She has given in five months and five days 6,130 lbs. 11 oz. of milk.

Dam of Lady Netherland was Gert Met 2d, which had a record of 71 lbs. 8 oz. in one day, and her grandam was Gert Met, a very fine cow and heavy milker, which was kept twenty years for breeding.

Lady Netherland is dam of Netherland Queen, No 104, Netherland Prince, No. 2, and Netherland Princess, No. 123.

Lady Netherland won Second Prize as best milch cow of any breed at New York State Fair, 1882 (Aaggie of same herd winning First Prize), and was one of the herd that won the Gold Medal.

No. 100.   DREAM OF HOLLAND.   No. 336.

(H. H. B. Vol. 6, No. 2,703.) Calved March 15, 1876. Imported by us Sept., 1882. Four-fifths black, star.

Sire, Wassenaer's bull.

Dam., Anna.

Dream of Holland gave just before importation, on fine grass feed exclusively 77 4-5 lbs. of milk in a day. She has given this season 11,820 lbs. 14 oz. in 10 months and 25 days to Sept. 26th.

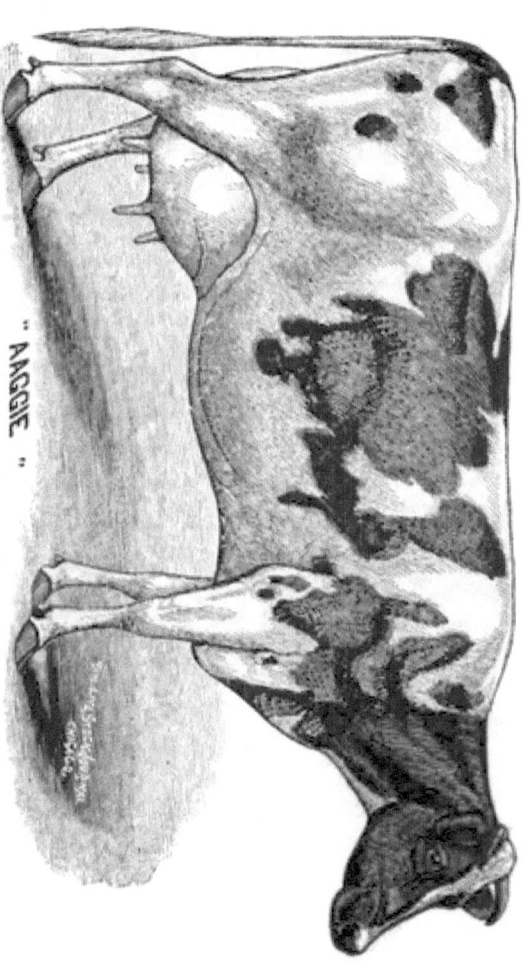

Imported Holstein Cow, "Aaggie." (No. 98.)

"AAGGIE."
MILK RECORD 16004 LBS. 15 OZ. IN ONE YEAR.

No. 101.　　　　　**LAMBERTINA.**　　　　　No. 770.

Lamberta (N. H. B. 576).

(H. H. B. Vol. 8, No. 6,889.) Calved March 15th, 1876. Imported by us May, 1884. One-half black, strip in face, large black saddle over back containing white spot on left side and three small white ones on right side, large black spot over left flank.

Sire, Rooker sire of Aaggie, (901), See No. 98 and milk records of Aaggie family, page 22.

Dam, Lamberta, a very choice cow.

Lambertina gave in Holland 68 2-5 lbs. of milk in a day. She is dam of Amy Alexander (4,328), Bettie Alexander (4,403), and Rothesay (3,302), See No. 53.

No. 102.　　　　　**AAGGIE CORNELIA.**　　　　　No. 610.

(H. H. B. Vol. 7, No. 4,410.) Calved March, 1877. Imported by us June, 1883. Two-thirds white, strip in face, large irregular black spot on each side containing several small white spots, black spots scattered over body, tail nearly all white.

Sire, Rooker, the sire of Aaggie (901), (See No. 98), See chart of Sir Henry 2d of Aaggie, also milk records of the Aaggie family, page 22.

Dam, Zwagerman, has a record of 77 4-5 lbs. in one day.

Aaggie Cornelia, gave in Holland, before importation, 73 1-5 lbs. in one day, and this season has given, the first year after importation 8,877 lbs. 10 oz in six months and twenty-five days to Sept. 26th. She is dam of Aaggie Cornelia 2d (4,341), (See No. 115,) which has given this season as a five-year-old, the first after importation 51 lbs. 12 oz. in one day, 7,985 lbs. 10 oz. in seven months and six days to Sept. 26th. She is also dam of Aaggie Cornelia 3d (4,342), (See No. 132,) which has given this season as a four-year-old, the first season after importation, 78 lbs. 12 oz. in one day, and 5,616 lbs. 3 oz in three months and two days to Sept. 26th. Also dam of Aaggie Cornelia 4th (4,343), (See No. 173,) which has given as a two-year-old this season 5,506 lbs. 9 oz. in seven months and ten days to Sept. 26th. Also dam of Somnambula (6,990). See No. 362.

No. 103.   NETHERLAND BARONESS.   No. 291.

(H. H. B. Vol. 6, No. 2,635.) Calved March 15, 1877. Imported by us, Sept., 1882.

Sire, District bull of Beemster.

Dam, Gert Met 3d, has a record of over 68 lbs. of milk in a in a day from three teats.

Grandam, Gert Met, a very fine cow and heavy milker. Was kept twenty years for breeding.

The dam of Netherland Baroness is a sister to the dam of Lady Netherland. See No. 99.

Netherland Baroness gave the first season after importation and before she was fully acclimated 72 lbs. in a day, 1,908 lbs. 4 oz. in one month and 11,249 lbs. 7 oz. in ten months, and made in one week 17 lbs. 5 oz. of butter. And this season has given 72 lbs. 11 oz. in one day, and 4,134 lbs. 4 oz. in two months and sixteen days to Sept. 26th.

Netherland Baroness is dam of Netherland Baroness 2d (2,636), (See No. 141), which has a record of 10,825 lbs. 9 oz. in one year, and made 8 lbs. 12 oz of butter in one week in January as a two-year-old, and this season, as a four-year-old, 4,950 lbs. 10 oz. in six months and twenty-one days to Sept. 22d. She is also the dam of Netherland Baroness 4th (2,638). See No. 186.

No. 104.   **NETHERLAND QUEEN.**

(See Group.)

(H. H. B. Vol. 3, No. 414.) Calved March 26th, 1877. Imported by us in 1878.

Sire, Schreuder ; also sire of Netherland Duchess No. 112.

Dam, Lady Netherland (See No. 99), with a record of 50 lbs. of milk in a day with first calf, at two years old, and 73⅜ lbs. as a four-year old.

Lady Netherland is also dam of Netherland Prince No. 2, Netherland Princess No. 123, and Netherland Aaggie No. 271.

G-dam, Gert Met 2d, gave 71 lbs. 8 oz. milk in one day.

Gert Met 2d is sister to Gert Met 3d, dam of Netherland Baroness No. 103.

G-g-dam, Gert Met, a very fine cow and heavy milker. Was kept twenty years for breeding.

Queen made a record when two years old of 58 lbs. 12 oz. in one day, 1,670 lbs. 9 oz. in one month, and 13,574 lbs. 3 oz. in 345 days. As a four-year-old, 76 lbs. in one day, 2,132 lbs. 6 oz. in one month, and 15,614 lbs. 9 oz. in one year. As a five-year-old she has given in seven months and eighteen days 10,046 lbs. 8 oz. In November, 1882, she made 20 lbs. of butter in one week, and without any change from her ordinary feed in quantity or quality. Butter weighed after working and before salting.

For full records of Netherland family, see page 27.

Queen took First Premium as yearling heifer at New York State Fair, 1878 ; also First Prize as a two-year-old in 1879, at both State and Onondaga County Fairs ; also Second Prize at New York State Fair, 1880, when three years old, in class with mature cows ; gained First Prize at New York State Fair in

1881, also at Onondaga County Fair same year; Second at at New York State Fair in 1882 and 1884, both years being beaten by animals from our own herd, and was five different years one of the herd that won the Gold Medal.

No. 105.　　　AAGGIE IDALINE.　　　No. 772.

(H. H. B. Vol. 7, No. 4,362.) Calved Feb. 28th, 1878. Imported by us August, 1883. Largely white, white cheeks, large black patches on neck and over body, small black spots over body.

Sire, Jacob, (N. H. B. 20), he by Rooker, the sire of Aaggie, (See No. 98). See chart of Sir Henry 2d of Aaggie, and milk records of the Aaggie family, page 22.

Dam, Naatje has a record of 68 2-5 lbs. in one day.

Naatje is also dam of Aaggie Idaline 2d (4,363), (See No. 114), and Aaggie Idaline 3d (4,364). See No. 128.

Aaggie Idaline gave as a five-year-old in Holland 68 2-5 lbs. in one day, and as a six-year-old the present season, the first after importation, 60 lbs. in one day, 9,557 lbs. 13 oz. in six months and thirty days to Oct. 1st.

No. 106.　　　VALLEY BEAUTY.　　　No. 592.

(H. H. B. Vol. 7, No. 4,562.) Calved Spring of 1878. Imported by us June, 1883. Two-thirds black, strip in face, large irregular black saddle over back, small black spot just forward of right fore leg, legs, belly and two-thirds of tail white.

Sire, District bull of Beemster.

Dam, Van Dort.

Valley Beauty is a fine, large, handsome cow and has a record in Holland of 77 4-5 lbs. in one day, and has given this

AAGGIE ROSA 3d.
(No. 2,611, H. H. B. Born March 25th, 1882.)

{ DE RUITER, (N. H. 89.)

AAGGIE ROSA 2d 2,610, H. H. B.) called Wemeltie N. H. B. 686.

(. B., 56.) { JACOB (N. H. B . 20.) { ROOKER.
{ DE GOEDE, a Prize cow at the Paris Exposition. Milk record, 91 lbs. 8 oz. in a day.
TRINTJE, (N. H. B., 35.) Milk record, 80 lbs. in a day.

N. H. B., cord, 80 ay. { ROOKER.
OUDE PORCELEIN.

I. B., 56.) { JACOB, (N. H. B. 20.) { ROOKER.
{ DE GOEDE, a Prize cow at the Paris Exposition. Milk record, 91 lbs. 8 oz. in a day.
TRINTJE, (N. H. B., 35.) Milk record, 80 lbs. in a day.

A. (2605.)
N. H. B., ord at 5 n a day. Irst year on 16,156
{ JACOB, (N. H. B., 20.) { ROOKER.
{ DE GOEDE, a Prize cow.
JANSJE, (N. H. B., 88.) Milk record, 68 lbs. in a day. Jansje took First Prize at Zaandam, two First Prizes at Amsterdam, silver medal at Rotterdam. Beef wgt. dressed was 1,150 lbs.
{ ROOKER.
OUDE JANSJE.

season, the first after importation, 62 lbs. 11 oz. in one day, 3,900 lbs. 9 oz. in two months and eight days, to Sept. 26th. She is dam of Valley Beauty 2d, No. 203, who has given this season as a two year-old, the first season after importation, 55 lbs. 13 oz. in one day, 3,816 lbs. 14 oz. in two months and twenty-seven days, to Sept. 26th, is also dam of Valley Beauty 3d, No. 226, and Valley Beauty 4th, No. 443.

No. 107.   AAGGIE ROSA.   No. 154.

(H. H. B. Vol. 6, No. 2,605.) (Wemeltien, N. H. B., 323.) Calved March 15th, 1878. Imported by us, September, 1882.

Sire, Jacob (N. H. B. 20), he by Rooker, the sire of Aaggie. See milk records of the Aaggie family, page 22.

Jacob's dam, De Goede, a prize cow at the Paris Exposition, has a record of 91 lbs. 8 oz. of milk in a day.

Dam, Jansje (N. H. B. 88). Milk record, 68 lbs in a day on grass. Jansje took First Prize at Zaandam, two First Prizes at Amsterdam, and Silver Medal at Rotterdam. Beef weight dressed was 1,150 lbs.

Aaggie Rosa gave as a five-year-old in Holland 91 lbs. in a day. She gave the first season after importation 68 lbs. 8 oz. in one day, 1,920 lbs. 3 oz. in one month, and 16,156 lbs. 10 oz. in one year. This season she has given 70 lbs. in a day, and 4,637 lbs. 8 oz. in two months and eighteen days to Sept. 26th.

Aaggie Rosa is dam of Aaggie Rosa 2d No. 139, Aaggie Rosa 3d No. 197, Aaggie Rosa 4th No. 264, Sir Henry 2d of Aaggie (see chart) No. 4, and Aaggie Rosa's Prince No. 72.

For breeding, see chart of Sir Henry 2d of Aaggie.

No. 108. **NETHERLAND PAMELA.** No. 787.

(H. H. B. Vol. 8, No. 6,893.) Calved March, 1878. Imported by us May, 1884. Three-fourths black. Strip in face, white over shoulders and over hips to root of tail, white spots on right side of neck. Fore legs black to ankles. Hind legs black to gambrels.

Sire, Schreuder, the sire of Netherland Queen (414). See No. 104.

Dam, Zwarte Twenter, a great milker, in size and form like Netherland Pamela.

No. 109. **NETHERLAND DORINDA.** No. 788.

(H. H. B. Vol. 8, No. 6,894.) Calved March 15th, 1878. Imported by us May, 1884. Two-thirds black. Strip in face, small white spot on right cheek, white strip over shoulder to belly, left side, other spots on both sides.

Sire, Schreuder, the sire of Netherland Queen (414). See No. 104.

Dam, Boutje. Like daughter but is large and an *extra* milker.

No. 110. **NETHERLAND CHAPERONE.** No. 789.

(H. H. B. Vol. 8, No. 6,895.) Calved March 16th, 1878. Imported by us May, 1884. Three-fourths white. Cheeks and neck black, small white spot back of right ear, large black spot on right side and two on left, small black spots on both sides.

Sire, Schreuder, the sire of Netherland Queen (414). See No. 104.

Dam, Kuijper, an extra good cow, has a record of 64 lbs. in one day.

Netherland Chaperone has a record in Holland, before importation, of 59½ lbs. in one day.

No. 111. AAGGIE KATHLEEN. No. 771.

(H. H. B. Vol. 7, No. 4,492.) Calved March 17th, 1878. Imported by us August, 1883. Three-fourths white, black around right eye and under left eye, tips of ears black, irregular black on neck, large and small black spots scattered over body, two black spots on right fore leg.

Sire, Jacob, (N. H. B. 20), he by Rooker, sire of Aaggie (901), (See No. 98). See chart of Sir Henry 2d of Aaggie, and records of the Aaggie family, page 22.

Dam, Bontje Naatje, has a record of 80 1-6 lbs. in one day.

Aaggie Kathleen, has given this season the first after importation, 56 lbs. 8 oz. in one day, and 8,432 lbs. 4 oz. in six months and five days, to Oct. 1st. She is dam of Aaggie Kathleen's Marquis, No. 45.

Bred to Syracuse (822), Aug. 8th.

No. 112. NETHERLAND DUCHESS.
(Lady of the Lake, 574.) (See cut.)

(H. H. B. Vol. 6, No. 2,498.) Calved March 30th, 1878. Imported by us in 1879.

Sire, Schreuder, the sire of Netherland Queen (414). See No. 104.

Dam, a sister to Lady Netherland, (See No. 99), with record of 60 2-3 lbs. of milk in one day.

G-dam, Gert Met 2d, has a record of 71 lbs. 8 oz. of milk in one day.

G-g-dam, Gert Met, a very fine cow and a heavy milker. She was kept twenty years for breeding.

Netherland Duchess dropped her first calf when twenty-two and one-half months old, and before she was two years old gave 45 lbs. 13 oz in one day, 1,284 lbs. 9 oz. in one month, and 12,200 lbs. 4 oz. in one year. She dropped her second calf within a few weeks of the above record, and gave as a three-year-old 55 lbs. 6 oz. in one day, 1,588 lbs. 10 oz. in one month, 11,401 lbs. 12 oz in one year. She gave as a four-year-old 61 lbs. 4 oz. in one day, 1,667 lbs. 4 oz. in one month, and 16,520 lbs. 7 oz in one year. She made in one week 14 lbs. 12 oz. of butter. She has given as a five-year-old this season 6,295 lbs. 5 oz. in four months and twenty-five days, to Sept. 26th. It will be observed that this cow is by the same bull and her dam was a sister to the dam of Netherland Queen.

No. 113.   ÆGIS 2d.   No. 33.

(H. H. B. Vol. 3, No. 235.) Calved May 24th, 1878.

Sire, Uncle Tom (163), by Rip Van Winkle (35), imported, &c., sire of Echo, who has a record of 18,120 lbs. 8 oz. in one year, followed by 23,775 lbs. 8 oz. the next year. For extended pedigree of Uncle Tom, see Netherland King No. 15.

Dam, Ægis (69). See No. 96.

Ægis 2d dropped her first calf before she was two years old, and gave 44 lbs. 10 oz. in one day, 1,288 lbs. in one month, 5,613 lbs. 6 oz. in six months, 9,612 lbs. 5 oz. in one year. When three years old she gave in nine and one-half months 10,897 lbs. 12 oz. As a four-year-old she has given 68 lbs. in one day, 1,951 lbs. 9 oz. in one month, and 14,596 lbs. 11 oz. in one year, and made 15 lbs. 8 oz. of butter in one week. She has given this season in eight months and seven days, to Sept. 26th, 10,638 lbs. 14 oz.

No. 114.   **AAGGIE IDALINE 2d.**   No. 773.

(H. H. B. Vol. 7, No. 4,363.) Calved February 10th, 1879. Imported by us August, 1883. Two-thirds black, strip in face, irregular white over shoulders and hips to belly both sides, black spot on left hip, one black spot on right and three on left rump, numerous white spots on left side, two black spots on right fore leg.

Sire, Jacob 2d (N. H. B. 56). See chart of Sir Henry 2d of Aaggie, and milk records of the Aaggie family, page 22.

Dam, Naatje, same as dam of Aaggie Idaline No. 105. Record 68 2-5 lbs. in a day.

Aaggie Idaline 2d gave as a four-year-old in Holland 64 lbs. of milk in a day. She has given this season, the first after importation, 53 lbs. 12 oz. in a day, and 8,879 lbs. 4 oz. in seven months and twenty-two days to Oct 1st.

No. 115.   **AAGGIE CORNELIA 2d.**   No. 611.

(H. H. B. Vol. 7, No. 4,341.) Calved March, 1879. Imported by us June, 1883. One-half black, long star, snip, white over shoulders to belly on both sides, connected by very fine line on right side, white over hips to flanks on both sides, and extending forward nearly to shoulders, two black spots on each side, legs, belly and switch white.

Sire, Alexander, (N. H. B. 83).

Dam, Aaggie Cornelia (4,410). See No. 102.

Grandam, Zwagerman, has a record of 73 1-5 lbs. in one day.

Aaggie Cornelia 2d has given this season in seven months and eleven days to Oct. 1st, 8,130 lbs. 3 oz.

Aaggie Cornelia 2d is full sister to Aaggie Cornelia 3d, (See No. 132), Aaggie Cornelia 4th, (See No. 173), and half sister to

Aaggie Cornelia 5th, (See No. 250), and dam of Somnambula, No. 362.

Bred to Netherland Prince, No. 2, July 31st.

No. 116.   NETHERLAND PEERESS.   No. 342.

(H. H. B. Vol. 6, No. 2,640.) Calved March, 1879. Imported by us September, 1882.

Sire, District bull of Heilo.

Dam, Gert Met 9th, grandam of Netherland Jewel, No. 160.

Grandam, a sister to Lady Netherland (1,263). See No. 99.

G-g-dam, Gert Met 2d, has a record of 71 lbs. 8 oz. in one day.

G-g-g-dam, Gert Met, a very fine cow and heavy milker, which was kept twenty years for breeding.

She gave in nine months, the first season in this country, 6,352 lbs. 7 oz. of milk, and this season has given 52 lbs. 7 oz. in one day, and 8,529 lbs. 2 oz. in six months and twenty-three days, to Sept. 26th.

Netherland Peeress is dam of Netherland Peeress 2d, No. 421.

No. 117.   AAGGIE BEAUTY.   No. 149.

(H. H. B. Vol. 6, No. 2,907.) (Marijtje 2d, N. H. B. 572.) Calved March, 1879. Imported by us September, 1882

Sire, Jacob 2d (N. H. B. 56). See cut. See chart of Sir Henry 2d of Aaggie, and milk records of the Aaggie family, page 22.

Dam, Marijtje (N. H. B. 570) has a record of 80 1-6 lbs. of milk in a day.

Sire of Marijtje is Rooker (sire of Aaggie). See No. 98.

Dam, Oude Marijtje.

Aaggie Beauty made a record in Holland of 68 lbs. 8 oz. of milk in one day as a three-year-old, and made in one week in February, 1883, 10 lbs. 3 ounces of butter.

She gave as a four-year-old 51 lbs. 6 oz. in a day, 1,461 lbs. 14 oz. in one month, and 13,573 lbs. 15 oz. in one year, and has given this season 5,574 lbs. 3 oz. in five months and twenty-five days to Sept 26th.

Aaggie Beauty is dam of Aaggie Beauty 2d No. 154, and Aaggie Beauty 3d No. 259.

Bred to Netherland Prince, No. 2, July 26th.

No. 118.   **CLOTHILDE.**   No. 39.

(H. H. B. Vol. 5, No. 1,308.) Calved March, 1879. Imported by us October, 1880.

Sire, Dirk.

Dam, Stijl, gave 65 lbs. in a day.

Clothilde, dropped her first calf when twenty-two months old, just after coming out of quarantine, and gave in eleven and one-half months 8,964 lbs. 2 oz As a three-year-old she gave 60 lbs. in one day. 1,733 lbs. 10 oz. in one month, 8,703 lbs. 7 oz. in six months, and 15,622 lbs. 2 oz. in one year. She made in one week 12 lbs. 3½ oz. of butter. As a four-year-old she has given 67 lbs. 14 oz. in one day, 1,942 lbs. 7 oz. in one month, and 17,970 lbs. 3 oz. in one year, and 18,004 lbs. 4 oz. in 365 days, by omitting two days when sick, and adding two days at end of record.

Her daughter, Clothilde 2d (1,451), (See No. 147), commencing when two years old, has given 53 lbs. 9 oz. in one day, 1,429 lbs. 1 oz. in the month of January, and 10,244 lbs. 6 oz. in 9 months to Oct. 1st.

Clothilde 3d, See No. 198, Clothilde 4th No. 269, are also daughters of Clothilde.

Clothilde won First Prize at New York State Fair in 1883, competing in a class of twenty-one, and was one of the herd that won the Gold Medal.

No. 119.   CARLOTTA.   No. 59.

(See Cut.)

(H. H. B. Vol. 5, No. 1,266.) Calved March, 1879. Imported by us October, 1880.

Sire, District bull of Beemster.

Dam, a fine cow, gave 60½ lbs. of milk in one day.

Carlotta gave as a two-year-old 35 lbs. 14 oz. in one day, 1,018 lbs. in one month, and 7,227 lbs. 10 oz. in ten and one-half months. As a three-year-old she gave 57 lbs. 8 oz. in one day, 1,637 lbs. 8 oz. in one month, 7,824 lbs. 14 oz. in six months, and 11,886 lbs. 4 oz. in one year. She has a butter record of 12 lbs. 1 oz. in one week on winter feed. She gave as a four-year-old 1,544 lbs. 6 oz. in one month, and 10,509 lbs. 7 oz. in ten months and nineteen days.

She has given this season, as a five-year-old, 70 lbs. 3 oz. in one day, and 2,948 lbs. 11 oz. in one month and eighteen days, to Sept. 26th.

Carlotta is dam of Prince Imperial, No. 5, Netherland Carl, No. 76, and Carlotta 2d (3,555), which we sold for $1,000.

No. 120.   CAMEO.   No. 69.

(H. H. B. Vol. 5, No. 1,267.) Calved March 15th, 1879. Imported by us October, 1880.

Sire, District bull of Wognum.

Dam, Vriend.

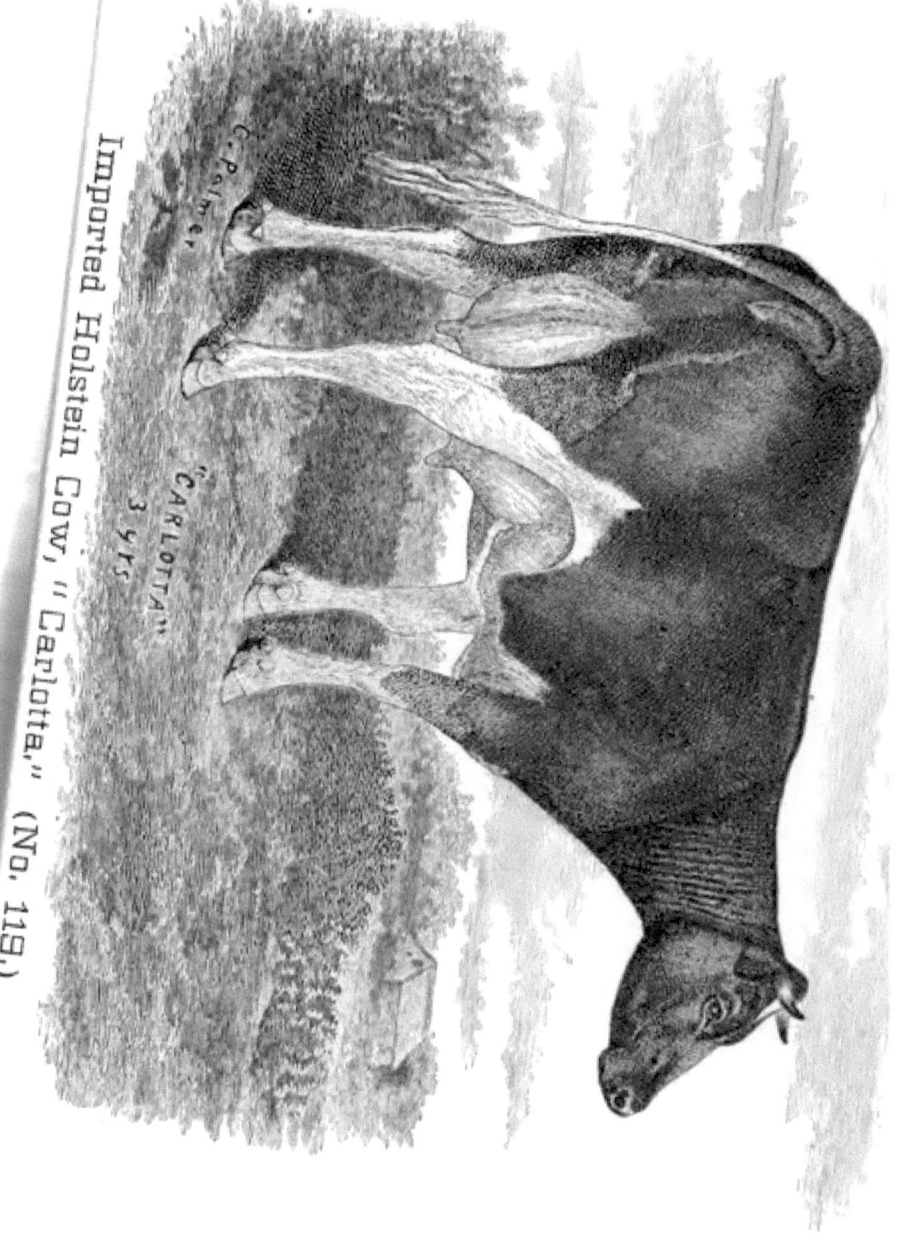

Imported Holstein Cow, "Carlotta." (No. 119.)

Cameo came in before she was two years old, just after coming out of quarantine, and gave 36 lbs. 11 oz. in one day, 1,062 lbs. 10 oz. in one month, and 8,166 lbs. 3 oz. in ten months and eighteen days. As a three-year-old she gave 55 lbs. 15 oz. of milk in one day, 1,604 lbs. 2 oz. in one month, 7,016 lbs. 10 oz. in six months, and 11,475 lbs. in one year. She gave as a four-year-old 57 lbs. 3 oz. in one day, 1,541 lbs. in one month, and 10,837 lbs. 13 oz in ten months.

She has given as a five-year-old, this season, 63 lbs. 3 oz. in one day, and 6,361 lbs. 6 oz. in four months and eight days to Sept. 26th.

No. 121. **AAGGIE BELLE.** No. 305.

(H. H. B. Vol. 6, No. 2,607.) (Antje 2d, N. H. B. No. 487.) Calved March 20th, 1879. Imported by us September, 1882.

Sire, Jacob 2d, (N. H. B. 56), (See cut). See chart of Sir Henry 2d of Aaggie, and milk records of the Aaggie family, page 22.

Dam, Antje, (N. H. B. 36), has a milk record of 80 lbs. in one day.

Aaggie Belle gave in eleven months 9,673 lbs. 14 oz. of milk, the first season after importation.

She has given this season 5,423 lbs. 14 oz. in six months and two days, to Sept. 26th.

Bred to Netherland Prince, No. 2, Aug. 18th.

No. 122. **ADDIE.** No. 77.

(H. H. B. Vol. 4, No. 873.) Calved April 2d, 1879. Imported by us September, 1879.

Sire, District bull of Edam.

Dam, Zwarte Greitje, has a four-year-old record of 57 1-5 lbs.

Addie as a two-year-old gave 41 lbs. 10 oz. of milk in one day, 1,131 lbs. 12 oz. in one month, 10,600 lbs. 13 oz. in one year, and as a three-year-old has given 50 lbs. in one day, 1,527 lbs 4 oz. in one month, and 7,652 lbs 9 oz. in six months, and 14,130 lbs. 11 oz. in one year. After completing her year's records she gave 40 lbs. in one day, and her record for fourteen months was 16,190 lbs. 2 oz. As a four-year old she has given 51 lbs. 2 oz. in one day, and in seven months and twenty-four days, to July 8th, 1884, 10,132 lbs. 4 oz. She has been milked continually since she had her first calf and has never been dry from that date.

No. 123.   **NETHERLAND PRINCESS.**   No. 75.

(See Group)

(H. H. B. Vol. 4, No. 862.) Calved April 6th, 1879. Imported by us July, 1879.

Sire, Schemmel, he by Schreuder. Schreuder is the sire of Netherland Queen (414). See No. 104.

Schemmel is son of Netherland Dowager. See No. 97.

Dam, Lady Netherland (See No. 96), gave as a four-year-old 73½ lbs. of milk in a day on grass alone. She gave in five months and six days, ending with February, 1883, 6,130 lbs. 11 oz.

G-dam, Gert Met 2d, a beautiful cow that gave 71 lbs. 8 oz. of milk in one day, on grass alone.

G-g-dam, Gert Met, an elegant cow that was kept twenty years for breeding.

Netherland Princess is sister to Netherland Queen, No. 104, also to Netherland Prince No. 2. She gave in one day, as a three-year old, 55 lbs. 14 oz. of milk ; 1,639 lbs. 11 oz. in one month, 8,400 lbs. 9 oz. in six months, and 14,101 lbs. 2 oz. in one year. She made before she was three years old 14 lbs.

4 oz of butter in one week, and when she was three years old 14 lbs. 11½ oz. in one week on winter feed. As a four-year-old she gave 60 lbs 9 oz. in one day, 1,687 lbs. 7 oz. in one month, and 12,789 lbs 13 oz. in one year. She made in one week 17 lbs. 11 oz. of butter. She has given this season 64 lbs. 3 oz. in one day, and 4,440 lbs. 2 oz. in two months and fourteen days to Sept. 26th, as a five-year-old. See records of the Netherland family, page 27.

Bred to Netherland Prince, No. 2, Aug. 17th.

No. 124.　　　　　　**LADY FAY.**　　　　　　No. 720.

Marie, (N. H. B. 1061).

(H. H. B. Vol. 7, No. 4,470.) Calved March, 1879. Imported by us August, 1883. Two-thirds black, large star, snip, very irregular white spots over shoulders and hips, two small white spots back of right eye, small white spots scattered over body, black spot at roots of tail.

Sire, District bull of Twisk.

Dam, Marie, has a record of 84½ lbs. in one day.

Lady Fay has given this season as a five-year-old, the first season after importation, and before she was fully acclimated, 80 lbs. 4 oz. in one day, and 2,326 lbs. in one month and eight days, to Sept. 26th She is dam of Netherland Statesman No. 77.

No. 125.　　　　　**MEADOW LILY.**　　　　　No. 58.

(H. H. B. Vol. 4, No. 863.) Calved March 28th, 1879. Imported by us July, 1879.

Sire, Son of Schreuder. Schreuder is the sire of Netherland Queen (414). See No. 104.

Dam, Dirk Jonges.

Meadow **Lily** came in before she was two years old, and gave 41 lbs. 2 oz. in one day, 1,174 lbs. 14 oz. in one month, and 7,233 lbs. 10 oz. in ten months and eleven days. As a three-year-old she gave 53 lbs. 8 oz. of milk in one day, 1,470 lbs. 8 oz in one month, 6,705 lbs. in six months, 9,238 lbs. 2 oz. in ten months and eight days. She made in one week on winter feed, 12 lbs. 10 oz. of butter. She has given this season, as a five-year-old, 53 lbs. 8 oz. in one day, and 2,549 5 oz. in one month and twenty-eight days, to Sept. 26th. She is milking from only two teats and we believe if it were not for her misfortune she would be one of our deepest milkers. In form and breeding she is one of our choicest cows. She is dam of Meadow Lily's Prince No. 69.

Bred to Netherland King, No. 15, July 25th.

No. 126.   **NETHERLAND QUEEN 2d.**   No. 110.

(H. H. B. Vol. 4, No. 560.)   Calved April 3d, 1879.

Sire, Uncle Tom.   See pedigree in No. 15.

Dam, Netherland Queen.   See No. 104.

Grandam, Lady Netherland.   See No. 99.

Netherland Queen 2d was awarded First Prize at Onondaga County Fair, 1879. As a two-year-old she gave 40 lbs 4 oz. in one day, 1,102 lbs. 7 oz. in one month. As a three-year-old she has given 49 lbs. 4 oz. in one day, 1,307 lbs. 11 oz. in one month, 6,569 lbs. 7 oz. in six months, and 10,471 lbs. 15 oz in eleven months. This season she has given 68 lbs. 8 oz. in one day and 3,670 lbs. 4 oz. in two months and one day to Sept. 26th.

She is the dam of Netherland Queen 2d's Heiress No. 444, and Netherland Queen 4th No. 211.

No. 127.   **LADY GRISWOLD.**   No. 869.

(H. H. B. Vol. 8, No. 6,878.) Calved March, 1879. Imported by us May, 1884. Three-quarters white, black around eyes, tips of ears black, large black on sides of neck, sides spotted.

Sire, Jacob (N. H. B. 20), he by Rooker, sire of Aaggie (901). See milk records of the Aaggie family, page 22.

Dam, Pleuster, looked much like the daughter, and was a superior milker.

Lady Griswold gave in Holland, just before importation, 77 4-5 lbs. of milk in a day. She is the dam of Jacob Wit's Frank No. 36.

Bred to Netherland King, No. 15, Sept. 10th.

No. 128.   **AAGGIE IDALINE 3d.**   No. 776.

(H. H. B. Vol. 7, No. 4,364.) Calved Feb. 20th 1880. Imported by us August, 1883. Two-thirds white, strip in face, black around eyes connecting with black on neck, black saddle over back very irregular and containing several white spots, black spots on various parts of body and fore legs.

Sire, Jacob 2d, (N. H. B. 56), he by Jacob, (N. H. B. 20), he by Rooker. See milk records of the Aaggie family, page 22.

Dam, Naatje, same as dam of Aaggie Idaline, (See No. 105) and Aaggie Idaline 2d, (No. 114). She has a record of 68 2-5 lbs. of milk in one day.

Aaggie Idaline 3d gave 57 1-5 lbs. in one day as a three-year-old, before importation. She has given this season, the first after importation, 55 lbs. 12 oz. of milk in one day, and 8,315 lbs. 11 oz. in seven months and nine days, to Sept. 26th.

She is dam of Aaggie Idaline 4th, No. 190, Aaggie Idaline 5th (4,425), and Aaggie Idaline 3d's Ruth No. 415.

Bred to Netherland Prince No. 2, Aug. 15th.

No. 129.   **KAPPIJNE.**   No. 1,156.

(H. H. B. Vol. —, No. ——.) Calved March 25th, 1879. Imported by us August, 1884. One-half black, strip in face, white over shoulders to belly on right side, and over hips to flank on right side, legs, belly and switch white.

Sire, District bull of Twisk.

Dam, Kappijne 1st, an extra milker.

Kappijne has given in Holland 64 lbs. in one day as a four-year-old. She is dam of Aaggie Constance No. 182.

Bred to P. Slot's bull May 5th, 1884.

No. 130.   **AAGGIE HANNAH.**   No. 775.

(H. H. B. Vol. 7, No. 4,361.) Calved Feb. 23d, 1880. Imported by us August, 1883. One-half black, small black spot around each eye, black over neck both sides and extending down on left fore leg nearly to ankle, large irregular black spot over body on both sides containing numerous small white spots, numerous black spots over body and on fore legs.

Sire, Jacob 2d, (N. H. B. 56), he by Jacob, (N. H. B. 20) he by Rooker. See chart of Sir Henry 2d of Aaggie, and milk records of the Aaggie family, page 22.

Dam, Stippeld Naatje, has a record of 68 2-5 lbs. in one day.

Aaggie Hannah gave as a three-year-old 57 1-5 lbs. in one day before importation, and this season, the first after importation, 71 lbs. 15 oz. in one day, and 3,635 lbs. in two months to Oct. 1st. She is the dam of Aaggie Hannah's Prince No. 75.

No. 131.   **AAGGIE ISADORA.**   No 774.

(H. H. B. Vol. 7, No. 4,493.) Calved Feb. 26th, 1880. Imported by us August, 1883. Two-thirds black, black around left eye and back of left ear, black over and below right eye, two spots on cheek, very irregular white over shoulder and hips, white and black spots all over body.

Sire, Jacob 2d (N. H. B. 56), he by Jacob (N. H. B. 20), he by Rooker. See milk records of the Aaggie family, page 22.

Dam, Trijntje, by Jacob (N. H. B. 20), etc., See chart of Sir Henry 2d of Aaggie. Trijntje has a record of 68 2-5 lbs. in one day, and is the dam of Aaggie Isadora 3d No. 249.

Aaggie Isadora gave in Holland, before importation, 57 1-5 lbs. in a day as a three-year-old. She has given this season, the first after importation, 54 lbs. 4 oz. in one day, and 8,008 lbs. 1 oz. in seven months and eleven days to Oct. 1st.

Bred to Netherland Prince No. 2, July 26th.

No. 132.   **AAGGIE CORNELIA 3d**   No. 612.

(H. H. B. Vol. 7, No. 4,342.) Calved March, 1880. Imported by us June, 1883. One-half black, star, snip, white over shoulders to belly both sides, over hips to flanks both sides, black on back side of both forelegs to knees, hind legs, belly and switch white.

Sire, Alexander (N. H. B. 83).

Dam, Aaggie Cornelia (4,410). See No. 102.

Grandam, Zwagerman has a record of 77 4-5 in a day.

Aaggie Cornelia 3d, has given this season, the first since importation, 78 lbs. 12 oz. in one day, and 5,890 lbs. 13 oz. in three months and seven days to Oct. 1st.

She is full sister to Aaggie Cornelia 2d No. 115, Aaggie Cornelia 4th No. 173, Aaggie Cornelia 5th No. 250, and Aaggie Cornelia 6th No. 426, and dam of Aaggie Cornelia 3d's Neptune No. 432.

No. 133. **NETHERLAND COUNTESS.** No. 269.

(H. H. B. Vol. 6, No. 2,634.) Calved March 8th, 1880. Imported by us August, 1882.

Sire, Schemmel, also called Koning, a son of Netherland Dowager, (See No. 97), by Schreuder, the sire of Netherland Queen (414). (See No. 104). He was sire of Netherland Prince, (See No. 2), Netherland Princess, No. 123, Netherland Belle, (See No. 138), and Netherland Dowager 2d, (See No. 153).

Dam, a two-year-old sister to Netherland Queen, now dead, (See No. 104).

Grandam, Lady Netherland, (See No. 99).

G-g-dam, Gert Met 2d, gave 71 lbs. 8 oz. of milk in one day.

G-g-g-dam, Gert Met, a very fine cow and heavy milker, that was kept twenty years for breeding.

Netherland Countess is a remarkably handsome cow, and has given as a two-year-old 40 lbs. 9 oz. in one day, 1,186 lbs 4 oz. in one month, and 9,481 lbs. 12 oz. in one year, and made in one week in January 10 lbs. 4 oz. of butter.

She has given this season 50 lbs. 7 oz. in one day, and 9,008 lbs. 14 oz. in eight months and two days, to Sept. 25th.

She is dam of Netherland Countess 3d, No. 410.

No. 134. **AAGGIE SARAH.** No. 628.

(H. H. B. Vol. 7, No. 4,412.) Calved March 15th, 1880. Imported by us June, 1883. White and black, black around right eye and under left eye, tips of ears black, seven black

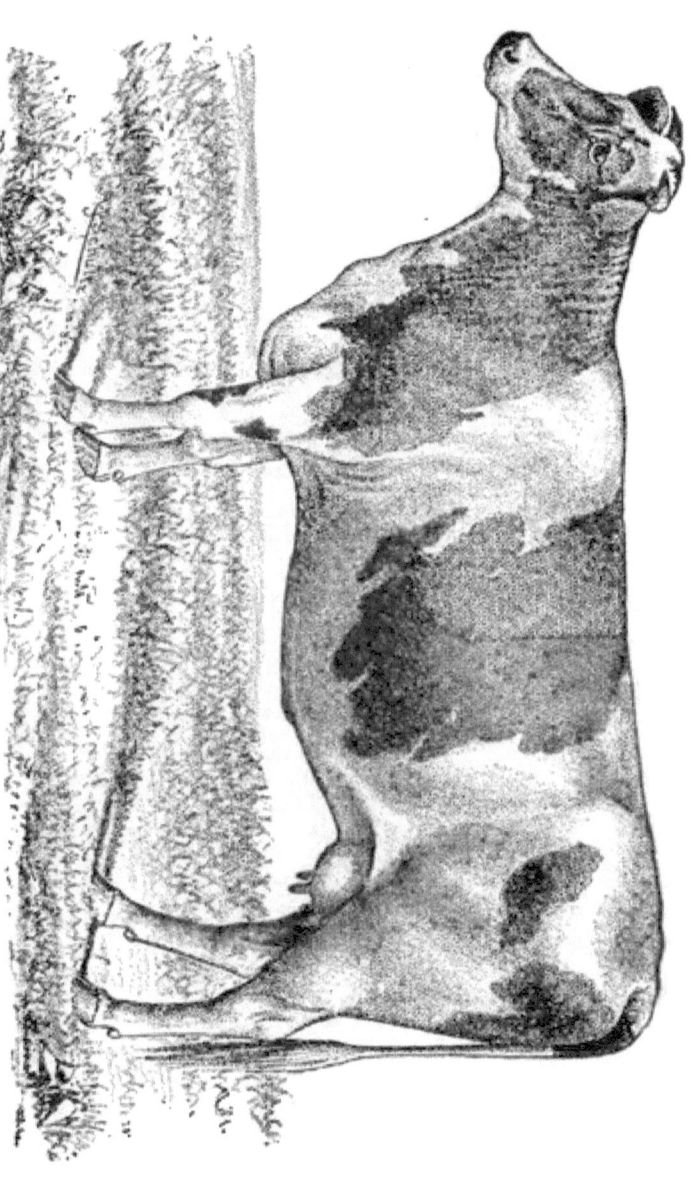

Netherland Countess, 2 years old. (No. 133.)

spots on left side, and seven on right side back of shoulder, others on neck, right fore leg and rump.

Sire, Jacob 2d (N. H. B. 56), (See cut), he by Jacob (N. H. B. 20), he by Rooker. See chart of Henry 2d of Aaggie and milk records of the Aaggie family, page 22.

Dam, Blokker, has a record of 82¼ lbs of milk in a day.

Grandam, Oude Blokker, a great milker.

Aaggie Sarah has given this season, as a four-year-old, the first season after importation and before she was fully acclimated, 80 lbs. 8 oz. in one day, and 3,009 lbs. in one month and sixteen days to Sept. 26th. She is dam of Aaggie Sarah 2d. See No. 253.

No. 135. **NETHERLAND CONSORT.** No. 292.

(H. H. B. Vol. 6, No. 2,639.) Calved March 15th, 1880. Imported by us September, 1882.

Sire, District bull.

Dam, Gert Met 3d, has a record of over 68 lbs. of milk in a day from three teats. See her sister, Netherland Baroness, No. 103.

Grandam, Gert Met, a very fine cow and heavy milker. She was kept twenty years for breeding.

Netherland Consort calved in midwinter while in quarantine, and gave as a two-year-old 41 lbs. 2 ounces in one day, 1,175 lbs. 3 oz. in one month, and 10,238 lbs. 7 oz. in one year, and made in one week in January 8 lbs. 12 ounces of butter. She has given this season, as a three-year-old, 55 lbs. in a day, and 9,770 lbs. 11 oz. in seven months and twenty-five days to Sept. 26th.

118 HOLSTEIN CATTLE.

No. 136. **AAGGIE CORA.** No. 307.

(H. H. B. Vol. 6, No. 2,609.) (Aaltje 2d, N. H. B. 766.) Calved March 15, 1880. Imported by us September, 1882.

Sire, Jacob 2d (N. H. B. 56). See cut. See chart of Sir Henry 2d of Aaggie, and milk records of the Aaggie family, page 22.

Dam, Aaltje (N. H. B. 324), has a record of 82½ lbs. of milk in a day.

Grandam, Porcelein (N. H. B. 147), by Rooker, sire of Aaggie (901). See No. 98.

Sire of Aaltje was Jacob, (N. H. B. 20). See chart of Sir Henry 2d of Aaggie.

Aaggie Cora gave as a three-year old, the first season after importation, 8,451 lbs. 8 oz. in nine months and seven days; and this season has given 65 lbs. 8 oz. in one day and 8,196 lbs. 13 oz. in five months and seventeen days to Oct. 1st.

Aaggie Cora is dam of Aaggie Cora's Wilfred No. 56.

No. 137. **AAGGIE BONNIE.** No. 306.

(H. H. B. Vol. 6, No. 2,608.) (Blokker 3d, N. H. B. 718.) Calved March 20th, 1880, Imported by us September, 1882.

Sire, Jacob (N. H. B. 56). See cut. See chart of Sir Henry 2d of Aaggie and milk records of the Aaggie family, page 22.

Dam, Blokker (N. H. B. 390), by Rooker, the sire of Aaggie. See No. 98.

Grandam, Oude Blokker, a great milker.

Blokker has a record of 82½ lbs. of milk in one day.

Aaggie Bonnie gave as a three-year-old the first season in this country after importation 7,307 lbs. 10 oz. in nine months and eleven days ; and this season has given 66 lbs. in one day and 7,425 lbs. 6 oz. in five months and twelve days to Sept. 26th.

No. 138.   **NETHERLAND BELLE.**   No. 235.

(H. H. B. Vol. 6, No. 1,876.) Calved March 20th, 1880. Imported by us 1881.

Sire, Schemmel, son of Netherland Dowager. See No. 97.

Schemmel, the sire of Netherland Belle, is the sire of Netherland Prince. See No. 2.

Sire of Schemmel, Schreuder, the sire of Netherland Queen (414), (See No. 104), and Netherland Duchess (2,498), See No. 112.

Dam, Schotter, gave 65 lbs. of milk in one day, she by Schreuder, the sire of Netherland Queen (414), See No. 104.

Netherland Belle gave as a three-year-old 56 lbs. 13 oz. in one day, 1,649 lbs. 12 oz. in one month, and 13,649 lbs. 6 oz. in one year. She made 16 lbs. 7 oz. of butter in one week.

As a four-year-old she has given 77 lbs 1 oz. in one day, and 5,136 lbs 2 oz. in two months and 17 days, to Sept. 26th.

No. 138½.   **NETHERLAND WAUKESHA.**   No. 018.

(H. H. B. Vol. 8, No. 7,007.) Calved March 20th, 1880. One-half black, strip in face, white over hips and shoulders to belly, both sides, irregular black over back down both sides.

Sire, District bull of Purmer.

Dam, Gert Met (Heinis), gave as a five-year-old 72½ lbs. of milk in one day.

Gert Met is by Schreuder, sire of Netherland Queen, etc. See Netherland records, page 27.

Netherland Waukesha has given this season, the first after importation, 55 lbs 7 oz. in one day, and 7,370 lbs. 8 oz. in six months and five days, to Sept 26th, and is dam of Netherland Oconto, No. 254

Bred to Netherland Prince, Aug. 20th, 1884.

No. 139. **AAGGIE ROSA 2d.** No. 308.

(H. H. B. Vol. 6, No. 2,610.) (Wemeltien 2d, N. H. B. 686.) Calved March 30th, 1880. Imported by us September, 1882.

Sire, Jacob 2d, (N. H B. 56.) See cut. See chart of Sir Henry 2d of Aaggie, and milk records of the Aaggie family, page 22.

Dam, Aaggie Rosa (2,605). See No. 107. See chart of Sir Henry 2d of Aaggie.

Aaggie Rosa 2d gave as a three-year-old the first season in this country 7,030 lbs. 5 oz. in nine months and nineteen days; and this season has given 65 lbs. 4 oz. in one day, and 5,367 lbs. 5 oz. in three months and fifteen days to Sept. 26th

Aaggie Rosa 2d is dam of Aaggie Rosa 3d No. 197, and Aaggie Rosa 2d's Emperor No. 68.

No. 140. **EULA LEE.** No. 218.

(H. H. B. Vol. 6, No. 1,846.) Calved April 6th, 1880. Imported by us 1881. About four-fifths black, with star.

Sire, District bull of Swaag.

Dam, Homan, gave 60⅔ lbs. of milk in one day.

Eula Lee has given this season 45 lbs. in one day and 8,676 lbs. 1 oz. in eight months and twenty-five days to Sept. 26th.

She is the dam of Eula Lee 2d. See No. 273.

No. 141. NETHERLAND BARONESS 2d. No. 293.

(H. H. B. Vol. 6, No. 2,636.) Calved April 5th, 1880. Imported by us September, 1882.

Sire, District bull of Beemster.

Dam, Netherland Baroness (2,635) gave 73¼ lbs. in a day as a five-year-old. She won First Prize at the New York State Fair in the sweepstakes class, in 1883, and in 1884 won the same prize, competing with Shorthorns, Ayrshires, and Jerseys. See No. 103.

G-dam, Gert Met 3d, has a record of over 68 lbs. of milk in a day from three teats.

G-g-dam, Gert Met, a fine cow and heavy milker, that was kept for breeding twenty years.

Netherland Baroness 2d calved in winter while in quarantine, and gave as a two-year-old 38 lbs. 1 oz. in one day, 1,070 lbs. 2 oz. in one month, and 10,825 lbs. 9 oz. in one year, and made 8 lbs. 12 oz. of butter in one week in January. She has given this season 44 lbs. 8 oz. in one day, and 4,950 lbs. 10 oz. in six months and twenty-one days to Sept. 26th.

No. 142. ÆGIS 4th.

(H. H. B. Vol. 5, No. 1,276.) Calved May 11th, 1880.

Sire, Beaconsfield (401), imported by us September 1878.

Grandsire, Kees (N. H. B. No. 32.) See pedigree of Lee Morgan No. 16.

Dam, Ægis 2d. See No. 113.

G-gam, Ægis. See No. 96.

G-g-dam, Agoo (1).

G-g-g-dam, Dowager (7). Imported.

Ægis 2d's sire, Uncle Tom (163).

Ægis' sire, Rip Van Winkle (35).

Beaconsfield's dam gave 80 1-6 lbs. of milk in one day on grass alone.

Ægis 4th gave as a two-year-old in ten months and eighteen days 6,483 lbs. 14 oz. She gave as a three-year-old 8,486 lbs. 14 oz. in ten months and nineteen days, and this season has given 4,861 lbs. 3 oz. in four months and seven days to Sept. 19th.

Ægis 4th is sister to Ægis 2d No. 113, and dam of Netherland Chancellor No. 64.

No. 143. **LITTLE WONDER.** No. 151.

(H. H. B. Vol 6, No. 1,788.) Calved May 14th, 1880. Imported by us in 1881. About one-half white, with star.

Sire, District bull of Purmer.

Dam, Mietje, a young cow that gave 65 lbs of milk in one day.

Grandam, gave 82½ lbs. of milk in one day.

Little Wonder, gave as a two-year old in eleven months and twenty days, 6,262 lbs. 8 oz.

No. 144. **SIGNET.** No. 182.

(H. H. B. Vol. 6, No. 1,817.) Calved April 6th, 1880. Imported by us in 1881. Three-fourths black, star, splash from left arm pit to back, two small spots on left side, white over left rump and down to right flank.

Sire, District bull of Benningbroek.

Dam, Trintje, has a record of 60⅜ lbs. in one day.

No. 145.   CARENO.   No. 234.

(H. H. B. Vol. 6, No. 1,859.) Calved May 20th, 1880. Imported by us 1881. About three-fourths black, with star.

Sire, Feereman's bull.

Dam, Zwaartkop, gave in one day 73 1-5 lbs of milk.

Careno calved when twenty-three months old, and gave the day she was two years old 49 lbs. 4 oz. of milk, 1,350 lbs. 6 oz. in one month, and 12,115 lbs. 2 oz. in one year.

Bred to Netherland Prince, June 21st, 1884.

No. 146.   **MOTTLED BEAUTY.**   No. 224.

(H. H. B. Vol. 6, No. 2,828.) Calved January 5th, 1881. Imported by us August, 1882. Two-thirds black, large strip in face, handsomely marked.

Sire, District bull of Binnewysend.

Dam, Aafke, gave when five years old 87 lbs. in one day.

Mottled Beauty gave 7,789 lbs. 4 oz. of milk in eight months and twenty-three days as a two-year-old, and this season has given 54 lbs. 10 oz. in one day, and 7,314 lbs. 9 oz. in five months and nineteen days, to Sept. 26th.

She is sister to Mottled Beauty II. No. 205, and dam of Mottled Beauty 3d, No. 420.

No. 147.   CLOTHILDE 2d.

(H. H. B. Vol. 5, No. 1,451.) Imported by us in September, 1880, in dam. Calved January 24th, 1881. Black and white, star, spots on body, white legs, belly and end of tail.

Sire, Jonges' bull.

Dam, Clothilde (1,308). See No. 118.

Grandam, Stijl, has a record of 68 2-5 lbs. in a day.

Clothilde 2d dropped her first calf last December, and has given 53 lbs. 9 oz. in one day, and 1,429 lbs. 1 oz. in January, and 10,096 lbs. 1 oz. in eight months and twenty-five days to Sept. 26th.

No. 148.   **NETHERLAND GEM 2d.**   No. 404.

(H. H. B. Vol. 6, No. 2,115.) Calved Feb. 15th, 1882. Strip in face, large black spot on left side, smaller spot on right side, black at rump.

Sire, Koning's bull.

Dam, Netherland Gem (1,875), imported by us, and which gave as a two-year-old, the first season after importation, 39 lbs. 8 oz. in a day, and 7,695 lbs. 11 oz. in eight months and twenty days, when we sold her for $1,000.

G-dam, Netherland Dowager (2,632.)   See No. 97.

G-g-dam, Oude Schemmel, has a record of over 80 lbs. in a day.

Netherland Dowager gave in Holland, just before importation, 61 lbs. of milk in a day. She gave the first season after importation 12,784 lbs. 2 oz. in one year. She has given this season 73 lbs. 11 oz. in one day, and 4,548 lbs. 12 oz. in two months and fifteen days to Sept. 26th.

Netherland Gem 2d has given as a two-year-old, under very unfavorable circumstances, 4,117 lbs. 3 oz. in seven months and fourteen days to Sept. 26th.

No. 149.   **AAGGIE ANNA.**   No. 25.

(H. H. B. Vol. 6, No. 2 602.) Calved February 14th, 1881. Imported by us in August, 1882.

Sire, Jacob 2d, (N. H. B. 56). (See cut). See chart of Sir

Henry 2d of Aaggie, and milk records of the Aaggie family, page 22.

Dam, Porcelein, (N. H. B. 147), with a record of 80 lbs. of milk in one day.

Sire of Porcelein was Rooker, sire of Aaggie (901).

Grandam, Oude Porcelein.

Aaggie Anna gave as a two-year-old, the first season after importation, 7,437 lbs. in one year, and this season has given 5,564 lbs. 11 oz. in five months and twenty-one days, to Sept. 26th.

She is the dam of Aaggie Anna 2d, No. 260.

No. 150.   **NOONTIDE.**   No. 225.

(H. H. B. Vol. 6, No 2,843.) Calved February 28th, 1881. Imported by us August, 1882. Large strip in face, small horns, elegantly marked.

Sire, District bull of Binnewysend.

Dam, Truintje gave as a three-year-old 571-5 lbs. of milk in one day.

Noontide, gave as a two-year-old the first season after importation, 31 lbs. of milk in one day, 834 lbs. 1 oz. in one month, and 5,472 lbs. 12 oz. in nine months and twenty days, when record was discontinued.

No. 151.   **AAGGIE MAY.**   No. 24.

(H. H. B. Vol. 6, No. 2,601.) Calved March 2d, 1881. Imported by us August, 1882.

Sire, DeRuiter, (N. H. B. 89), (See cut.) See chart of Sir Henry 2d of Aaggie, and records of Aaggie family, page 22.

Dam, Blokker 2d, (N. H. B. 391), has a two-year-old record of 45 lbs. 8 oz. in one day on grass.

Blokker 2d's sire was Gerrit, (N. H. B. 31), and her dam was Blokker, (N. H. B. 390), by Rooker, the sire of Aaggie (901). See No. 98.

Sire of Gerrit was Cornelius, and dam deGoede, the dam of Jacob 1st (N. H. B. 20). A Prize cow at Paris Exposition, with a record of 91½ lbs. in one day.

Aaggie May gave 9,279 lbs. 6 oz. of milk in eleven months and eleven days as a two-year-old, the first season after importation.

She has given as a three-year-old 57 lbs. 13 oz. in one day, and 7,642 lbs. in five months and thirteen days to Sept. 26th.

No. 152.   **LILLA.**   No. 161.

(H. H. B. Vol. 6, No. 2,783.) Calved March 9th, 1881. Imported by us in August, 1882. Small star, small white spot on left shoulder, fore legs black to knee.

Sire, District bull of Beemster.

Dam, Kragt, gave 73 1-5 lbs. of milk in a day.

Grandam, a very fine cow.

Lilla gave the first season in this country, as a two-year-old, 6,730 lbs. 7 oz. of milk. She has given this season, as a three-year-old, 45 lbs. 7 oz. in one day, and 5,674 lbs. 13 oz. in five months and seventeen days to Sept. 26th.

No. 153.   **NETHERLAND DOWAGER 2d.**   No. 32.

(H. H. B Vol. 6. No. 2,633.) Calved March 10th, 1881. Imported by us in 1882. About two-thirds black with star.

Sire, Schemmel, son of Netherland Dowager. See No. 97.

Schemmel is the sire of Netherland Prince (See No. 2), Netherland Princess No. 123, Netherland Belle No. 138, and Netherland Countess No. 133.

Dam, Netherland Dowager. See No. 97.

Grandam, Oude Schemmel, has a record of over 80 lbs. in a day.

Schemmel was sired by Schreuder, the sire of Netherland Queen (414), (See No. 104), and Netherland Duchess (2,498). See No. 112.

Netherland **Dowager 2d,** gave as a two-year-old the first season after importation 31 lbs. 1 oz. in one day. 835 lbs. 9 oz. in one month, and 7,066 lbs. 10 oz. in eleven months and eleven days. She has given this season as a three-year old 55 lbs. 1 oz. in a day, and 6,185 lbs. 7 oz. in five months and four days to Sept. 26th.

No. 154.   **AAGGIE BEAUTY 2d.**   No. 333.

(H. H. B. Vol. 6, No. 2,631) Calved March 12th, 1881. Imported by us September, 1882.

Sire, Jacob 2d, (N. H. B. 56), (See cut). See chart of Sir Henry 2d of Aaggie, and records of Aaggie family, page 22.

Dam, Aaggie Beauty (2,907.) (Maritje 2d, N. H. B. 572). See No. 117.

Grandam, Maritje, (N. H. B. 570), has a record on grass, as a three-year-old, of 68 lbs. 4 oz. in one day.

Aaggie Beauty 2d came in the last of February, 1883, and gave 48 lbs. 4 oz. of milk in one day, 1,117 lbs. in one month, and 9,642 lbs. 3 oz. in eleven months and seven days, and made 7 lbs. 15½ oz. of butter in one week as a two-year-old.

She has given this season, as a three-year-old, 49 lbs. 4 oz. in one day, and 6,895 lbs. 14 oz. in six months, to Sept. 26th.

Bred to Netherland Prince, No. 2, Aug. 27th.

No. 155.   **SUSIE LEE.**   No. 298.

(H. H. B. Vol. 6. No. 2,900.) Calved March 15th, 1881. Imported by us September, 1882. Two-thirds black, strip in face.

Sire, Hogatoorn's bull.

Dam, Bowman, gave as a four-year-old 68 2-5 lbs. of milk in one day.

Grandam, a fine cow and splendid milker.

Bowman is dam of Rosa Bonheur (890), which has a record as a two-year-old of 57 lbs. 4 oz. of milk in one day, 1,646 lbs. 13 oz. in one month, and 13,411 lbs. 4 oz. in one year.

Susie Lee gave as a two-year-old, the first season after importation, 5,653 lbs. 12 oz. of milk in six months and twenty-six days.

She has given this season, as a three-year-old, 43 lbs. 12 oz. in one day, and 4,625 lbs. 6 oz. in four months and nine days, to Sept. 26th. She is dam of Susie Lee 2d, No. 428.

Bred to Netherland Prince, No. 2, Sept. 20th.

No. 156.   **PRUNELLA.**   No. 254.

(H. H. B. Vol. 6. No. 2,871.) Calved March 15th, 1881. Imported by us in August, 1882. Two-thirds black, medium star, neatly marked.

Sire, Doet's Bull.

Dam, Amerikan, gave as a three year-old 54 6-7 lbs. of milk in a day.

Grandam, a fine cow, with a record of 68 2 5 lbs. of milk in a day.

Prunella gave as a two-year-old, the first season after importation, 31 lbs. 13 oz. of milk in a day, 842 lbs. in month, and 6,472 lbs. 13 oz. in nine months and twenty-three days. She has given this season as a three-year-old 49 lbs. 10 oz. in one day, and 7,981 lbs. 6 oz. in six months and fifteen days to Sept. 26th.

No. 157.   LYRA.   No. 181.

(H. H. B. Vol. 6, No. 2,801.) Calved March 16, 1881. Imported by us in August, 1882. Medium star, little white dot over left shoulder, white under chin and throat.

Sire, Sijmen 2d, winner of First Prize at Uythoorn, Alkmaar and Mydrecht.

Grandsire, Prince (N. H. B. 59), winner of First Prize at London and Second at Paris.

G-grandsire, Sijmen (N. H. B. 23).

G-g-grandsire, Graaf Adolph winner of First Prize at The Hague.

Dam, Dirkje, has a record of 77 4-5 lbs. in a day.

Grandam, a great milker.

Lyra made in one week, on winter feed, 9 lbs. 3 oz. of butter when only two years old. She gave in ten months and nineteen days as a two-year-old 7,476 lbs. 15 oz. She has given this season, as a three-year-old, 46 lbs. 7 oz. in one day, and 6,117 lbs. 2 oz. in five months and nine days to Sept. 26th. She is dam of Lyra's Prince No. 55.

No. 158.   LIGHTSOME.   No. 162.

(H. H. B. Vol. 6, No. 2.784.) Calved March 16th. 1881. Imported by us August, 1882. Strip in face, white back of jaws up to both ears, well marked.

Sire, District bull of Beemster.

Dam, Tyme gave 68 2-5 lbs. in one day.

Lightsome gave as a two-year-old the first season after importation, 7,629 lbs. 5 oz. in ten months. She is sister to Ristori (1.890), which gave as a two-year old 38 lbs. 12 oz. in one day, and 8,774 lbs in nine months and twenty-five days, when she was sold.

Lightsome has given this season as a three-year-old 49 lbs. 2 oz. in one day, and 7,275 lbs. 4 oz. in five months and twenty-eight days, to Sept. 26th. She is dam of Lightsome 2d, No. 424.

No. 159.   MISS NANNA.   No. 204.

(H. H. B. Vol. 6, No. 2,824.) Calved March 25th, 1881. Imported by us August, 1882. Two-thirds black, strip in face and white around nose, legs, belly and switch white, very nicely marked.

Sire, District bull of Hem.

Dam, Sijtje, gave as a three-year-old 52 2-5 lbs. in one day

Grandam, a great milker.

Miss Nanna calved when only twenty-three months old just after importation, and gave 35 lbs. 7 oz. of milk in one day, 1,015 lbs. 9 oz. in one month, and 7,022 lbs. 1 oz. in ten months, and made in one week on winter feed, 7 lbs. 13½ oz. of butter. She won Second Prize at New York State Fair in 1883.

She has given this season as a three-year-old 1,995 lbs. 3 oz. in three months, to Sept 26th.

Bred to Netherland Prince No. 2, August 26th.

No. 160.   NETHERLAND JEWEL.   No. 341.

(H. H. B. Vol. 6, No. 2,642.) Calved March 25th, 1881. Imported by us in September, 1882.

Sire, District bull of Heilo.

Dam, Gert Met 10th, a fine milker.

G-dam, Gert Met 9th, a great milker.

G-g-dam was a sister to Lady Netherland (1,263). See No. 99.

G-g-g-dam, Gert Met 2d, has a record of 71 lbs. 8 oz. in a day.

G-g-g-g-dam, Gert Met, a very fine cow and heavy milker, was kept twenty years for breeding.

Netherland Jewel has given this season 5,508 lbs. 10 oz. in seven months and fourteen days to Sept 26th. She is dam of Netherland Jewel 2d, No. 263, and Netherland Jewel 3d's Princess No. 414.

Bred to Netherland Prince No. 2 April 22d.

No. 161.   **SILENE.**   No. 278.

(H. H. B. Vol. 6, No. 2,890.) Calved March 28th, 1881. Imported by us in September, 1882. Long star, two thirds black.

Sire, Bakker's bull.

Dam, Kossen, gained First Prize at Schagen for most and best milk. Record $82\frac{1}{3}$ lbs in a day.

Silene has given as a two-year old, the first season after importation, 945 lbs. of milk in one month, and 7,735 lbs. 3 oz. in ten months and nine days; and this season has given 46 lbs. 10 oz. in one day and 6,658 lbs. 3 oz in five months and seventeen days to Sept. 26th She is dam of Silene 2d, No. 419.

No. 162.   **ALBINO.**   No. 268.

(H. H. B. Vol. 6, No. 2,654.) Calved April 5th, 1881. Imported by us in August, 1882. Mostly white, strip in face.

Sire, District bull of Hoogcarspel.

Dam, Klasina Hengeveld (N. H. B. 656), gave 102 lbs of milk in one day, and 956 lbs. 8 oz. in ten consecutive days.

Grandam, a great milker.

Albino calved when twenty-two months old, just after imimportation, and gave 35 lbs. 11 oz. of milk in one day, 1,024 bs. 7 oz. in one month, and 7,516 lbs. 11 oz. in eleven months; and this season has given 6,043 lbs. 1 oz. in six months to Oct. 1st. She is dam of Albino 2d No. 258.

Bred to Netherland Prince No. 2, July 25th.

No. 163.   **MILLICENT.**   No. 205.

(H. H. B. Vol. 6, No. 2,825.) Calved April 5th, 1881. Imported by us August, 1882. Two-thirds black, medium star, white over nose, white switch, legs and belly.

Sire, District bull of Hem.

Dam, Mooike, gave as a three-year-old 57 1-6 lbs. in one day.

Grandam, an extra milker.

Millicent has given this season 4,460 lbs. 15 oz. in seven months and eleven days, to Sept. 26th. Owing to an accident this heifer has not made the record we think she was capable of making under more favorable circumstances.

Bred to Neptune No. 1 April 18th.

No. 164.   **AAGGIE LEILA.**   No. 151.

(H. H. B. Vol, 6, No. 2,603).) Calved April 25th, 1881. Imported by us August, 1882. One-half black, strip in face, white around nose, four black spots on left side, and one on left flank, irregular white over left shoulder, two black spots on right shoulder, large irregular black spot on right side surrounding small white spot.

Sire, deRuiter, (N. H. B. 89), (See chart of Sir Henry 2d of Aaggie). See milk records of Aaggie family, page 22.

Dam, Aaggie Flora, (2,606), (No. 10 N. H. B. 574), she by Jacob 2d, (N. H. B. 56). (See cut). See chart.

G-dam, DeSchot, (N. H. B. 573), she by Rooker, the sire of Aaggie, (901). See No. 98.

DeSchot has a milk record of 76 lbs. in one day.

G-g-dam, Oude Schot,

Aaggie Flora gave in Holland before importation, when three-year-old, 68 lbs. 8 oz. of milk in one day. She gave as a four-year-old, just after importation, 3,001 lbs. 14 oz. in two months and eleven days when we sold her.

She made in February, 1883, 11 lbs. 13 oz. of butter in one week.

Aaggie Leila has given this season, (her first in milk), 44 lbs. in one day, and 6,486 lbs. 4 oz. in seven months and sixteen days, to Sept. 26th. Owing to sickness and other causes her record is much smaller than it would have been had her health and condition been perfect. Early in the season she bid fair to make an unusual record.

Bred to N. Prince No. 2, April 16th.

No. 165.　　　　　**MIGNONETTE.**　　　　　No. 206.

(H. H. B. Vol. 6, No. 2,826.) Calved April 30th, 1881. Imported by us August, 1882. Three-fourths black, medium star, white on left side of nose, legs, belly and switch white, well marked.

Sire, Peter, (N. H. B. 103), gained First Prize at Schagen, Alkmaar, London and Kullemburger, also First Prize at Leyden as the best bull and best animal.

Peter's dam a deep milker.

Peter is the sire of Nundine (2,845), imported by us, and which gave as a two-year-old 63 lbs. 5 oz in one day, and 1,802 lbs. 10 oz. in one month.

Dam, Anna, gave as a four-year-old 68 2-5 lbs. in one day.

Mignonette gave as a two-year-old 7,242 lbs. 9 oz. in one year.

Bred to Netherland Prince, No. 2, January 18th.

No 166.   **NETHERLAND QUEEN 3d.**

(H. H. B. Vol. 5, No. 1,466.) Calved May 16th, 1881. Beautifully marked, star, white spot on shoulder, and one on hips, legs, belly and switch white.

Sire, Uncle Tom (163), he by Rip Van Winkle (35). See No. 66 for pedigree of Uncle Tom.

Dam, Netherland Queen (414), by Schreuder. See No. 104.

G-dam, Lady Netherland, No. 99.

G-g-dam, Gert Met 2d, gave 71 lbs. 8 oz. in one day.

G-g-g-dam, Gert Met, a very fine cow and heavy milker, was kept twenty years for breeding.

Netherland Queen 3d calved when twenty-two months old and gave in ten months and four days 7,260 lbs. and 4 oz. and this season has given 47 lbs. 2 oz. in one day, and 6,514 lbs. 2 oz. in five months and seventeen days, to Sept. 26th.

No. 167.   **ÆGIS 6th.**

(H. H. B. Vol. 6, No. 2,088.) Calved October 12th, 1881. Star, small spot on left shoulder, spot on hip, white legs, belly and switch.

Sire, Neptune (711), (See No. 1), he by Jacob 2d, (N. H. B. 56). See milk records of the Aaggie family, page 22.

Neptune's dam, Aaggie (No. 98), by Rooker.

Dam, Ægis 2d, (235), (See No. 113), by Uncle Tom, (163), he by Rip Van Winkle, (35).

G-dam, Ægis (69), No 96.

G-g-dam, Agoo (1).

G-g-g-dam, Dowager (7).

Ægis 6th calved in December and gave as a two-year-old 44 lbs. 9 oz. of milk in one day, 1,196 lbs. 10 oz. in one month and 9,053 lbs. in nine months and seventeen days, to October 1st. She is the dam of Netherland Conqueror, No. 19.

Bred to Netherland Prince, No. 2, July 11th.

No. 168. **SOLDENE.** No. 285.

(H. H. B. Vol. 6, No. 2,896.) Calved Feb. 6th, 1882. Imported by us in 1882 Two-thirds black, long star well marked.

Sire, Willem (N. H. B. 82), winner of First Prize at Alkmaar and Schagen ; also winner of First Prize as best bull at Gouda in September, 1882

Dam, Martje, has given 73 1-5 lbs of milk in a day as a four-year-old.

No. 169. **ALDINE.** No. 1.

(H. H. B. Vol. 6, No. 2,643.) Calved Feb. 10th, 1882. Imported by us August, 1882. Two thirds black, large star and snip, well marked.

Sire, Peter, (N. H B. 103, gained First Prize at Schagen, Alkmaar, London and Kullemburger, also First Prize at Leyden as best bull and best animal. See No. 165.

Peter's dam, a deep milker.

Dam, Tiel, (N. H. B. 647), gained First Prizes at Haarlem, Schagen, Leyden and Alkmaar.

She gave 54 6-7 lbs. of milk in one day.

Aldine has given this season 5,867 lbs. 14 oz. in eight months and ten days, to Sept. 26th.

Bred to Neptune No. 1, August 9th.

No. 170. **AAGGIE LEE.** No. 312.

(H. H. B. Vol. 6, No. 2,613.) Calved Feb. 18th, 1882 Imported by us September, 1882. Two-thirds black, strip in face.

Sire, Napoleon, (N. H. B. 129,) he by Jacob 2d, (N. H. B. 56, (See cut). See chart of Sir Henry 2d of Aaggie, and milk records of the Aaggie family, page 22.

Napoleon's dam, Porcelein 2d, (N. H. B. 392), by Gerrit, (N. H. B. 31), he by Cornelius.

Porcelein's 2d's dam, Porcelein, (N H. B. 147), by Rooker, the sire of Aaggie (901). See No. 98.

Porcelein has a record of 80 lbs. 1 oz. of milk in one day. Her dam was Oude Porcelein.

Gerrit's dam, deGoede, the dam of Jacob 1st. See chart of Sir Henry 2d of Aaggie.

Aaggie Lee's dam, Marie, (N. H. B. 373), has a four-year-old record of 64 lbs. of milk in one day.

Aaggie Lee has given as a two-year-old 4,094 lbs. 2 oz. in four months and twenty-five days, to Sept. 26th. She is sister to Aaggie Lee 2d, No. 232.

No. 171.   **COMEDIA.**   No. 1,055.

(H. H. B. Vol. 8, No. 6,997.) Calved Feb. 24th, 1882. Imported by us May, 1884. Two-thirds black, star, snip, white over shoulders to belly, left side and over hips to flanks, black at rump.

Sire, Alexander (N. H. B. 83), a very superior animal; his dam, an excellent cow and a great milker.

Alexander is also sire of Belle Alexander No. 179, Esther Alexander No. 184, Alexander's Queen No. 172, etc.

Dam, Geertje, gave $74\frac{1}{2}$ lbs. of milk in a day.

No. 172.   **ALEXANDER'S QUEEN.**   No. 1,056.

(H. H. B. Vol. 8, No. 6,998.) Calved Feb. 27th, 1882. Three-fourths black, star, snip, white over shoulders, large white over hips and rump.

Sire, Alexander (H. H. B. 83.) See No. 171.

Dam, Zijp, gave 73 1-5 lbs. of milk in a day as a six-year-old.

G-dam, a good cow and good milker.

No. 173.   **AAGGIE CORNELIA** 4th.   No. 609.

(H. H. B. Vol. 6, No. 4,343.) Calved March, 1882. Imported by us in June, 1883. Two-thirds white, strip in face, irregular white over shoulders to leg on left side, mostly white from shoulders back, little black on rump and tail.

Sire, Alexander (N. H. B. 83). See No. 171.

Dam, Aaggie Cornelia (4,410). See No. 102.

Aaggie Cornelia 4th has given this season, the first after importation, commencing before she was two years old, 5,506 lbs. 9 oz. in seven months and ten days to Sept. 26th. She is sister to Aaggie Cornelia 2d No. 115, and Aaggie Cornelia 3d No. 132

No. 174.   ST. CATHARINE.   No. 763.

(H. H. B. Vol. 7, No. 4,488.) Calved March 2, 1882. Imported by us in August, 1883. Two-thirds white, white in face, black spots all over body, large black patch on each side filled with white spots, legs, belly and nearly all of tail white.

Sire, District bull of Venhuisen, same as sire of Strathmore. See No. 3.

Dam, Jacoba (N. Hol. H. B. 95), a very fine cow, which has a record of 77 4-5 lbs of milk in a day.

St. Catharine has given this season, coming in before she was two years old, 35 lbs. 14 oz. in one day, and 4,527 lbs. 13 oz. in six months and twenty-five days to Sept. 26th. She is sister to Dorrice No. 299.

Bred to Neptune No. 1 July 16th.

No. 175.   DIVINIA.   No. 1,054.

(H. H. B. Vol. 8, No. 6,996.) Calved March 3d, 1882. Imported by us in May, 1884. One-half black, star, snip, long black saddle over back.

Sire, Alexander (N. H. B. 83). See No. 171.

Dam, Ellerbroek gave 68 2-5 lbs. of milk in a day as a five-year old.

G-dam and g-g-dam, choice cows and fine milkers.

No. 176.   AAGGIE SADIE.   No. 723.

(H. H. B. Vol. 7, No. 4,472.) Calved March 5th, 1882. Imported by us in August, 1883. Mostly black, small star, fore legs black nearly to ankles, hind legs black to gambrels.

Sire, de Ruiter (N. H. B. 89), by Jacob 2d (N. H. B. 56),

&c. See chart of Sir Henry 2d of Aaggie and milk records of the Aaggie family, page 22.

Dam, Polly, a fine cow, which has a record of 77 4-5 lbs. of milk in a day.

Aaggie Sadie has given this season, commencing when she was just two years old, 46 lbs. 5 oz. in one day, 5,184 lbs. 5 oz. in six months and twenty days to Sept. 26th.

Bred to Netherland Prince No. 2, July 21st.

No. 177.   **LADY de RUITER.**   No. 900.

(H. H. B. Vol. 8, No. 6,942.) Calved March 15th, 1882. Imported by us in May, 1884. Three-fourths white, strip in face, irregular black spot over back and down to belly, both sides, black at rump.

Sire, de Ruiter (N. H. B. 89), he by Jacob 2d (N. H. B. 56). See chart of Sir Henry 2d of Aaggie and milk records of the Aaggie family, page 22.

Dam, Teunisje, has given 64 lbs of milk in a day.

Grandam has given 68 2-5 lbs. in a day.

Teunisje is dam of Sir Henry of Aaggie's Phlox No. 325.

Bred to Netherland King No. 15, Sept. 2d.

No 178.   **AAGGIE MERREL.**   No. 329.

(H. H. B. Vol. 6, No. 2,628.) Calved March 8th, 1882. Imported by us in September, 1882. Three-fourths black, with strip in face.

Sire, de Ruiter (N. H. B. 89), (See chart of Sir Henry 2d of Aaggie). See milk records of the Aaggie family, page 22.

Dam, Bregger 3d gave 64 lbs. of milk in a day as a three-year-old.

G-dam, Bregger 2d.

G-g-dam, Bregger.

Aaggie Merrel has given this season, as a two-year old, 46 lbs. 1 oz in a day, and 5,771 lbs. 3 oz. in five months and fifteen days to Sept. 26th. She is sister to Jacob Wit's Belva No. 380, and is dam of Netherland Leo No. 52.

No. 179.　　　**BELLE ALEXANDER.**　　　No. 607.

(H. H. B. Vol. 7, No. 4,408.) Calved March 8th, 1882. Imported by us in June, 1883. Mostly black, small star, white over right hip, fore legs black nearly to ankles, and hind legs black to gambrels, belly and switch white.

Sire, Alexander (N. H. B. 83). See No. 171.

Dam, Forrest, gave 54 6-7 lbs. of milk in a day.

Belle Alexander has given this season, the first after importation, as a two-year-old, 46 lbs. 11 oz. in a day, and 4,003 3 oz. in four months and eight days to Oct. 1st. She is dam of Belle Alexander 2d No. 433.

No. 180.　　　**AAGGIE KATE.**　　　No. 548.

(H. H. B. Vol. 7, No. 4,516.) Calved March 10th, 1882. Imported by us in June, 1883. Two-thirds black, large star, nose and under jaw white, white strip from shoulder to right fore leg, four small white spots on left side, belly and switch white.

Sire, Lincoln (N. H. B. 120), he by Jacob 2d (N. H. B. 56). For extension, see Clovis No. 13, and milk records of the Aaggie family, page 22.

Dam, Mathilda 2d, gave as a three-year-old 54 6-7 lbs. of milk in one day.

G-dam, Mathilda (N. H. B. 444), has a five-year-old record of 68 2-5 lbs. of milk in one day.

G-g-dam, a fine cow, with a record of 80 lbs. in a day.

Aaggie Kate has given this season 1,805 lbs. 13 oz. in two months and twenty-three days to Sept. 24th.

No. 181.   **BEAUTY OF WALTHAM.**   No. 634.

(H. H. B. Vol 7, No. 4,546.) Calved March 10th, 1882. Imported by us June, 1883. Two-thirds white, medium star, snip, long black saddle over back, containing small white spot on right side, small black spot just above right gambrel, legs, belly and two thirds tail white.

Sire, District bull of Nieuwe Niedorp.

Dam, Trijntje.

Bred to Chesterfield No. 6, June 20th.

No. 182.   **AAGGIE CONSTANCE.**   No. 330.

(H. H. B. Vol. 7, No. 2,629.) Calved March 10th, 1882. Imported by us in September, 1882. Five-sixths black, very small star, snip, black to left knee outside, irregular white between left hip and roots of tail, small white splash on right shoulder, small white spot at point of right hip.

Sire, deRuiter, (N. H. B. 89), (See cut). See chart of Sir Henry 2d of Aaggie, and milk records of the Aaggie family, page 22.

Dam, Kappijne 2d,. No. 129, imported by us in May, 1884, gave as a two-year-old 41 1-6 lbs. in one day.

Aaggie Constance has given this season as a two-year-old 76 lbs. 6 oz. in one day, and 6,392 lbs. 9 oz. in four months and twelve days, to Sept. 26th. She is dam of Aaggie Constance's Sir Henry No. 65.

142   HOLSTEIN CATTLE.

No. 183.   **AAGGIE BEATRICE.**   No. 605

(H. H. B. Vol. 7, No. 4,336) Calved March 10th, 1882 Imported by us in June, 1883. Seven eighths black, star, white over left shoulder and over hips, black on fore legs to below knees and to gambrels, belly and switch white.

Sire, Alexander (N. H. B. 83). See No. 171.

Dam, Neeltje, by Jacob 2d (N. H. B. 56). See chart of Sir Henry 2d of Aaggie and milk records of the Aaggie family, page 22.

Neetje gave as a four-year-old 73 1-5 lbs. of milk in one day.

Aaggie Beatrice has given this season, the first after importation, commencing before she was two years old, 4,320 lbs. 10 ounces in six months and twenty-five days to Sept. 26th.

No. 184.   **ESTHER ALEXANDER.**   No. 604.

(H. H. B. Vol. 7, No. 4,407.) Calved March 12, 1882. Imported by us in June, 1883. Three-fourths black, star, snip, white over shoulders to belly on left side, large white over hips extending forward to middle of back, two black spots on right fore leg, one on right hind leg.

Sire, Alexander (N. H. B. 83). See No. 171.

Dam, Trintje, gave as a four-year-old 64 lbs. of milk in one day.

Bred to Sir Henry 2d of Aaggie, No. 4, January 25th, 1884.

No. 185.   **AAGGIE PAULINE**   No. 324.

(H. H. B. Vol. 6, No. 2,622.) Calved March 13th, 1882. Imported by us in September, 1882. Two-thirds black, white head, black around and under each eye, black strip between horns, two black spots at point of right hip, irregular black along middle of right side, two black spots on left thigh, legs, belly and most of tail white.

Sire, de Ruiter (N. H. B. 89), (See cut). See chart of Sir Henry 2d of Aaggie and milk records of the Aaggie family, page 22.

Dam, De Schot, gave 68 lbs. 8 oz. of milk in a day.

Aaggie Pauline has given this season, as a two-year-old, 35 lbs. 1 oz. in a day, and 3,796 lbs. 13 oz in four months and seventeen days to Sept. 26th.

No. 186. **NETHERLAND BARONESS 4th.** No. 295.

(H. H. B. Vol. 6, No. 2,638.) Calved March 14th, 1882. Imported by us in September, 1882. Two-thirds white, strip in face, black spot on outside of left fore leg near body, two black spots on left side, nine black spots on right side and two on right fore leg, legs, belly and switch, white

Sire, Noome.

Dam, Netherland Baroness (2,635). See No. 103.

Netherland Baroness 4th, has given this season, as a two-year-old, 46 lbs. 11 oz. in one day, and 2,780 lbs. in two months and eighteen days to Sept. 26th. She is a sister to Netherland Baroness 2d, No. 141, and Netherland Baroness 5th, No. 265.

No. 187. **NETHERLAND PRIDE.** No. 344.

(H. H. B. Vol. 6, No. 2,641.) Calved March 15th, 1882. Imported by us in September, 1882. Four-fifths black, small star, irregular white over left shoulder, black to knees and to left gambrel, belly and switch white.

Sire, District bull of Purmer.

Dam, Heinis, gave as a five-year-old $72\frac{1}{2}$ lbs. of milk in one day.

Heinis is a sister to Netherland Queen (414) See No. 104.

Netherland Pride has given this season as a two-year-old 49 lbs. 4 oz. in one day, and 6,190 lbs. 3 oz. in five months and eighteen days, to Oct. 1st. She is sister to Netherland Waukesha No. 138½.

No. 188. **EASTER MAID.** No. 500.

(H. H. B. Vol. 7, No. 4,511.) Calved March 15th, 1882. Imported by us in June, 1883. Five-sixths black, small star, small white spot on left shoulder, large white spot over hips, legs, belly and switch white.

Sire, Uitentuis' bull.

Dam, Bleeker, has a record of 68 2-5 lbs. of milk in one day. She is the dam of Meadow Maid (1,793), imported by us in 1881.

Meadow Maid dropped her first calf before she was two years old, just after importation, and gave 37 lbs. 15 oz. in one day, and 7,260 lbs. 7 oz. in nine months and fifteen days when she was sold. She made in one week on winter feed 9 lbs. 4¼ oz. of butter.

Bred to Sir Henry 2d of Aaggie No. 4, May 22d.

No. 189. **BONANZA MAID.** No. 630.

(H. H. B. Vol. 7, No. 4,544.) Calved March 15th, 1882. Imported by us in June, 1883. Five-sixths black, star, left fore leg black to ankle, right fore leg black to knee, white on right hip, small white spot near right fore leg, small black spot on right flank, hind legs black to gambrels.

Sire, District bull of Oosterblokker.

Dam, Klasina Hengeveld 2d.

G-dam, Klasina Hengeveld, (N. H. B. 656), gave 102 lbs. of milk in one day, and 956 lbs. 8 oz. in ten consecutive days.

G-g-dam, a great milker.

Klasina Hengeveld is the dam of Albino. See No. 162.

Bonanza Maid has given this season, the first after importation, as a two-year-old, 55 lbs. 14 oz. in one day, and 5,557 lbs. 6 oz. in four months and twenty-eight days, to Sept. 26th. She is dam of Bonanza King No. 60.

No. 190.   **AAGGIE IDALINE 4th.**   No. 779.

(H. H. B. Vol. 7, No. 4,365.) Calved March 16th, 1882. Imported by us in August, 1883 One half black, black cheeks, white around nose, irregular black saddle over back, containing two white spots on each side, three black spots, one near each hip, legs, belly and switch white.

Sire, Willem, (N. H. B. 84), a very fine bull with strip in face. Also sire of Executrix, No. 196. His dam a very fine cow.

Dam, Aaggie Idaline 3d, (4,364), (See No. 128). She by Jacob 2d, (N. H. B. 56), etc. See milk records of the Aaggie family, page 22.

Grandam, Naatje, gave 68 2-5 lbs. of milk in one day.

Aaggie Idaline 4th has given this season, the first after importation, commencing before she was two years old, 3,642 lbs. 8 oz. in seven months and six days, to Sept. 26th.

No. 191.   **AAGGIE EVA.**   No. 597.

(H. H. B. Vol. 7, No. 4,354.) Calved March 16th, 1882. Imported by us in June, 1883. Three-fourths white, black cheeks, irregular black surrounding seven white spots on neck and running nearly back to shoulders, black spots on each side, small black spot at roots of tail, legs, belly and tail white.

Sire, de Ruiter, (N. H. B. 89), (See cut). See chart of Sir Henry 2d of Aaggie, and milk records of the Aaggie family, page 22.

Dam, Agatha, gave as a five-year-old 68 2-5 lbs. of milk in one day, and is unquestionably a descendant of Rooker, sire of Aaggie (901), although the exact relationship has not been established.

Aaggie Eva has given this season, the first after importation, commencing before she was twenty-three months old, 36 lbs. 11 oz. in one day, and 6,716 lbs. 12 oz. in seven months and sixteen days, to Sept. 26th.

Aaggie Eva is dam of Aaggie Eva's Rufus, No. 24.

Bred to Netherland Prince, No. 2, August 6th

No. 192.   **LADY ARTIS.**   No. 575.

(H. H. B. Vol. 7, No. 4,525.) Calved March 19th, 1882. Imported by us in June, 1883. Mostly white, two large black spots on left side of neck, one on right side, small black spots scattered over body.

Sire, Artis (N. H. B. 127). See No. 8.

Dam, Jansje (N. H. B. 596), has a record of 80 1-6 lbs. of milk in one day. She is a fine elegant cow, with fine escutcheon and milk veins.

G-dam, Johanna, has a record of 77 4-5 lbs. of milk in one day.

G-g-dam, Jacoba, has a record of 93 4-5 lbs. of milk in one day.

G-g-g-dam, Oude Zwart, gave 109 4-5 lbs. per day for twelve consecutive days.

Lady Artis has given this season, the first after importation, as a two-year-old, 41 lbs. 11 oz. in one day, and 1,815 lbs. 15 oz. in one month and eighteen days to Sept 24th.

No. 193.   **AAGGIE CLEORA.**   No. 637.

(H. H. B. Vol. 7, No. 4,567.) Calved March 20th, 1882. Imported by us in June, 1883. Three-fourths black, large star, large white spot over hips, small white spot on left side, very small white spot on rump, left side, legs, belly and most of tail white.

Sire, Jacob 2d (N. H B. 56), (See cut) See chart of Sir Henry 2d of Aaggie, and milk records of the Aaggie family, page 22.

Dam, Geertruida, gave as a four-year-old 64 lbs. of milk in one day.

Aaggie Cleora has given this season, the first after importation, commencing before she was two years old, 4,501 lbs. 12 oz. in six months and twelve days to Sept. 24th.

No. 194.   **SIMPLICITY.**   No. 1,053.

(H. H. B. Vol. 8, No. 6,995.) Calved March 20th, 1882. Imported by us in May, 1884. Two-thirds black, star, white over shoulders and hips and down to belly on both sides.

Sire, Alexander (N. H. B. 83). See No. 171.

Dam, Antje, gave 68 2-5 lbs. of milk in a day.

Grandam, a good cow.

No. 195.   **CARRIE FAIR.**   No. 632.

(H. H. B. Vol. 7, No. 4,415.) Calved March 25th, 1882. Imported by us in June, 1883. Three-fourths white, wide strip in face, black cheeks and black neck, large black patch on left side, one large irregular and one small black spot just above left fore arm, three black spots on right side.

Sire, Duin's bull.

Dam, Mooike.

Carrie Fair has given this season, the first after importation as a two-year-old, 36 lbs. 10 oz in one day, and 2,767 lbs. 14 oz. in four months and twelve days to Sept. 26th.

No. 196.   **EXECUTRIX.**   No. 595.

(H. H. B. Vol. 7, No. 4,401.) Calved March 15th, 1882. Imported by us in June, 1883. Two-thirds black, large star, snip, large irregular white over shoulders to belly on left side and nearly to belly on right side, large irregular white spot over hips and rump, small white spot on each side, legs, belly and switch white.

Sire, Willem (N. H. B. 84), a very fine bull with strip in face; also sire of Aaggie Idaline 4th, No. 190. His dam a very fine cow.

Dam, Stapel, has a record of 68 2-5 lbs. of milk in a day.

Executrix has given this season, the first after importation, as a two-year-old, 47 lbs. 1 oz. in a day, and 1,673 lbs. 13 oz. in one month and nine days to Sept. 24th. She also won First Prize at the New York State Fair in 1884, competing with a large number of meritorious animals.

No. 197.   **AAGGIE ROSA 3d.**   No. 309.
(See Chart.)

(H. H. B. Vol. 6, No. 2,611.) Calved March 25th, 1882. Imported by us in September, 1882. Three-fourths black, strip in face, two white spots on left side, one white spot just forward of left flank, irregular white from belly to back just back of right shoulder, four black spots on outside of right fore leg.

Sire, deRuiter (N. H. B. 89.) (See cut). See chart of Sir Henry 2d of Aaggie, and milk records of the Aaggie family, page 22.

Dam, Aaggie Rosa 2d, (2,610). See No. 139.

Grandam, Aaggie Rosa No. 107, also dam of Sir Henry 2d of Aaggie No. 4. See chart.

No. 198.   **CLOTHILDE 3d.**

(H. H. B. Vol. 6, No. 2,091.) Calved March 29th 1882. Star, snip, strip of white over right shoulder to belly, spot on hips to flank on right side, legs, belly and switch white.

Sire, Uncle Tom (163), he by Rip Van Winkle (35). For extension, see No. 66.

Dam, Clothilde. (See No. 118,) she by Dirk.

Grandam, Stijl gave 65 lbs. in one day.

Clothilde 3d was sold when a calf, and so highly did we esteem the animal and her family, that we purchased her at a high figure in order to have all the known living relatives of Clothilde in our herd.

No. 199.   **BETSY TROTWOOD.**   No. 643.

(H. H. B. Vol. 7, No. 4,418.) Calved March 31st. 1882. Imported by us in June, 1883. Three-fourths black, star, snip, white over shoulders, white over hips and rump extending to middle of back and flank on left side, black spot on left flank, nest of white spots just above left fore arm, three black spots on right flank.

Sire, Willem, (N. H. B. 82), winner of First Prizes at Alkmaar and Schagen, also First Prize at Gouda as best bull in September, 1882.

Dam, Kathrina, gave as a four-year-old 52 2-5 lbs. of milk in one day.

Betsy Trotwood has given this season, the first after importation, 4,151 lbs. 10 oz. in six months and eleven days, to Sept. 26th. She is dam of Betsy Trotwood 2d, No. 425.

Bred to Netherland Prince, No. 2, August 2d.

No. 200.   **DeRUITER'S BONA.**   No. 776.

(H. H. B. Vol. 8, No. 6,887.) Calved March, 1882. Imported by us in May, 1884. Three-fourths white, strip in face, large black spot on left side and two on right, larger one on each side containing small white spot, small black spots on sides, flanks, and below rump.

Sire, de Ruiter, (N. H. B. 89), he by Jacob 2d, (N. H. B. 56). See milk records of the Aaggie family, page 22.

Dam, Cornelia, a splendid milker and looks like her daughter.

Bred to Netherland King, No. 15, Sept. 16th.

No. 201.   **De RUITER'S BEATUS.**   No. 777.

(H. H. B. Vol. 8, No. 6,888.) Calved March, 1882. Imported by us in May, 1884. Two-thirds white, strip in face, large irregular black spot on left side, several large spots on right side.

Sire, de Ruiter (N. H. B. 89), he by Jacob 2d (N H. B 56). See milk records of the Aaggie family, page 22.

Dam, Catharina.

Bred to Netherland King No. 15, August 22d.

No. 202.   **FATINITZA 2d.**   No. 3.

(H. H. B. Vol. 6, No. 2,724.) Calved April 14th, 1882. Imported by us in 1882. Three-quarters black, strip in face, white nose, white over shoulders to belly, both sides, white on left hip, small white spot over right hip and one at root of tail.

Sire, de Valk (N. H. B. 160). Prize bull at Leyden. De Valk is brother to Marie Wortel (1,867), (Marie, N. H. B. 463), imported by us.

Dam, Fatinitza (2,723), (de Jood, N. H. B. 653), imported by us in 1882. She gave as a four-year-old 7,645 lbs. 3 oz. in six months, when she was sold.

G-dam Koning, a splendid milker.

Fatinitza's sire, Kohne's bull.

No. 203.   **VALLEY BEAUTY 2d.**   No. 613.

(H. H. B. Vol. 7, No. 4,532.) Calved April 15th, 1882. Imported by us in June, 1883. Two-thirds black, long star, white on nose, white over shoulders to belly both sides, white over hips to flank on right, black spot on left hind leg.

Sire, de Valk, (N. H. B. 160), Prize bull at Leyden. See No. 202.

Dam, Valley Beauty, (4,562.) See No. 106.

Grandam, Van Dort.

Valley Beauty 2d has given this season, the first after importation, as a two-year-old 55 lbs. 13 oz. in one day, and 3,816 lbs. 14 oz. in two months and twenty-seven days, to Sept. 26th.

She is the dam of Valley Beauty 2d's Marchioness, No. 435, and sister to Valley Beauty 3d, No. 226, and Valley Beauty 4th, No. 443.

No. 204.   **SINCERITY.**   No. 282.

(H. H. B. Vol. 7, No. 2,892.) Calved April 16th, 1882. Imported by us in September, 1882. Four-fifths black, small star, no white on left side, irregular white between hips and roots of tail, black to left gambrel, white strip from belly right side up to point of right shoulder.

Sire, Willem, (N. H. B. 82). Winner of First Prizes at Alkmaar and Schagen, also First Prize at Gouda as best bull in September, 1882.

Dam, Zwart Vries, a splendid cow, has a record of 77 4-5 lbs. of milk in one day.

Sincerity has given this season as a two-year-old 40 lbs. 15 oz. in one day, and 5,569 lbs. 5 oz. in six months and ten days, to Sept. 24th.

No. 205.   **MOTTLED BEAUTY 2d.**   No. 223.

(H. H. B. Vol. 6, No. 2,829.) Calved April 20th, 1882. Imported by us in September, 1882. Two-thirds black, strip in face, black nose, irregular white and black on both sides, no black crosses back bone, most of tail white.

Sire, District bull of Binnewysend.

Dam, Aafke, has a record of 87 lbs. of milk in one day.

Grandam, a fine milker.

Mottled Beauty 2d has given this season as a two-year-old 49 lbs. 7 oz. in one day, and 5,284 lbs. 14 oz. in four months and seventeen days, to Sept. 26th. She is sister to Mottled Beauty, No. 146, and dam of Mottled Beauty 2d's Pride, No. 436.

No. 206.   **CROWN JEWEL 2d.**   No. 18.

(H. H. B. Vol. 6, No. 2,697.) Calved April 20th, 1882. Imported by us in September, 1882. Five-sixths black, small star, white on right shoulder, small white spot on back between hips and roots of tail, black to left gambrel and below right gambrel.

Sire, Italy, he by Kees (N. H. B. 32). See Italy in pedigree of Lee Morgan No. 16.

Dam, Crown Jewel (2,690), (See cut), gave in Holland $82\frac{1}{2}$ lbs. of milk in one day, and won the First Prize in the sweepstakes class as best cow of any age or breed at Wageningen,

Holland, in a very large class. She gave the first season in this country, before being fully acclimated, 81 lbs. 13 oz. in one day, 2,119 lbs. 5 oz. in one month, and 14,724 lbs. 1 oz. in one year, and made in one week 19 lbs. 9 oz. of butter. This season she has given 4,765 lbs. 1 oz. in two months and nineteen days, to Sept. 26th, and was sold with her bull calf by her side for $2,500.

Crown Jewel 2d has given this season, commencing before she was two years old, 41 lbs. in one day, and 5,151 lbs. 6 oz. in five months and fifteen days, to Sept. 26th. She is dam of Crown Jewel 2d's Princess No. 423.

Bred to Netherland Prince No. 2, Sept. 15th.

No. 207. **BEAUTY OF NINON.** No. 622.

(H. H. B. Vol. 7, No. 4,541.) Calved April 24th, 1882. Imported by us in June, 1883. Three-fourths black, medium star, broad white from hips and rump to flank on right side, two small white spots near right flank and two on left side low down, legs, belly and most of tail white.

Sire, District bull of Beemster.

Dam, Pietje has a record of 61 4-5 lbs. of milk in one day.

Beauty of Ninon has given this season the first after importation commencing before she was 22 months old, 28 lbs. 15 oz. in one day, and 5,360 lbs. 4 oz. in seven months and thirteen days, to Sept. 26th. She is dam of Beauty of Ninon 2d, No. 416.

Bred to Netherland Prince No. 2, May 9th.

No. 208. **AAGGIE AURELIA.** No. 150.

(H. H. B. Vol. 6, No. 2,630.) Calved April 24th, 1882. Imported by us in September, 1882. Two-thirds black, star, snip, narrow white half way up back of jaws, irregular white over shoulders surrounding large black spot on right shoulder, large irregular white over hips to roots of tail, black spot on left flank, large black running from point of right hip to middle of right thigh, black spot right side of tail half way down.

Sire, Napoleon (N H. B. 129), he by Jacob 2d (N. H. B. 56), (See cut.) See chart of Sir Henry 2d of Aaggie.

Dam of Napoleon was Porcelein 2d (N. H. B. 392), by Gerrit (N. H. B. 31) he by Cornelius.

Dam of Porcelein 2d was Porcelein (N. H. B. 147), which has a record of 80 lbs. of milk in one day.

Dam of Gerrit was DeGoede, the dam of Jacob 1st. See chart.

Aaggie Aurelia's dam was Porcelein (N. H. B. 147). See chart and milk records of the Aaggie family, page 22.

Aaggie Aurelia has given this season as a two-year-old 2,203 lbs. 4 oz. in three months and sixteen days to Sept. 26th.

No. 209.   **TOPAZ 3d.**   No. 403.

(H. H. B. Vol. 6, No. 2,106.) Calved April 28th, 1882. Black and white, white face, black spot on under jaw, black spot on left fore knee, black spot on left flank, two white spots on left side, one small white spot on right shoulder, black at rump.

Sire, Netherland Prince (716), (See No 2). See records of the Netherland family, page 27.

Dam, Topaz (870), imported, she by Kees (N. H. B., 32), winner of First Prizes at Zaandam, Scheidam, Alkmaar, Haarlem, Rotterdam and Amsterdam; also Second Prizes at Amsterdam and Purmerende.

Kees' dam, Olje, a splendid cow and superior milker.

Grandam, Matedor (N. H. B. 263), has a record of 65 lbs. of

milk in one day, and was winner of six First Prizes at the Fairs of Holland.

Topaz gave as a two-year-old, under unfavorable conditions, 37 lbs. 13 oz. of milk in a day, 1,031 lbs. in one month, 9,811 lbs 4 oz. in a year, and 45 lbs. 11 oz. in one day as a three-year-old. When four years old she gave 57 lbs. 2 oz. in one day, 1,544 lbs. 14 oz. in one month, and 14,630 lbs. 2 oz. in one year.

She made 13 lbs. 3½ oz. of butter in one week on winter feed.

Italy, a son of Kees (N. H. B. 32), and therefore half brother to Topaz, is the sire of Molly Bawn (1,298), imported by us and sold when a yearling. She has given as a three-year old 70 lbs. 11 oz. of milk in a day, 2,012 lbs. 4 oz. in one month, and 16,391 lbs. 6 oz. in one year.

This is the highest three-year-old record yet made for same time by any cow of any breed of which we have knowledge.

Topaz 3d has given this season as a two-year-old 3,325 lbs. 2 oz. in four months and twenty-three days to Sept. 26th.

No. 210.   **ANTIQUE.**   No. 8.

(H. H. B. Vol. 6, No. 2,648.) Calved May 2d, 1882. Imported by us in September, 1882. Two-thirds black, star, snip, broad white up left shoulder, over and to belly on right side in narrow strip, irregular white over hips, legs, belly and switch white.

Sire, Van Beer's fine two-year-old bull.

Dam, Platform, a splendid cow, with a record of 87 lbs. of milk in one day.

Van Beer's bull's dam, a fine cow, with a record of 73 1-5 lbs. in one day.

Bred to Prince Imperial, No. 5, Feb. 29th.

No. 211.   NETHERLAND QUEEN 4th.

(H. H. B Vol. 6. No. 2,105.) Calved May 3d, 1882. Black and white, star, white spot on left shoulder, spot on hip, black spot on left gambrel, black spot on left fore knee, legs, belly and switch white.

Sire, Neptune, (711), (See No. 1), he by Jacob 2d, (N. H. B. 56), he by Jacob, (N. H. B. 20), he by Rooker, sire of Aaggie.

Neptune's dam, Aaggie (901). See milk records of the Aaggie family, page 22.

Dam, Netherland Queen, 2d, (560), (See No. 126). See records of the Netherland family, page 27.

G-dam, Netherland Queen, No. 104.

G-g-dam, Lady Netherland, No. 99.

G-g-g-dam, Gert Met 2d, gave 71 lbs. 8 oz. in one day.

G-g-g-g-dam, Gert Met, a very fine cow and heavy milker, was kept twenty years for breeding.

Netherland Queen 4th has given this season, commencing before she was two years old, 3,641 lbs. 10 oz. in five months and eleven days, to September 26th. She is dam of Netherland Queen 4th's Princess, No. 434.

No. 212.   ÆGIS 9th.   No. 179.

(H. H. B. Vol. 6, No. 3,014.) Calved Nov. 4th, 1882. Three-fourths black, small star, strip from left shoulder, over and down right side to belly, white over rump to belly both sides, black spots on left flank and on legs.

Sire, Neptune, (711.) See No. 1.

Dam, Ægis, (69). See No. 96.

Ægis 9th won First Prize at the New York State Fair in 1883.

Bred to Netherland Prince No. 2, June 18th.

Yearling Heifers.

No. 213.   **AAGGIE ETHEL.**   No. 512.

(H. H. B. Vol. 7, No. 4,353.) Calved Feb. 16th, 1883. Imported by us in August, 1883. Two-thirds white, strip in face, large irregular black spot on each side with several small ones, two small white spots on left side of neck and one on right side

Sire, Sir Henry of Aaggie (1,450). For extension, see Sir Donald of Aaggie No. 7, and milk records of the Aaggie family, page 22.

Dam, Grietje, a fine four-year-old with a record of 57 1-5 of milk in one day.

No. 214.   **GOLDEN ERA.**   No. 514.

(H. H. B. Vol. 8, No. 6,738.) Calved March 18th, 1883. Imported by us in August, 1883. Mostly black, small star, small white spot over shoulders, fore legs black to below knees.

Sire, Henri, a fine bull, black and white, star.

Henri's dam Rency 3d gave 73 1-5 lbs. in one day, an extra milker.

G-dam, Rency 2d, gave 75½ lbs. in one day.

G-g-dam, Rency, gave 77 4-5 lbs. in one day, she has extra milk veins, good escutcheon and was a deep milker.

Dam, Wijdehorn, a fine heifer, black and white, strip in face, gave as a three-year-old 57 1-5 lbs. in one day.

Bred to Sir Henry 2d of Aaggie No. 4, August 1st.

No. 215. **LADY EMMA.** No. 529.

(H. H. B. Vol. 7, No. 4,381.) Calved April 25th, 1883. Imported by us in August, 1883. One-half black, strip in face, irregular white on right shoulder, four small white spots on right side, black at rump and roots of tail, several small black spots on left fore leg.

Sire, District bull of Binnewysend.

Dam, Trijntje, has a milk record as a five-year-old of $75\frac{1}{2}$ lbs. in one day. She is a great milker, unusually fine form, not large, but a model; escutcheon good.

Bred to Sir Henry 2d of Aaggie No. 4, July 28th.

No. 216. **LADY ELMWOOD.** No. 531.

(H. H. B. Vol. 7, No. 4,383.) Calved April 29th, 1883. Imported by us August, 1883. Five-sixths black, medium star, small white spot on right jaw, left foreleg black to ankle, right fore leg black to knee, flanks, belly and two-thirds of tail white.

Sire, Jan (Friesland).

Dam, Emma, a fine cow with very superior skin, fine crumpled horns, escutcheon first class. She gave as a four-year-old 91 3-5 lbs. of milk in a day.

Bred to Sir Henry 2d of Aaggie No. 4, August 3d.

No. 217.   **LADY GLADSTONE.**   No. 532.

(H. H. B. Vol. 7, No. 4,384.) Calved April 1st, 1883. Imported by us in August, 1883. Five-eighths black, strip in face, black cheeks, small white spot on right side of neck, black spots on right side of rump, and on roots of tail, two small white spots on left side of neck, legs, belly and tail white.

Sire, District bull of Binnewysend.

Dam, Aafje, a very fine cow, with a milk record of 68 2-5 lbs. in one day as a five-year old.

Bred to Sir Henry 2d of Aaggie No. 4, July 26th.

No. 218.   **AAGGIE SOPHIE.**   No. 555.

(H. H. B. Vol. 7, No. 4,394.) Calved Feb. 27th, 1883. Imported by us in August, 1883. Two-thirds black, strip in face, large, irregular white over back, shoulders and hips to belly and flank on right side, small white spots on both sides, black spots on gambrels.

Sire, Sir Henry of Aaggie (1,450). For extension, see Sir Donald of Aaggie No. 7.

Dam, Groote Wit, (N. H. B. 2,545), (De Groot,) a fine four-year-old, has a record of 68 2-5 lbs of milk in one day.

Aaggie Sophie is sister to Jacob's Wit's Maylie No. 373.

Bred to Prince Imperial No. 5, June 22d.

No. 219.   **RUTH ARTIS.**   No. 562.

(H. H. B. Vol. 7, No. 4,517.) Calved April 19th, 1883. Imported by us in August, 1883. Three-fourths black, strip in face, broad white over hips to belly, both sides, black spot at roots of tail, black spot on left gambrel, several small white spots on both sides.

Sire, Artis, (N. H. B. 127). For extension, see Prince of Artis, No. 8.

Dam, Jansje 2d, (N. H. B. 1,022), a fine two-year-old heifer, with a record of 36 4-7 lbs. of milk in one day.

G-dam, Jansje, (N. H. B. 596), has a milk record of 80 1-6 lbs. in one day. She is dam of Lady Artis, No. 192.

G-g-dam, Johanna, has a record of 77 4-5 lbs. of milk in one day.

G-g-g-dam, Jacoba, has a milk record of 93 4-5 lbs. in one day.

G-g-g-g-dam, Oude Zwart, gave 109 5-7 lbs. of milk per day for twelve successive days.

Bred to Netherland Prince, No. 2, August 8th.

No. 220. **ELSIE ARTIS.** No. 563.

(H H. B. Vol. 7, No. 4,518.) Calved April 11th, 1883. Imported by us in August, 1883. Three-fourths black, star, two white spots on left shoulder, one over hips, black spot on right flank, small white spot just above right knee, black spot on left hind leg, small white spot on left flank, small black spot on each fore foot.

Sire, Artis, (N. H. B. 127). For extension, see Prince of Artis, No. 8.

Dam, Zwaantje, (N. H. B. 599), has a milk record of 77 4-5 lbs. in one day. She is a very large, fine cow.

Elsie Artis is sister to Zwaantje 2d, dam of Artis' Edmonia, No. 408, and Bessie Artis, No. 224.

No. 221.   **STELLA ARTIS.**   No. 564.

(H. H. B. Vol. 7, No. 4,557.) Calved Feb. 13th, 1883. Imported by us in June, 1883. Black predominating, small star, fore legs black to ankles, hind legs black to below gambrels, belly and one-half of tail white.

Sire, Artis, (N. H. B. 127). For extension see Prince of Artis, No. 8.

Dam, Princesje, (N. H. B. 520), gave 48 lbs. of milk in one day.

G-dam, Peternella, (H. H. B. 540), imported. Won Third Prize at Zaandam, and has a record of 82½ lbs. of milk in one day.

G-g-dam, Paulina, has a record of 77 4-5 lbs. of milk in one day.

G-g-g-dam, Peternella, has a record of 75½ lbs. of milk in one day.

G-g-g-g-dam, Paulina, has a record of 80 1-6 lbs. of milk in one day.

The sire of Princesje is "Kas" out of "Klaasje," which has a record of 70 8-9 lbs of milk in one day.

"Kroeza," the sire of "Kas," won First Prize at Hoorn and Second at Zaandijk.

Bred to Netherland Prince, No. 2, June 30th.

No. 222.   **BELLA ARTIS.**   No. 569.

(H. H. B. Vol. 7. No. 4,520.) Calved Feb. 17th, 1883. Imported by us in June, 1883. Four-fifths black, long star, snip, white over shoulders to belly on right side by fine line, white spot on left rump, right fore leg black to below knee.

Sire, Artis, (N. H. B. 127). For extension, see Prince of Artis No. 8.

Dam, Doortje, (N. H. B. 598), has given as a five-year-old 66¼ lbs. of milk in one day.

G-dam, Duife, has a record of 73 1-5 lbs. of milk in one day.

G-g-dam, Daatje, has a record of 61 4-5 lbs. of milk in one day.

Bred to Netherland Prince No. 2, June 2d.

No. 223. **CORA ARTIS.** No. 571.

(H. H. B. Vol. 7, No. 4,521.) Calved April 9th, 1883. Imported by us in August, 1883. Four-fifths black, star, snip, white spot at roots of tail, fore legs black to ankles, flanks, belly and switch white.

Sire, Artis, (N. H. B. 127). For extension, see Prince of Artis No. 8.

Dam, Haarlemmermeer, (N. H. B. 1,020), gave as a three-year-old 57 1-5 lbs. of milk in one day.

No. 224. **BESSIE ARTIS.** No. 572.

(H. H. B. Vol. 7, No. 4,522).) Calved March 29th, 1883. Imported by us in June, 1883. Mostly black, star, fore legs black to ankles, hind legs black to below gambrels, two small white spots on left flank, one crescent-shaped, one-half of tail white.

Sire, Artis (N. H. B. 127). For extension, see Prince of Artis No. 8.

Dam, Zwaantje 2d, gave as a two-year-old 32 lbs. of milk in day.

Grandam, Zwaantje (N. H. B. 599), has a milk record of 32 lbs. in a day. She is dam of Eisie Artis No. 220.

Bessie Artis is sister to Artis' Edmonia No. 408.

No. 225.   **CLARA HAMILTON.**   No. 587.

(H. H. B. Vol. 7, No. 4,560.) Calved March 12th, 1883. Imported by us in August, 1883. Mostly black, small star, white spot over hips, fore legs black to below knees, hind legs black to below gambrels, belly and switch white.

Sire, Poel's bull.

Dam, Poel, gave 70 8-9 of milk in a day.

No. 226.   **VALLEY BEAUTY 3d.**   No. 590.

(H. H. B. Vol. 7, No. 4,533.) Calved March 18th, 1883. Imported by us in June, 1883. Two-thirds white, strip in face, irregular black saddle over back, small black spot on right rump, one on left side, and one on left flank, two small white spots on left fore arm.

Sire, DeValk (N. H. B. 160), Prize bull at Leyden. See No. 202.

Dam, Valley Beauty (4,562). See No. 106.

Grandam, VanDort.

Valley Beauty 3d, is sister to Valley Beauty 2d No. 203, and to Valley Beauty 4th No. 443.

Bred to Sir Henry 2d of Aaggie No. 4, July 26th.

No. 227.   **AAGGIE BEATRICE 2d.**   No. 601.

(H. H. B. Vol. 7, No. 5,243.) Calved March 1, 1883. Imported by us in June, 1883. Two-thirds black, strip in face, large irregular white over shoulders to belly on left side, white over hips and rump to flanks both sides, large triangular white spot on left side, black spot on left fore knee.

Sire, Tromp (N. H. B. 188), he by "Mr. Wit," he by Jacob 2d (N. H. B. 56), (See cut.) See chart of Sir Henry 2d of Aaggie.

Tromp's dam, Zwart, has a milk record of 77 4-5 lbs. in a day.

"Mr. Wit's" dam is Berkhout, and his grandam a fine cow sold to go to Russia.

Dam, Neeltje, by Jacob 2d, (N. H. B. 56), etc), (See chart). She has a four-year-old milk record of 73 1-5 lbs. in a day.

She is dam of Aaggie Beatrice No. 183.

Bred to Netherland Prince No. 2, July 12th.

No. 228.   **AAGGIE LOTTA.**   No. 602.

(H. H. B. Vol. 7, No. 4,405.) Calved March 15th, 1883. Imported by us in June, 1883. Three-fourths white, black around each eye, and on neck to fore legs, numerous black spots on right side, three on left side, black at rump and spot on tail, legs, belly and tail white.

Sire, Tromp. (N. H. B. 188). See No. 227.

Dam, Grietje, by Jacob 2d (N. H. B. 56), etc., has a record of 68 2-5 lbs. of milk in a day as a four-year-old.

Bred to Netherland Prince No. 2, July 14th.

No. 229.   **AAGGIE IDALINE 6th.**   No. 655.

(H. H B. Vol. 7, No. 4,366) Calved Feb. 15th, 1883. Imported by us in August, 1883. Two-thirds white, strip in face, black neck containing one white spot on left side, two large irregular black spots on right side and one on left side, each containing one or more small white spots.

Sire, Willem, (N. H. B. 84), a very fine bull with a strip in face. His dam a very fine cow. See No. 106.

Dam, Aaggie Idaline, (4,362). See No. 105.

Bred to Prince Imperial, No. 5, June 28th.

No. 230. **HIGHLAND IDA.** No. 662.

(H. H. B. Vol. 7, No. 4,432.) Calved April 1st, 1883. Imported by us in August, 1883. Three fourths white, black around right eye, left cheek black, neck nearly black, large spots on side and over back.

Sire, District bull of Twisk.

Dam, Schaagen 2d, gave as a two-year old 43½ lbs. of milk in one day.

G-dam, Schaagen, a choice cow with a milk record of 68 2-5 lbs. in one day.

G-g-dam, a fine cow.

No. 231. **BOMBA.** No. 664

(H. H. B. Vol. 7, No. 4,433.) Calved Feb. 13th, 1883. Imported by us in August, 1883. Two-thirds black, large star, small snip, large white over shoulders to belly both sides, irregular white over hips and back from roots of tail, four small white spots on each side, small black spot on left side.

Sire, District bull of Twisk. His sire is a fine bull, very straight and square. His dam, a fine cow, gave 68 2-5 lbs. of milk in one day.

Dam, Krelisje, has a record of 73 1-5 lbs. of milk in one day. She is a very fine cow with fine horns and extra veins.

Bred to Netherland Prince, No 2, July 22d.

No. 232.   **AAGGIE LEE 2d.**   No. 666.

(H. H. B. Vol. 7, No. 4,435.) Calved Feb. 13th, 1883. Imported by us in August, 1883. Three-fourths black, large star, snip, white band over shoulders, white over hips to flank and belly on left side, white spot near belly on right side, legs, belly, flanks and most of tail white.

Sire, Napoleon, (N. H. B. 129), by Jacob 2d, (N H. B. 56), &c. For extension, see Aaggie Lucille, No. 233.

Dam, Marie, (N. H. B. 373), has a four year old record of 64 lbs. of milk in one day.

This heifer is a full sister to Aaggie Lee, No. 127.

Bred to Netherland Prince, No. 2, July 19th.

No. 233.   **AAGGIE LUCILLE.**   No. 668.

(H. H. B. Vol. 7, No. 4,570.) Calved Feb. 12th, 1883. Imported by us in August, 1883. Two-thirds white, black cheeks and neck, four large and five black spots on right side, two large and three small black spots on left side, black at rump, legs, belly and most of tail white.

Sire, Napoleon (N. H. B. 129), he by Jacob 2d (N. H. B. 56), he by Jacob (N. H. B. 20), he by Rooker, the sire of Aaggie (901). See No. 98, and milk records of the Aaggie family, page 22.

Napoleon's dam, Porcelein 2d (N. H. B. 392), by Gerrit, (N. H. B. 31), he by Cornelius.

Porcelein 2d's dam, Porcelein (N. H. B. 147), has a record of 80 lbs. in a day. She was sired by Rooker, the sire of Aaggie (901)

Porcelein's dam, Oude Porcelein.

Gerrit's dam, De Goede, the dam of Jacob 1st. (See chart). She was a Prize Cow at the Paris Exposition, and has a milk record of 91 lbs. 8 oz in one day.

Jacob 2d's dam, Trintje (N. H. B. No. 35), has a milk record of 80 lbs. in one day.

Jacob 1st's dam, De Goede. See above.

Dam, Coba, gave as a four-year-old 64 lbs. of milk in a day. She is a straight and square cow, with fine head and horns and good escutcheon.

Bred to Netherland Prince No. 2, July 17th.

No. 234.   **AAGGIE PEERESS.**   No. 671.

(H. H. B. Vol. —, No. ——.) Calved April 29th, 1883. Imported by us in August, 1883. Two-thirds black, star, snip, white over left shoulder, white over hips extending to belly and flanks both sides, black at rump.

Sire, Jan Wit (2,524), Jacobson (N. H. B. 251), he by Jacob 2d (N. H. B. 56) See milk records of the Aaggie family, page 22.

Dam, Dankbaare.

Jan Wit is a beautiful animal, star, snip, spot on shoulder and one on hip, very fine head and horns, broad back, straight and square with a good escutcheon.

His dam, Amie, has a six-year old milk record of 91 3-5 lbs. in one day. She is dam of Aaggie Rachel No. 243.

No. 235.   **AAGGIE ROXANA.**   No. 674.

(H. H. B. Vol. 7, No. 4,438.) Calved March 28th, 1883. Imported by us in August, 1883. Two-thirds white, large star, and fine line to snip, arrow-head shaped black below left shoulder, large irregular black spots on both sides.

Sire, Jan Wit (2,524). Jacobson (N. H. B. 251), (See No. 234), he by Jacob 2d, (N. H. B. 56), (See No. 234), he by Jacob (N. H. B. 20). See milk records of the Aaggie family, page 22.

Jan Wit's dam, Amie, has a six-year-old milk record of 91 3-5 lbs. in one day. She is the dam of Aaggie Rachel No. 243.

Dam, Sophie, a fine three-year-old, with good escutcheon, has a record of 64 lbs. in one day.

Bred to Netherland Prince No. 2, August 25th.

No. 236.   **AAGGIE ALICE.**   No. 678.

(H. H. B. Vol. 7, No. 4,333.) Calved Feb. 16th, 1883. Imported by us in August, 1883. Mostly white, black around each eye, some black on neck, irregular black spot on right side and one on back, several black spots on left side, small black spot on tail and one on right side of rump.

Sire, Sir Henry of Aaggie (1.450). For extension, see Sir Donald of Aaggie No 7 and page 22.

Dam, Groote Wit (N. H. B. 2,545), (de Groot), has given 77 4-5 lbs. of milk in one day. She is called by her owner the best cow in his herd. See No. 218.

Bred to Netherland Prince No. 2, August 8th.

No. 237.   **AAGGIE FIDELIA.**   No. 682.

(H. H. B. Vol. 7, No. 4,357.) Calved March 17th, 1883. Imported by us in August, 1883. Two-thirds black, star and snip, irregular white over shoulders and hips to belly on both sides, white spot just above right fore arm, black spot on back side of right fore leg.

Sire, Jacob Wit (2,662), Jacob 4th, (N. H B. 210), he by Jacob 2d, (N. H. B. 56). For extension, see Jacob Wit's Volunteer No. 22 and page 22..

Jacob 4th's dam, Heiltje (N. H. B. 1,006).

Dam, Neeltje, has a two-year-old milk record of 36 4-7 lbs. in one day. Her sire is de Ruiter (N. H. B. 89)   See chart.

Bred to Pionis No. 10, July 25th.

No. 238.   **HAPPY THOUGHT.**   No. 683.

(H. H. B. Vol. 7, No. 4,440.) Calved March 16th, 1883. Imported by us in August, 1883. Mostly white, black on cheeks and neck, black spot on right fore arm, three black spots on left side, and four on right, small black spot at roots of tail and on rump.

Sire, Nico, (N. H. B. 207), a fine, large straight and square bull, good head and horns, star in forehead, now district bull of Sijbecarspel.

Dam, Trijntje (N. H. B. 602), a very fine cow, with elegant escutcheon, good udder and veins. She has a milk record of 68 2-5 lbs. in one day.

Bred to Sir Henry 2d of Aaggie No. 4, August 2d.

No. 239. **JOSIE LYLE.** No. 694.

(H. H. B. Vol. 7, No. 4,450.) Calved Feb. 15th, 1883. Imported by us in August, 1883 Two-thirds white, strip in face, black over neck extending to fore arm on left side, two large irregular black spots over back and down on each side, black spot on each fore arm and on left knee.

Sire, Jan, (Bakker's) a very fine bull. His dam is fine, and a superior milker.

Jan's dam a fine black and white cow.

Dam, Groote Bles, a fine cow with a milk record of 54 6-7 lbs. in a day as a four-year-old.

Bred to Neptune, No. 1, July 23d.

No. 240. **KATIE LANDER.** No. 700.

(H. H. B. Vol. 7, No. 4,456.) Calved March 12th, 1883. Imported by us in August, 1883. Three-fourths black, narrow white strip over back to belly on both sides, large irregular white spot over hips, legs, belly and half of tail white.

Sire, Jan, (Bakker's). See No. 239.

Dam, Wieringer, by Graaf Adolf, (N. H B. 98). She has a milk record of 59½ lbs. in one day as a three-year-old.

Grandam, Wieringer, a fine milker.

Bred to Netherland Prince, No. 2, July 16th.

No. 241. **VIROQUA.** No. 714.

(H. H. B. Vol. 8, No. 7,009.) Calved April 7th, 1883. Imported by us in August, 1883. Five-sixths black, star, snip, group of white spots on right shoulder, white spot on left shoulder, white over hips, fore legs black to knees.

Sire, Porcelein. (N. H. B. 142), sold to go to Cape of Good Hope. His dam gave 82¼ lbs. in one day.

Dam, Boterijk, star, fine head and horns, veins fair, escutcheon fine, tail long. She has given as a three-year-old 54 6-7 lbs. in one day.

No. 242.　　　　　　**NOURMAHAL.**　　　　　　No. 715.

(H. H. B. Vol. 8, No. ——.) Calved Feb. 4th, 1883. Imported by us in August, 1883. Five-sixths black, star, snip, white strip over shoulders, white on rump, narrow white spot on left hip and one on right shoulder, fore legs black to knees backside.

Sire, Porcelein (N. H. B. 142). See No. 241.

Dam, Porceleine, a handsome cow ; good veins, fine horns, fair escutcheon. She gave as a three-year-old 54 6-7 lbs. of milk in a day.

Bred to Netherland Prince, No. 2, July 15th.

No. 243.　　　　　　**AAGGIE RACHEL.**　　　　　　No. 724.

(H. H. B. Vol. 7, No. 4,473.) Calved Feb. 11th, 1883. Imported by us in August, 1883. Mostly white, black below each eye, and a large number of black spots scattered over body.

Sire, Sir Henry of Aaggie (1,450). For extension, see pedigree of Sir Donald of Aaggie No. 7, and page 22.

Dam, Amie, a very fine cow, extra veins, good udder. She has a record of 91 3-5 lbs. of milk in one day. She is dam of Jan Wit (2,524). See No. 234.

Bred to Netherland Prince, No. 2, June 23d.

No. 244. **SIR HENRY OF AAGGIE'S UINTAH.** No. 726.

(H. H. B. Vol. 8, No. 7,004.) Calved Feb. 1st, 1883. Imported by us in August, 1883. Two-thirds black, star, white over shoulders to belly left side, and over hips to flanks and belly both sides, black at rump.

Sire, Sir Henry of Aaggie (1,450). For extension, see Sir Donald of Aaggie, No. 7, and page 22.

Dam, Ida, a fine cow which gave 66¼ lbs. of milk in one day.

Bred to Clovis, No. 13, August 18th.

No. 245. **AAGGIE JULIET.** No 730.

(H. H. B. Vol. 7, No. 4,474.) Calved March 5th, 1883. Imported by us in August, 1883. Two-thirds white, broad strip in face, small white spot on each side of neck, long irregular black saddle over back and down both sides, numerous small black spots scattered over body.

Sire, Sir Henry of Aaggie, (1,450). For extension, see Sir Donald of Aaggie, No. 7, and page 22.

Dam, Blokker, (N. H. B. 390), by Rooker, the sire of Aaggie, (901). See No. 98.

Grandam, Oude Blokker, a great milker.

Blokker has a record of 82½ lbs. of milk in one day.

Aaggie Juliet is from same dam as Aaggie Bonnie, No. 137, and Aaggie Ida, (2,600), imported by us in 1882, which has given as a three-year-old 47 lbs. in one day, and 1,494 lbs. in thirty-five days.

Bred to Netherland Prince, No. 2, Sept. 11th.

No. 246.   **AAGGIE CAMILLE.**   No. 731.

(H. H. B. Vol. 7, No. 4.349) Calved Feb. 28th, 1883. Imported by us in August, 1883. Two-thirds white, broad white strip in face, large irregular black spot over back and down both sides, several small black spots scattered over body, black spots on both fore legs.

Sire, Sir Henry of Aaggie (1,450). For extension, see Sir Donald of Aaggie No. 7. See page 22.

Dam, De Schot (N. H. B. 573), she by Jacob (N. H. B. 20), he by Rooker, the sire of Aaggie (901.) See No. 98.

Jacob's dam, De Goede, a Prize cow at the Paris Exposition. has a milk record of 91 lbs. 8 oz in one day, She was the dam of Sir Henry of Aaggie (1,450), which we sold at two years old for $1,500.

Bred to Netherland Prince No. 2, July 24th.

No. 247.   **JACOB WIT'S MINELLA.**   No. 737.

(H. H. B. Vol. —, No. ——.) Calved Feb. 14th, 1883, Two-thirds black, star, white over shoulders to belly right side, white over hips to flanks left side, small white spot near left shoulder, fore legs black to knees.

Sire, Jacob Wit (2,662), Jacob 4th (N. H. B. 210). See Jacob Wit's Volunteer No. 22, and page 22.

Dam, Lak, which gave 52 2-5 lbs. of milk in a day.

No. 248.   **AAGGIE CARENO.**   No. 760.

(H. H. B. Vol. 7, No. 4,344.) Calved March 26th, 1883. Imported by us in August, 1883. Two-thirds black, strip in face, two small white spots on neck right side, white over shoulders to belly right side and nearly connected on left side, large black spot on left fore leg, white over hips to flank and belly right side containing two black spots, two small white spots on left side and three on right side, tail nearly white.

Sire, Tromp (N. H. B. 188), he by "Mr. Wit," he by Jacob 2d (N. H. B. 56). See cut and chart, also page 22.

Tromp's dam, Zwart has a milk record of 77 4-5 lbs. in a day.

"Mr. Wit's" dam, Berkhout, and grandam, a fine cow, sold to go to Russia.

Dam, Pleuster 2d, has a two-year-old milk record of 45 4-5 lbs. in one day.

G-dam, Lady Griswold No. 127, a fine cow with fine horns, good udder and veins. She was sired by Jacob (N. H. B. 20), &c. See chart.

G-g-dam, a fine wedge-shaped cow, with fine horns and extra veins.

Bred to Netherland Giant, August 9th.

No. 249.　　　**AAGGIE ISADORA 3d.**　　　No. 781.

(H. H. B. Vol. 7, No. 4,340.) Calved Feb. 19th, 1883. Imported by us in August, 1883. Three-fourths black, strip in face, small white spot behind right ear, white over shoulders to belly right side, irregular white over hips to flanks on both sides, one large and two small black spots on right flank, one large and one small black spot on left side, two small white spots on right side and one on left.

Sire, Willem, (N. H. B. 84), a very fine bull, with strip in face. His dam a very fine cow. See No. 229.

Dam, Trijntje by Jacob (N. H. B. 20), &c., See chart, has a record of 68 2-5 lbs. of milk in one day. She is dam of Aaggie Isadora No. 131.

Bred to Prince Imperial No. 5, June 21st.

No. 250. **AAGGIE CORNELIA 5th.** No. 011.

(H. H. B. Vol. 8, No. 6,733.) Calved March 20th, 1883. Imported by us in November, 1883. Two-thirds white. spotted, black cheeks, two large black spots on right side.

Sire, Tromp (N. H. B. 188). See No. 248.

Dam, Aaggie Cornelia (4,410), (See No. 102), which is also dam of Aaggie Cornelia 2d, No. 115, Aaggie Cornelia 3d, No. 132, Aaggie Cornelia 4th, No. 173 and Aaggie Cornelia 6th, No. 426.

Bred to Netherland Prince No. 2, Sept. 1st.

No. 251. **NETHERLAND LASS.** No. 012.

(H. H. B. Vol. 8, No. 6,736.) Calved March 22d, 1883. Imported by us in November, 1883. Three-fourths black, small star, white over shoulders to belly right side, small white spot on left side, black on outside left fore leg to ankle.

Sire, J. Tol's bull.

Dam, Tol, (Zwartbek) which gave 68 2-5 lbs. of milk in one day. She is large, square, fine veins, long but fine horns, very broad and square.

Tol's sire, Schreuder, the sire of Netherland Queen. See No. 104.

No. 252. **AAGGIE CORNELIA 3d's LASS.** No. 013.

(H. H. B. Vol. 8, No. 6,735.) Calved March 15th, 1883. One-half white, large star, black saddle over back containing two small white spots on right side, two black spots on right side, black spot on right fore leg, back side.

Sire, Tromp, (N. H. B. 188). See No. 248.

Dam, Aaggie Cornelia 3d, (4,342). Imported. See No. 132.

Grandam, Aaggie Cornelia, (4,410), (See No. 102), which is also dam of Aaggie Cornelia 2d, (See No. 115), Aaggie Cornelia 4th, No. 173, and Aaggie Cornelia 6th, No. 426.

No. 253.   **AAGGIE SARAH 2d.**   No. 014.

(H. H. B. Vol. 8, No. 7,142.) Calved April 5th, 1883. Imported by us in November, 1883. White predominating, black around each eye, two black spots on left side, one above the other, numerous black spots scattered over body.

Sire, Jacob 3d, by Jacob 2d, (N. H. B. 56,) (See cut). See chart and page 22.

Jacob 3d's dam, Porcelein, (N. H. B. 147), she by Rooker, the sire of Aaggie, (901).

Porcelein's dam, Oude Porcelein.

Dam, Aaggie Sarah, (4,412). See No. 134.

No. 254.   **NETHERLAND OCONTO.**   No. 015.

(H. H. B. Vol. 8, No. 7,010.) Calved April 15th, 1883. Imported by us in November, 1883. Three-fourths black, star, large white spot on left shoulder, small white spot back of right shoulder, white spot over hips and rump, black spot on right flank.

Sire, District bull of Purmer.

Dam, Netherland Waukesha (7,007). See No. 138½.

Grandam, Gert Met (Heinis), a sister to Netherland Queen (414) See No. 104, and dam of Netherland Pride (2,641), See No. 187. She gave as a five-year-old 73 1-5 lbs. of milk in one day.

No. 255. **NETHERLAND MAID.** No. 016.

(H. H. B. Vol. 8, No. 6,737.) Calved April 18th, 1883. Imported by us in November, 1883. One-half black, strip in face, white over neck and shoulders to belly left side, white over hips and rump to flanks both sides, three white spots on left side.

Sire, District bull of Beemster.

Dam, Hil, she by Schreuder, the sire of Netherland Queen (414). See No. 104.

Hil gave on grass alone 68 2-5 lbs. of milk in one day.

No. 256. **NETHERLAND WAUPACA.** No. 017.

(H. H. B. Vol. 8, No. 7,011.) Calved May 19th, 1883. Two-thirds black, strip in face, white on top of shoulders, small black spot on left fore leg and two on right, and two white spots on left side, large black spot on each side near hip, black spot on right gambrel.

Sire, District bull of Beemster.

Dam, Gert Met 3d has a record of 87 lbs. in one day on grass, and is a sister to the Grandam of Netherland Queen (414). See No. 104.

Grandam, Gert Met, a very fine cow and heavy milker, was kept twenty years for breeding.

No. 257. **AAGGIE MAY 2d.** No. 345.

(H. H. B. Vol 7, No. 3,501.) Calved Feb. 14th, 1883. Imported in dam by us in August, 1882. Two-thirds white, strip in face, large black over neck and shoulders, large black spot on each side, smaller spots on each side, small black spot below left gambrel, three small black spots on left fore leg.

Sire, Sir Henry of Aaggie (1,450). For extension, see Sir Donald of Aaggie No. 7.

Dam, Aaggie May (2,601), See No. 151, she by de Ruiter, (N. H. B. 89), by Jacob 2d (N. H. B. 56), (See cut). See chart, and page 22.

G-dam, Blokker 2d (N. H. B. 391), gave as a two-year-old 45 4-5 lbs in one day, she by Gerrit (N. H. B. 31), he by Cornelius.

Gerrit's dam, De Goede the dam of Jacob 1st.

G-g-dam, Blokker (N. H. B. 390), by Rooker.

Bred to Netherland Prince No. 2, June 29th.

No. 258. **ALBINO 2d.** No. 347.

(H. H B. Vol. 7, No. 3,500.) Imported in dam by us in August, 1882. Calved Feb. 15th, 1883. Two-thirds black, star and snip, irregular white strip over shoulders connecting with white on belly right side, white over hips to flanks and belly, black spot on left gambrel, two small white spots on left side, three white spots on right side.

Sire, District bull of Hoogcarspel.

Dam, Albino (2,654). See No. 162.

Bred to Netherland Prince No. 2.

No. 259. **AAGGIE BEAUTY 3d.** No. 351.

(H. H. B. Vol 7, No. 3,505.) Calved Feb. 16th, 1883. Two-thirds white, strip in face, large irregular black spot on each side, numerous small white spots, and black spots on each side, white spot on left shoulder, four small black spots on left fore leg.

Sire, Sir Henry of Aaggie, (1,450). For extension see Sir Donald of Aaggie, No. 7, and page 22.

Dam, Aaggie Beauty, (2,907). See No. 117.

Bred to Netherland Prince, No.   Sept. 25th.

No. 260.   **AAGGIE ANNA 2d.**   No. 353.

(H. H. B. Vol. 4, No. 3,504.) Imported by us in dam, in August, 1882. Calved Feb. 19th, 1883. Two-thirds white, strip in face, two small white spots on right side of neck, fifteen black spots on right side, and seven on left side, long, narrow black spot on left fore leg, narrow white spot just above it.

Sire, Sir Henry of Aaggie, (1,450). For extension, see Sir Donald of Aaggie, No. 7, and page 22.

Dam, Aaggie Anna, (2,602). See No. 149.

No. 261.   **AAGGIE BEAUTY 4th.**   No. 61.

(H. H. B. Vol. 7, No. 3,508.) Imported in dam by us in September, 1882. Calved Feb. 20th, 1883. White predominating, strip in face, two white spots under right ear, two black spots on right fore leg, eleven black spots on right side, black spot on left fore leg, white spot just above it, large irregular black spot and four smaller ones on left side, five small spots on left flank, black on rump.

Sire, Willem, (N. H. B. 84), a very fine bull with strip in face. His dam a very fine cow. See No. 229.

Dam, Aaggie Beauty 2d, (2631). See No. 154.

Bred to Netherland Prince, No. 2, July 1st.

No. 262.   **MERCEDES 3d.**   No. 493

(See Cut.)

(H. H. B. Vol. 7, No. 3,769.) Calved Feb. 24th, 1883. Three-fourths black. star, strip up right shoulder, patch on left hip, legs, from knees and gambrels, belly and switch white.

Sire, Mahomet (289), he by Pluto (133), he by Rip Van Winkle (35), imported in cow Fraulein (9).

Mahomet's dam, Ægis (69). See No. 96.

Pluto's dam, Topsey (61), by Hollander (20), imported, and out of Dowager (7). Topsey is also dam of Uncle Tom (163). (See No. 15.)

Fraulein (9), has a record of 70 lbs. of milk in one day, and 1,873 lbs. in one month.

Topsey (61), has a record of 40 lbs. 8 oz. of milk in one day when less than two years old. In the season of 1879 she gave as high as 70 lbs. in one day, 64 lbs. per day for thirty consecutive days, and 6,005 lbs. in five months.

Dowager (7), has a record of 12,681 lbs. 8 oz. of milk in one year.

Echo (121), half sister to Ægis (69), the grandam of this calf on sire's side, has a milk record of 18,120 lbs. 8 oz. in one year, and gave the following year 23,775 lbs. 8 oz.

Dam, Mercedes (723), imported by Mr. T. B. Wales, Jr. She has given as a five year old 88 lbs. of milk in one day, 2,534 lbs in thirty-one days, 8,025 lbs. in three months and seventeen days, being an average of 81 lbs 12 oz. per day.

Mercedes won the CHALLENGE SILVER CUP offered by the *Breeders' Gazette* of Chicago, for the largest thirty day butter record, open for one year to July 1st, 1883, to all breeds, and

(Mercedes III,--8 Months old. No. 262.)

the world. She made 3 lbs. 10 oz. in one day, 24 lbs. 6 oz. in seven days, and 99 lbs. 6½ oz. in thirty days, butter being weighed before salting.

At the Public Sale of Holsteins held at Chicago, Ill., in October, 1883, we secured this calf at a cost of $4,200, the highest price ever paid for a Holstein calf.

Bred to Netherland Prince No 2, Sept. 29th.

No. 263.   **NETHERLAND JEWEL 2d.**   No. 411.

(H. H. B. Vol. 7, No. 3,492.) Imported by us in dam in September, 1882. Calved March, 13th, 1883. Three-fourth black, star, irregular white strip over hip and to belly on right side, two white spots on left shoulder, small white spot on left flank, right fore leg black to knee, left hind leg black to gambrel, black spots on both fore feet.

Sire, District bull of Heilo.

Dam, Netherland Jewel (2,642). See No. 160.

Bred to Netherland Prince No. 2, August 27th.

No. 264.   **AAGGIE ROSA 4th.**   No. 427.

(H. H. B. Vol. 7, No. 3,485.) Imported by us in dam in September, 1882. Calved April 1st, 1883. One-half white, black cheeks, two small white spots on right shoulder, two on right side near flank, two small and one large black spot on right side, four small and one large black spot on left side, one small white spot on left side, black around rump at roots of tail.

Sire, Sir Henry of Aaggie (1,450). For extension, see Sir Donald of Aaggie No. 7, and page 22.

Dam, Aaggie Rosa (2,605). See No. 107.

Bred to Netherland Prince No. 2, August 11th.

No. 265.   **NETHERLAND BARONESS** 5th.   No. 430.

(H. H. B. Vol. 7, No. 3,483.) Imported by us in dam in September, 1882. Calved May 5th, 1883. Two-thirds white, black spots around eyes, nine small white spots on left side, five small black spots on left side.

Sire, District bull of Beemster.

Dam, Netherland Baroness (2,635). See No. 103.

No. 266.   **NETHERLAND PRINCESS** 3d.   No. 433.

(H. H. B. Vol. 7, No. 3,481.) Calved May 12th, 1883. One-half black, star, snip, large black saddle over back, black spot on right flank, right fore leg black to ankle, small white spot on left side, black spot on left flank, black at rump.

Sire, Neptune (711). See No. 1.

Dam, Netherland Princess (862). See No. 123.

No. 267.   **IMOGENIA** 2d.   No. 478.

(H. H. B. Vol. 7, No. 3,923.) Calved May 20th, 1883. Three-fourths black, star, white on throat, white over hips and shoulders, legs, belly and two thirds of tail white.

Sire, St. Elmo (714), he by Uncle Tom (163). See No. 15.

St. Elmo's dam, Porceleintje (568), (N. H. B. 218), imported by us in 1878. She gave when six years old 64 ℔s. 9 oz. in one day, 1,891 ℔s. 3 oz. in one month, 8,004 ℔s. 13 oz. in six months, and 10,893 ℔s. 3 oz. in ten months and sixteen days. She won First Prize at the Onondaga County Fair in 1879, and was one of the herd that won the Gold Medal at the New York State Fair the same year.

St. Elmo is a very choice, elegant bull, with a first-class escutcheon, wide on thighs and running well up with thigh-ovals, thin skin and velvety coat. He won First Prize at the Nebraska State Fair in September, 1883, and also won First Prize at Otoe Co. Fair, Nebraska, same year.

Dam, Imogenia, (500), by Stentor, (316), he by Rip Van Winkle, (35), imported in cow Fraulein, (9).

Stentor's dam, Dowager, (7), imported, has a milk record of 12,681 lbs. 8 oz. in one year.

Rip Van Winkle's dam, Fraulein, has a milk record of 70 lbs. in one day, and 1,873 lbs in one month.

Rip Van Winkle is the sire of Ægis, (69), (See No. 96), which has a record of 16,823 lbs. 10 oz. in one year. He is also the sire of Echo, (121), which has a record of 18,120 lbs. 8 oz. in one year, and gave the following year 23,775 lbs. 8 oz.

Imogenia gave as a two-year-old $47\frac{1}{4}$ lbs. of milk in one day, and 10,925 lbs. 9 oz. in three hundred and fifty days.

She is a grand show cow and one of the choicest cows of the breed At the Nebraska State Fair at Omaha, in September, 1883, she won the sweepstakes for the best Holstein milch cow and also the sweepstakes for the best milch cow of any age or breed. She also won First Prize at Otoe Co. Fair, Nebraska, the same month.

Grandam, Isis, (148), is full sister to Uncle Tom, (163), (See No. 57.) She has a milk record of 4,140 lbs. 11 oz. in four months, milking from only two teats.

G-g-dam, Topsey, (61), &c.

G-g-g-dam, Dowager, (7). For extension, records, &c., see No. 15.

Isis' daughter, Isis 2d, gave as a two-year-old 9,114 lbs. 12 oz. of milk in one year.

No. 268.   **MEADOW MAID 2d.**   No. 443.

(H. H. B. Vol. 7, No. 3,559.) Calved June 1st, 1883. Three fourths black, large star, snip. right fore leg black to ankle, small white spot on right shoulder, larger one on top of left shoulder, large white spot on top of rump with narrow white line running down left flank.

Sire, Netherland Prince (716). See No. 2.

Dam, Meadow Maid (1,793), imported by us, she by District bull of Beemster. Meadow Maid dropped her first calf before she was two years old and soon after importation. She gave 37 lbs. 15 oz. in one day, and 7,260 lbs. 7 oz. in nine months and fifteen days, when she was sold. When only twenty-three months old she made 9 lbs. 4½ oz. of butter in one week.

Grandam, Bleeker, has a record of 69¼ lbs. in one day.

No. 269.   **CLOTHILDE 4th.**   No. 439.

(H. H. B. Vol. 7, No. 3,480.) Calved June 2, 1883. One-half black, tips of ears black, black spots at and near eyes, black over neck and down to fore legs, black spot on right fore leg. large irregular black saddle over back, large irregular black spot on left side, small black spot on left fore leg, seven white and three black spots on right side.

Sire, Netherland Prince (716). See No. 2.

Dam, Clothilde (1,308). See No. 118

No. 270.   **TOPAZ 4th.**   No. 450.

(H. H. B. Vol. 7, No. 3,577.) Calved July 8th, 1883. Four-fifths black, small star, two small white spots on right shoulder, one each side back bone at rump, fore legs black to ankles, hind legs black to gambrels. one-half tail white.

Sire, Neptune (711). See No. 1.

Dam, Topaz (870). See dam of Topaz 3d, No. 209.

No. 271.   **NETHERLAND AAGGIE.**   No. 459.

(H. H. B. Vol. 7, No 3,948.) Calved August 29th, 1883. Three-fourths black, star, small snip, and small white spot on under lip, large irregular white spot over shoulder to belly on left side, black spot on right fore leg, two on right flank, three small white spots on right side, two small black spots near left fore leg one in front and one behind.

Sire, Neptune (711). See No. 1.

Dam, Lady Netherland (1,263). See No. 99.

No. 272.   **IDOL 2d.**

(H. H. B. Vol. 7, No. 3,949.) Calved Sept. 19, 1883. Three-fourths white, large black around each eye, large irregular black over back, numerous smaller spots on each side.

Sire, Fearless (1,463), he by Italy, he by Kees (N. H. B. 32), winner of First Prize at Zaandam, Scheidam, Alkmaar, Haarlem, Rotterdam and Amsterdam, also Second Prizes at Amsterdam and Purmerende.

Fearless' dam, Cornelia (N. H. B. 483), has a milk record of $82\frac{1}{4}$ lbs. in a day.

Italy's dam, Jannek (871), (N. H. B. 151), imported by us. She made a record in Holland of 78 lbs. in one day, and in August, 1879, nearly six months after calving and just before importation, one of our firm saw her milk 62 lbs. 12 oz. in a day. Although not fully acclimated, she gave in 1880, 71 lbs. 12 oz. in one day, 2,110 lbs. 8 oz. in one month, 9,250 lbs. in six months, and 13,015 lbs. 15 oz. in one year. In 1881 she gave 75 lbs. in one day, 2,132 lbs. 3 oz. in one month, and 11,980 lbs. 3 oz. in nine months and fourteen days. In the nine months and twenty days ending January 31st, 1882, she gave 12,028 lbs. 4 oz. of milk. In 1880, when giving 48 lbs. of milk in a day, she made 2 lbs. $2\frac{1}{2}$ oz. of butter per day. In

1881 she made 19 lbs. 15 oz. of butter in seven days, and 28 lbs. 6¼ oz. in ten days.

Kee's dam Olje, a splendid cow and superior milker.

Italy is the sire of Molly Bawn (1,278), imported by us and sold when a yearling. She has given as a three-year-old 70 lbs. 11 oz. of milk in one day, 2,012 lbs. 4 oz. in one month, and 16,391 lbs. 6 oz. in one year. This is the largest three-year-old record yet made by any cow of any breed of which we have knowledge.

Kees (N. H. B. 32), was the sire of Topaz (870). She made a two-year-old milk record of 9,811 lbs. 4 oz. in one year. As a three-year-old she gave 45 lbs. 11 oz. in one day, and as a four-year-old she gave 57 lbs. 2 oz. in one day, 1,544 lbs. 14 oz. in one month, and 14,630 lbs. 2 oz. in one year.

Dam, Idol (892), imported.

Grandam, Arisje, has a milk record of 82½ lbs. in a day.

Idol is full sister to Maartje (584), imported, which has a two-year-old record of 48 lbs. 8 oz. of milk in one day, and 8,886 lbs. 4 oz. in 276 days.

No. 273.   **EULA LEE 2d.**   No. 494.

(H. H. B. Vol. 7, No. 4,783.) Calved Dec. 9th, 1883. Two-thirds white, medium star, large irregular black spot over back and on both sides, black to shoulders and on rump, black spot on right fore leg, and one on side just back of right fore leg, two-thirds tail white.

Sire, General Herkimer Jr. (1,363), he by General Herkimer (252), he by Hasselman (106), he by Prince of Orange (137), imported in dam Maid of Zuid (183).

General Herkimer Jr's dam Marguerite (185), by Prince of Orange (137).

Marguerite's dam Gertrude, imported.

General Herkimer's dam, Annitje (245), imported.

Hasselman's dam, Catrina (106), imported.

Dam, Eula Lee (1,846), imported, (See No. 140). She has given 40 lbs. 4 oz. of milk in one day, and 1,105 lbs. 9 oz. in one month.

Grandam, Homan, gave 60¾ lbs. of milk in one day.

No. 274.   **CLOTHILDE 2d's DUCHESS.**   No. 480.

(H. H. B. Vol. 8, No. 6,401.) Calved Dec. 30th, 1883.

Sire, Duke of Manheim (2,118) he by Uncle Tom (163). See No. 15.

Duke of Manheim's dam, Octoroon (916), imported by us. She calved May 20th, 1883, and gave as a four-year-old 79 lbs. 12 oz. of milk in one day, 1,981 lbs. 12 oz. in June, and 2,178 lbs. in July, a total of 4,159 lbs. 12 oz. in two months, an average of over 68 lbs. 3 oz per day. She gave in seven months and eight days 10,212 lbs. 12 oz.

Octoroon's dam, Tiger, gave as a three-year-old 45 4-5 lbs. of milk in one day.

Dam, Clothilde 2d (1,451). See No. 147.

Grandam, Clothilde (1,308). See No. 118.

N6. 275.   **CHARLENE.**   No. 752.

(H. H. B. Vol. 8, No. 6,845.) Calved May 14th, 1883. Imported by us in May, 1884. Three-fourths black, strip in face, white over shoulders to belly on right side, white over hips to flanks and belly both sides, two black spots on left side and three on right.

Sire, Kohne, son of Fatinitza (2,723), DeJood (N. H. B. 653), imported by us in September, 1882.

Fatinitza's dam, Koning, a splendid milker.

Fatinitza gave as a four-year-old, the first season after importation, 59 lbs. 5 oz. in one day, 1,640 lbs. 15 oz. in one month, and 7,645 lbs. 3 oz. in six months, when we sold her.

Dam, Cornelia 2d, a large, low, straight and square cow; has an extra escutcheon and a milk record of 68 2-5 lbs. in a day as a four-year-old.

Grandam, Cornelia, a very straight and square cow, with a record of 77 4-5 lbs in a day.

Bred to Clovis No. 13, August 6th.

No. 276. **ABDALETTA.** No. 758.

(H. H. B. Vol. 8, No. 6,847.) Calved April 1st, 1883. Imported by us in May, 1884. Four-fifths black, small star, white spot over hips, right fore leg black to knee outside.

Sire, de Wit's fine two-year-old bull; now District bull of Edam.

Dam, Marie 1st, a fine straight and square heifer, with fine head and horns. She gave as a two-year-old 45 4-5 lbs. of milk in one day.

G-dam, Marie, a fine black and white cow, fine head and horns, a good escutcheon and a long milker. She has a record of 82½ lbs. in one day.

G-g-dam has a record of 77 4-5 lbs. in one day.

Bred to Clovis No. 13, July 10th.

No. 277. **APPOLINE.** No. 760.

(H. H B. Vol. 8. No. ——.) Calved April 10th, 1883. Imported by us in May, 1884. Three-fourths black, strip, long white spot on right shoulder and small one above right fore leg, white over hips to flank on right side.

Sire, District bull of Beemster, a fine two-year-old bull, with fine escutcheon.

His dam has a record of 80 1·6 lbs. in one day.

Dam, Overtje, a fine cow, with fine horns and large milk veins, has a record of 82¼ lbs. in a day as a four-year-old.

G-dam had a record of 82¼ lbs. in a day. All this family were long milkers.

Bred to Clovis No. 13, June 26th.

No. 278.　　　**ALEXIA OF LAKESIDE.**　　　No. 762.

(H. H. B. Vol. 8, No. 6,880.) Calved March 26th, 1883. Imported by us in May, 1884. One-half black, star, snip, large black saddle over back containing two small white spots on right side, black spot on right hind leg, black spot on left fore leg, one on left side and two on left flank.

Sire, District bull of Nieuwe Niedorp.

Dam, Mina, gave as a four-year-old 68 2-5 lbs. in one day.

Bred to Prince Imperial, No. 5, July 13th.

No. 279.　　　**ALMARTHA.**　　　No. 763.

(H. H. B. Vol. 8, No. 6,849.) Calved March 31st, 1883 Imported by us in May, 1884. Three-fourths white, strip in face, black saddle over back containing small white spot on right side, black spot on left fore leg.

Sire, District bull of Berkhout, a fine two-year-old bull.

Dam, Willig, a fine two-year-old heifer, with fine horns and extra milk veins, has a milk record of 45 4 5 lbs. in one day.

Bred to Prince of Artis, No. 8, Sept. 17th.

No. 280. **AGNACE.** No. 764.

(H. H. B. Vol. 8, No. 6,850.) Calved March 15th, 1883. Imported by us in May, 1884. Three-fourths black, star, narrow white spot over shoulder, broad white over hips to flanks both sides, black at rump.

Sire, District bull of Benningbroek.

Dam, Geertje, gave 68 2-5 lbs. in a day.

G-dam gave 91 3-5 lbs. in a day.

Bred to Robertus No 17, August 6th.

No. 281. **AMBRONETTA.** No. 765.

(H. H. B. Vol. 8, No. 6,851.) Calved March 15h, 1883. Imported by us in May, 1884. Mostly white, tips of ears black, black around eyes, large black spot on left shoulder, numerous spots scattered over body.

Sire, Napoleon (N. H. B. 129). See No. 233, also page 22.

Dam, Charlotte, gave as a three-year-old 64 lbs. in a day.

G-dam gave 80 1-6 lbs. in a day.

Bred to Netherland King No. 15, Sept. 9th.

No. 282. **AZULEAH.** No. 766.

(H. H. B. Vol. 8, No. 6,881.) Calved April 6th, 1883. Imported by us in May, 1884. Two-thirds black, star, white from shoulders to belly left side, small white spot back of right shoulder, right fore leg black to below knee, white over hips to flanks both sides, black to rump.

Sire, Henri. See No. 214.

Dam, Zwartje, a fine large heifer with good milk veins, gave as a three year-old 52 2-5 lbs.

Grandam gave 91 3-5 lbs. in one day.

Bred to Prince Imperial No. 5, July 19th.

No. 283.   **ASPASIA.**   No. 767.

(H. H. B. Vol. 8, No. 6,852.) Calved May 28th, 1883. Two-thirds black, large star, snip, white over shoulders to belly left side, white over hips to flanks both sides.

Sire, deGraaff (N. H. B. 166).

De Graaff's dam Maria (N. H. B. 369), a very fine straight cow, large crooked milk veins, escutcheon 3d class 3d order, gave 82¼ lbs, of milk in one day.

Dam, Trijntje (N. H. B. 1,080), she was a very choice cow.

Grandam, a great milker.

Bred to Clovis No. 13, August 7th.

No. 284.   **MISS LINCOLN.**   No. 768.

(H. H. B. Vol. 8, No. 6,853) Calved March 1st, 1883. Imported by us in May, 1884. One-half black, large star, muzzle and lower jaw white, white from shoulder to belly left side, white over hips to flanks both sides, four small white spots left side.

Sire, Lincoln, (N. H. B. 120). See No. 13.

Dam, Boertje, a fine heifer, straight and square, fine bone, yellow skin, good escutcheon, a superior milker, gave as a three-year-old 80 1-6 lbs. in one day.

Bred to Prince Imperial, No. 5, July 22d.

No. 285.   **BLACK QUEEN.**   No. 769.

(H. H. B Vol. 8. No. 6,854.) Calved April 2d, 1883. Imported by us in May, 1884. Mostly black, small star, hind legs black to below gambrels, fore legs black nearly to knees.

Sire, Van der Meer's fine two-year-old bull. He was selected by the District as the best out of sixty bulls.

Dam, Jantje, a fine cow, gave as a four-year-old 73 1-5 lbs. in one day.

Grandam, gave as a five-year-old 77 4-5 lbs in one day.

No. 286.   **ORPHAN QUEEN.**   No. 771.

(H. H. B. Vol. 8, No. 6,855.) Calved March 16th, 1883. Imported by us in May, 1884. Four-fifths black, star, strip over shoulders to belly right side, white from left hip to flank, one-half tail white.

Sire, Van der Meer's bull. See No. 285.

Dam, Jaapje, marked like heifer, and has a record of 64 lbs. in one day as a five-year-old.

No. 287.   **FONTANA.**   No. 772.

(H. H. B. Vol. 8, No. 6,883.) Calved May 2d, 1883. Imported by us in May, 1884. Three-fourths black, star, white over shoulders to belly left side, white over shoulders to belly left side, white over hips, right fore leg black to ankle, white spot near right knee.

Sire, Heuvel's bull.

Dam, Aafje, gave as a two-year old 50¼ lbs. in a day.

Bred to Robertus No. 17, August 1st.

No. 288.   **MALA.**   No. 773.

(H. H. B. Vol. 8, No. 6,884.) Calved April 2d, 1883. Imported by us in May, 1884. Three-fourths black, star, strip over shoulders to belly left side, white over hips.

Sire, Heuvel's bull. See No. 287.

Dam, Heuvel, gave as a four-year-old 73 1-5 lbs. in one day.

Bred to Robertus No. 17, July 12th.

No. 289.   **CELY.**   No. 774.

(H. H. B. Vol. 8, No. 6,885.) Calved April 20th, 1883. Imported by us in May, 1884. Four-fifths black, star, white spot on right shoulder, small white spot near root of tail, hind legs black to gambrels.

Sire, Heuvel's bull. See No. 287.

Dam, Geertruida gave as a three-year-old 48 lbs. in one day.

Bred to Clovis No 13, June 20th, 1884.

No. 290. **SIR HENRY OF AAGGIE'S LUZELLE.** No. 775.

(H. H. B. Vol. 8, No. 6,886).) Calved April 5th, 1883. Imported by us in May, 1884. Mostly white, tips of ears black, large black spot on each side of neck, numerous black spots scattered over body.

Sire, Sir Henry of Aaggie (1,450). See Sir Donald of Aaggie No. 7, and page 22.

Dam, Porcelein II. (N. H. B. 392), by Gerrit (N. H. B. 31), he by Cornelius.

Gerrit's dam, de Goede, the dam of Jacob (N. H. B. 20), (See chart.) She has a record of $91\frac{1}{2}$ lbs. in a day.

G-dam, Porcelein (N. H. B. 147), by Rooker. She has a record of 80 lbs. 1 oz. in a day.

G-g-dam, Oude Porcelein.

Porcelein II. has a record of 68 2-5 lbs. in a day.

Bred to Netherland King No. 15, Sept. 2.

No. 291.   **GABUNA.**   No. 780.

(H. H. B. Vol. 8, No 6,890.) Calved March 20th, 1883. Imported by us in May, 1884. One-half black, star, snip, white over back, hips and rump to flanks and belly both sides, small black spot near left flank, and large one above it, white spot on right side, small black spot on right hind quarter.

Sire, Alexander 2d, (1,552), (N. H B. 171), by Alexander, (N. H. B. 83). See No. 171.

Alexander 2d's dam, Smit, has a record of 86 lbs. in one day.

Dam, Lamberta I. A., gave as a two-year-old 45 4-5 lbs. in one day.

G-dam, Lambertina, (6,889), imported, she by Rooker. See No. 101.

G-g-dam, Lamberta, a very choice cow.

Bred to Sir Henry 2d of Aaggie, No. 4, Aug. 24th.

No. 293.   **BENOLA FLETCHER.**   No. 782.

(H. H. B. Vol. 8, No. 6,891) Calved March 10th, 1883. Imported by us in May, 1884. Three-fourths black, star, white over hips and rump running down on left hind leg, right fore leg black to ankle, hind legs black to gambrels.

Sire, Alexander 2d, (1,552), (N. H B. 171), by Alexander, (N. H. B. 83). See No. 171.

Alexander 2d's dam, Smit, has a record of 86 lbs. in one day.

Dam, Bakker, (N. H. B. 1,266) gave as a two-year-old 50¼ lbs in one day, she by Visser.

Grandam, Koster, has a six-year-old record of 75½ lbs. in one day.

Bred to Prince Imperial, No. 5, July 14th.

No. 294. **BEATRIX.** No. 784.

(H. H. B. Vol. 8, No. 6,858.) Calved April 10th, 1883. Imported by us in May, 1884. Two-thirds black, large star, snip, white over shoulders to left fore leg, white over hips to flanks both sides, containing one black spot on left side and two on right.

Sire, District bull of Benningbroek

Dam, Anna, has a record of 82¼ lbs. in a day.

G-dam, gave 73 1-5 lbs. in a day.

No. 295. **BERTHALDA.** No. 786.

(H. H. B. Vol. 8, No. 6,860.) Calved April 5th, 1883. Imported by us in May, 1884. One-half white, strip in face, four large black spots on left side and one on fore leg, irregular black on right side, two small black spots on right flank.

Sire, Sluis' bull "Cornelius."

Dam, Pinkster, a fine cow, straight and square, good escutcheon and long tail, gave as a five-year-old 57 1-5 lbs in a day.

G-dam and G-g-dam, also fine cows and good milkers.

Bred to Sir Henry 2d of Aaggie No. 4, Sept. 2d.

No. 297. **SIR HENRY OF AAGGIE'S ELLAND.** No. 791.

(H. H. B. Vol. 8, No. 6,896.) Calved March 5th, 1883. Imported by us in May, 1884. One-half white, ears black, two black spots on left side, and three on right side of face, black over neck and on left side, large black spot on right side, numerous black spots on both sides.

Sire, Sir Henry of Aaggie (1,450). See No. 7 and page 22.

Dam, Mantel, a large straight and square cow with good escutcheon. She has a record of 75½ lbs. in one day.

No. 298. **LADY CASTLEWOOD.** No. 792.

(H. H. B. Vol. 8, No. 6,861.) Calved March 15th, 1883. Imported by us in May, 1884. Two-thirds black, strip in face, white over back from shoulder to roots of tail and to flank, and belly right side, large black spot on right side containing small white spot.

Sire, District bull of Schaardam.

Dam, Marguerite, a good cow, straight and square, with a record of 68 2 5 lbs. in one day.

Bred to Neptune No. 1, Sept. 1st.

No. 298½. **EGBERTA.** No. 793.

(H. H. B. Vol. 8, No. 6,897.) Calved March 1st, 1883. Imported by us in May, 1884. Two-thirds black, star, irregular white over shoulders to right fore leg, white spot on left shoulder, small one on back and large one over hips.

Sire, de Graaf (N. H. B. 166), Prize Bull at Leyden. See No. 202.

Dam, Geertje 1 A. A large straight and square cow with good head and neck, fine horns and is from a good family.

No. 299. **DORRICE.** No. 795.

(H. H. B. Vol. 8, No. 6,863.) Calved March 1st, 1883. Imported by us in May, 1884. Two-thirds black, strip in face, white over shoulders, narrow white strip from left shoulder to belly, white over hips and rump to belly both sides, black spot on left flank.

Sire, Doris, a fine bull, owned by C. Vis.

His dam has a record of 82½ lbs. in a day.

Dam, Jacoba (N. H. H. B. 95), has a record of 77 4-5 lbs. in one day, and is dam of St. Catharine No. 174.

No. 300. **EMBASSADRESS.** No. 796.

(H. H. B. Vol. 8, No. 6,864.) Calved March 10th, 1883. Imported by us in May, 1884. Three-quarters white, tips of ears black and black around eyes, one large and four small black spots on each side, small black spot below rump.

Sire, District bull of Ven Huisen.

Dam, Klomp (N. H. B.), has a four-year old record of 50½ lbs. in a day. She is straight, square and fine, good head and neck, fine amber horns, good udder, veins and escutcheon.

G-dam, a superior milker.

Bred to Clovis No. 13, June 27th.

No. 301. **CHELSEA MAID.** No. 797.

(H. H. B. Vol. 8, No. 6,865.) Calved March 5th, 1883. Imported by us in May, 1884. Two-thirds white, strip in face, very irregular black saddle over back, black at rump.

Sire, Schuurman's fine bull.

Dam, Bles, is a large, straight, square, fine cow, good escutcheon, good head, very fine horns, a grand cow. She gave 45 4-5 lbs. in one day, six weeks after calving.

Bred to Sir Henry 2d of Aaggie, No. 4, Sept. 13th.

No. 302.   **FLEECY CLOUD.**   No. 798.

(H. H. B. Vol. 8, No. 6,866.) Calved March 10th, 1883. Imported by us in May, 1884. Three-fourths white, black spot around each eye, long black over neck to fore leg both sides, large irregular black spot on each side, etc.

Sire, Schuurman's fine bull. See No 301.

Dam, Jacoba, is an extra heifer, fine, straight and square, good escutcheon and milk veins.

Grandam, an extra fine cow, straight and square, gave 68 2-5 lbs. in one day.

Bred to Prince Imperial, No. 5, July 29th.

No. 303.   **MYCALE.**   No. 799.

(H. H. B. Vol. 8, No. 6,898.) Calved March 8th, 1883. Imported by us in May, 1884. Two-thirds black, strip in face, white over shoulders to belly left side, and over hips to flanks both sides, black at rump, black on fore legs to knees.

Sire, Koster.

Dam, Dirkje, is a fine, large, straight, square cow, with good escutcheon, fine hair and hide, a handsome cow. She is dam of Koster. She gave 68 2-5 lbs. of milk in one day.

Bred to Clovis, No. 18, June 19th.

No. 304.   **ALHAMBRA.**   No. 800.

(H. H. B. Vol. 8, No. 6,899.) Calved March 25th, 1883. Imported by us in May, 1884. Two-thirds black, star, snip, white over hips and shoulders.

Sire, Koster. See No. 303.

Dam, Grietje, has a record of 50¼ lbs. in one day as a four-year-old.

Grietje is good size, straight, square and fine, with good milk veins and escutcheon.

Bred to Robertus, No. 17, July 2d.

No. 305. **DAME DURDEN.** No. 801.

(H. H. B. Vol. 8, No. 6,867.) Calved March 10th, 1883. Imported by us in May, 1884. Two-thirds black, strip in face, white over hips and shoulders.

Sire, Koster. See No. 303.

Dam, Dirkje 3d, gave as a three-year-old 45 4-5 lbs.

Grandam, Dirkje. See dam of No. 303.

Dirkje and Dirkje 5th, dam of No. 306 are sisters.

The dams of Nos. 303, 304, 305 and 306 are of good size, straight, square and fine, with good milk veins and escutcheon.

Bred to Clovis No. 13, July 18th.

No. 306. **AFRICAN MAID.** No. 802.

(H. H. B. Vol. 8, No. 6,900.) Calved April 2d, 1883. Imported by us in May, 1884. Two-thirds black, strip in face, white over hips and shoulders.

Sire, Koster.

Dam, Dirkje 5th, has a record of 57 1-5 lbs. Dirkje 5th is sister to dam of No. 303. See also No. 305.

Bred to Prince Imperial No. 5, July 31st.

No. 307. **GLAD TIDINGS.** No. 825.

(H. H. B. Vol. 8, No. 6,869.) Calved April 25th, 1883. Imported by us in May, 1884. Two-thirds white, strip in face, large irregular black saddle over back.

Sire, District bull of Medemblik.

Dam, Grootje, has a three-year-old record of 41 1-6 lbs.

Bred to Prince Imperial No. 5, July 25th.

No. 308. **CALISTRA.** No. 831.

(H. H. B. Vol. 8, No. 6,870.) Calved March 15th, 1883. Imported by us in May, 1884. Two-thirds white, black spot on each cheek, large irregular black saddle over back.

Sire, Nico (N. H. B. 207). See No. 238.

Nico's dam, a fine large cow, gave 75½ lbs. in one day.

Dam, Winkle, has a three-year-old record of 64 lbs., and is a fine heifer.

Grandam, a fine cow and good long milker.

Bred to Clovis No. 13, July 5th.

No. 309. **WIDE-AWAKE.** No. 861.

(H. H. B. Vol. 8, No. 6,875.) Calved Feb. 22d, 1883. Imported by us in May, 1884. Three-fourths black, star, black spot on left hind quarter, broad white over hips to flanks both sides.

Sire, Wonder's bull.

Dam, Bowman 2d (N. H. B. 1,077), has a record of 57 1-5 lbs. as a three-year-old. She is large and square, fine hair, good hide, head and neck, long, fine tail, good milk veins and very extra escutcheon.

Grandam, Bowman 1st, has a record of 77 4-5 lbs. A large square cow, light colored and handsome, with remarkable milk veins.

Bred to Sir Henry 2d of Aaggie, No. 4, Sept. 13th.

No. 310.   **JACOB WIT'S SOLACE.**   No. 867.

(H. H. B. Vol. 8, No. 6,916.) Calved April 2d, 1883. Imported by us in May, 1884. Three-fourths white, cheeks black, large irregular black spot over back, black spot over neck and down both sides.

Sire, Jacob Wit (2,662), Jacob 4th (N. H. B. 210). See Jacob Wit's Volunteer No. 22.

Dam, Meerhof, has a four-year-old record of 59½ lbs. in one day.

Bred to Clovis No. 13, August 12th.

No. 311.   **DAZIEL.**   No. 875.

(H. H. B. Vol. 8, No. 6,920.) Calved March 6th, 1883. Imported by us in May, 1884. One-half black, white face, black spot around right eye, large irregular black saddle over back.

Sire, District bull of Binnenwijzend.

Dam, Hausje, has a five-year-old record of 57 1-5 lbs. She is very straight square and fine, and a good milker. Her two-year and three-year-old daughters which we saw are also large and fine and good milkers.

Bred to Prince Imperial No. 5, July 16th.

No. 312. **POLIANTHUS.** No 876.

(H. H. B. Vol. 8, No. 6,921.) Calved March 20th, 1883. Imported by us in May, 1884. Three-fourths white, black on cheeks, large irregular black spot on each side.

Sire, District bull of Binnenwijzend.

Dam, de Jonge Jaapje, has a four-year-old record of 64 lbs. She is large, straight and square, fine bone, good horns, splendid milk veins and *extra* escutcheon.

Grandam has a record of 68 2-5 lbs She is handsomer than the dam, straight and square, fine bone, good head and neck, good milk veins running very far forward, *extra* escutcheon and very yellow skin.

Bred to Clovis No. 13, July 13th.

No. 313. **PANSYNE.** No. 878.

(H. H. B. Vol. 8, No. 6,923.) Calved April 14th, 1883. Imported by us in May, 1884. Two-thirds white, strip in face, large black saddle over back.

Sire, District bull of Binnenwijzend.

Dam, Vrouwtje Bowman, has a five-year-old record of 66¼ lbs., and is a long milker. She is straight and square.

No. 314. **MAXIMA.** No. 879.

(H. H. B. Vol. 8, No. 6,924.) Calved March 10th, 1883. Imported by us in May, 1884. Two-thirds white, small black spot under each eye, large irregular black saddle over back, black at rump.

Sire, District bull of Schellinkhout.

Dam, Sneek, has a record of 82½ lbs , and is a superior and very long milker.

Bred to Clovis No. 13, July 26th.

No. 315.   QUENITH.   No. 882.

(H. H. B. Vol. 8, No. 6,927.) Calved March 30th, 1883. Imported by us in May, 1884. One-half black, strip in face, broad white over hips to flanks both sides, white over shoulders to belly on left side.

Sire, District bull of Binnenwijzend.

Dam, Geertje, has a four-year-old record of 68 2-5 lbs.

Bred to Clovis No. 13, July 25th.

No 316.   QUEEN OF KENNETT.   No. 883.

(H. H. B. Vol. 8, No. 6,928.) Calved March 20th, 1883. Imported by us in May, 1884. Two-thirds black, white in face, white strip from right shoulder to belly, irregular white on back.

Sire, District bull of Schellinkhout.

Dam, Sneek 2d, a good milker, but we have no record. She is sister to Maxima No. 314.

Bred to Prince Imperial No. 5, July 29th.

No. 317.   ORANGE BUD.   No. 884.

(H. H. B. Vol. 8, No. 6,929.) Calved April 15th, 1883. Imported by us in May, 1884. One-half black, black on cheeks, white over shoulders and hips.

Sire, District bull of Blokker.

Dam, Maartje 3d, has a two-year-old record of 41 1-6 lbs.

Bred to Clovis No. 13, July 18th.

No. 318. **MANTISSA.** No. 886.

(H. H. B. Vol. 8, No. 6,931.) Calved Feb. 27th, 1883. Imported by us in May, 1884. Three-fourths white, black spots on face and scattered over body.

Sire, District bull of Blokker.

Dam, Trijntje, has a five-year-old record of 73 1-5 lbs.

Bred to Clovis No. 13, July 20th.

No. 319. **LÉONNE.** No. 887.

(H. H. B. Vol. 8, No. 6,932.) Calved Feb. 26th, 1883. Imported by us in May, 1884. Mostly white, large black spot around each eye, medium black spots on both sides.

Sire, District bull of Schellinkhout.

Dam, Bartje, (N. H. B.) has a five-year-old record of 68 2-5 lbs. She is a large white and black cow, very straight and square, fine bone, good head and neck, fine hair and hide, good milk veins, extra escutcheon.

Bred to Clovis No. 13, July 6th.

No. 320. **MADAME STAPEL.** No. 889.

(H. H. B. Vol. 8, No. 7,799.) Calved March 15th, 1883. Imported by us in May, 1884. Three-fourths black, star, white spot over shoulders and one over hips.

Sire, Willem 3d, (N. H. B. 190), District bull of Schellinkhout, a large, straight, square, good four year-old bull.

Willem 3d's dam gave 68 2-5 lbs. of milk in one day, and in 1880 won First Prize at Harlem.

Dam, Antje, (N. H. H. B. 107), has a six-year-old record of 77 4-5 lbs. and is dam of Duessa, No. 399.

Bred to Clovis, No. 13, July 30th.

No. 320½.   LA CAPATAINE.   No. 890.

(H. H. B. Vol. 8. No. 6,934.) Calved March 16th, 1883. Imported by us in May, 1884. Three-fourths white, strip in face, small white spot on left side of neck, two large black spots on each side, black at rump, two-thirds tail white.

Sire, Willem 3d, (N. H. B. 190). See No. 320.

Dam, Aagje, (N. H. H. B. 106), gave as a four-year-old 64 lbs. in one day. She is a fine straight and square cow, white and black, with large milk veins.

Grandam, white and black, has a record of 68 2-5 lbs. in one day.

Bred to Prince Imperial No. 5, July 20th.

No. 321.   AQUILA.   No. 895.

(H. H. B. Vol. 8, No. 6,937.) Calved April 3d, 1883. Imported by us in May, 1884. Two-thirds white, large star, snip, large irregular black saddle over back.

Sire, Willem 3d, (N. H. B. 190). See No. 320.

Dam, Gorter, has a three-year-old record of 45 4-5 lbs.

No. 322.   STELLETA.   No. 896.

(H. H. B. Vol. 8, No. 6,938.) Calved March 16th, 1883. Imported by us in May, 1884. Two-thirds black, star, snip, large black saddle over back.

Sire, Willem 3d, (N. H. B. 190). See No. 320.

Dam, Schuit, (N. H. H. B.), has a four-year-old record of 68 2-5 lbs. in one day, and is a large, straight, fine cow, good milk veins, splendid udder, good head and neck, fine horns and bone.

Bred to Prince Imperial, No. 5, August 4th.

No. 324. **ROZALIA SOMERS.** No. 898.

(H. H. B. Vol. 8, No. 6,940.) Calved March 3d, 1883. Imported by us in May, 1884. Three-fourths white, black around eyes, large irregular black spot on each side.

Sire, Willem 3d, (N. H. B. 190). See 320.

Dam, Palenstein (N. H. H. B.), has a six-year-old record of 64 lbs. and is a large fine cow, handsome, well marked, very fine hair and hide, extra escutcheon, amber horns, evidently an extra milker.

Bred to Prince of Artis No. 8, Sept. 17th.

No. 325. **SIR HENRY OF AAGGIE'S PHLOX.** No. 901.

(H. H. B. Vol. 8, No. 6,943.) Calved March 1st, 1883. Imported by us in May, 1884. Mostly white, black around eyes, black spots on sides.

Sire, Sir Henry of Aaggie (1,450). See Sir Donald of Aaggie No. 7.

Dam, Teunisje 1st, has a six-year-old record of 64 lbs. in one day.

Grandam has a record of 68 2-5 lbs. in one day. She is sister to No. 177.

Bred to Clovis No. 13, July 3d.

No. 326. **SIR HENRY OF AAGGIE'S CRESSA.** No. 902.

(H. H. B. Vol. 8, No. 6,944.) Calved Feb. 15th, 1883. Imported by us in May, 1884. One-half black, large star, snip, irregular white over shoulders to belly both sides, broad white over hips to flank left side.

Sire, Sir Henry of Aaggie (1,450). See Sir Donald of Aaggie No. 7.

Dam, Porcelein, has a record of 68 2-5 lbs.

Bred to Netherland Prince No. 2, August 20th.

No. 328. **COLIANTHUS.** No. 906.

(H. H. B. Vol. 8, No. 7,270.) Calved April 4th, 1883. Imported by us in May, 1884. Four fifths black, star, snip, white spot on left shoulder and on left rump.

Sire, Boxumer.

Dam, Lieuwkje 2d, has a four-year-old record of 61 4-5 lbs. and is very straight and square, fine head and bone, good horns, fine hair, mellow hide, good escutcheon and milk veins.

Bred to Prince of Artis No. 8, Sept. 15th.

No. 329. **VILLAGE LASS.** No. 909.

(H. H. B. Vol. 8, No. 6,947.) Calved March 12th, 1883. Imported by us in May, 1884. Two-thirds black, strip in face, broad white over shoulders to belly on each side, large white over left hip.

Sire, Boonstra, a black and white bull with star in the forehead.

Dam, Kalsbeek, has a record of 61 4-5 lbs. in one day, and is large, straight, square, with good head and horns, and fair escutcheon.

Bred to Clovis, No. 13, July 2d.

No. 330. **BOSTON QUEEN.** No. 910.

(H. H. B. Vol. 8, No. 6,948.) Calved March 10th, 1883. Imported by us in May, 1884. Two-thirds black, strip in face, white over shoulders to belly on left side, black at rump and roots of tail.

Sire, Boonstra. See No. 329.

Dam, Wiersma, has a record of 61 4-5 lbs. in one day.

Bred to Netherland Prince, No. 2, August 19th.

No. 331.   **POSTMISTRESS.**   No. 911.

(H. H. B. Vol. 8, No. 6,949.) Calved March 14th, 1883 Imported by us in May, 1884. One-half black, star, snip, large black spots on left side, left fore leg black to below knee.

Sire, Postman.

Antje, dam of Postman, has a record of 73 1-5 lbs. in one day as a five-year-old. She is of good size, straight, square, with good head, horns and udder.

Grandam has a record of 82¼ lbs. in one day.

Dam, Truij, has a five-year old record of 64 lbs. per day for ten consecutive weeks. She is a large white and black cow, fine bone, good milk veins and very extra escutcheon.

Bred to Prince Imperial, No. 5, July 16th.

No. 332.   **TWEEDLEDUM.**   No. 913.

(H. H. B. Vol. 8, No 6,951.) Calved May 3d, 1883. Imported by us in May, 1884. One-half black, star, snip, white over shoulders to belly both sides and over hips to flanks and belly on left side.

Sire, Johan.

Dam, Trijntje, gave as a five-year-old, 64 lbs. of milk in one day.

Bred to Prince of Artis No. 8, Sept. 11th.

No. 333.   **SPINAWAY.**   No. 915.

(H. H. B. Vol. 8, No. 6,953.) Calved April 5th, 1883. Imported by us in May, 1884. Three-fourths black, star, broad white over shoulders running in narrow line to belly on right side, white over hips to left flank.

Sire, Hallum is a large fine black and white bull.

Dam, Gjetje has a two-year-old record of 41 1-6 lbs.

No. 334.   **CLOVETTE.**   No. 916

(H. H. B. Vol. 8. No. 9,654.) Calved April 1st, 1883. Imported by us in May, 1884. Three-fourths black, small star, snip, white spot over shoulders, white over hips to flank on right side.

Sire, Hallum. See No. 333.

Dam, Bontje, has a two-year-old record of 41 1-6 lbs.

Bred to Robertus No. 17, July 25th.

No. 335.   **WARWICK MAID.**   No. 917.

(H. H. B. Vol. 8, No. 6,955.) Calved March 18th, 1883. Imported by us in May, 1884. Three-fourths black, star and snip, white over shoulders to belly both sides, white over hips to flank on left side by narrow line

Sire, Jan. Sold to go to Germany.

His dam has a record of 68 2-5 lbs. and is a fine cow. gave 64 lbs. per day for a long time.

A sister to Jan gave as a four-year-old $59\frac{1}{2}$ lbs. in one day.

Dam, Engeltje, has a five year old record of 68 2-5 lbs. She is a large fine cow, straight and square, long milk veins, extra escutcheon.

Bred to Robertus No. 17, July 14th.

No. 336. **LASS OF WINSUM.** No. 918.

(H. H. B. Vol. 8, No. ——.) Calved May 5th, 1883. Imported by us in May, 1884. Four-fifths black, large star, large triangular white spot on left side near shoulder.

Sire, Jan. See No. 335.

Dam, Slotsum. Sold to go to Germany. She has a five-year-old record of 73 1-5 lbs.

No. 337. **WIKOLIS.** No. 919.

(H. H. B. Vol. 8, No. 6,956.) Calved April 28th, 1883. Imported by us in May, 1884. Two-thirds white, large star, snip, large irregular black saddle over back.

Sire, Siersma, a fine black and white bull.

Dam, Jacoba, as a four-year-old gave 64 lbs. per day for a long time. She is large, straight, square, fine hair, good hide, good milk veins and escutcheon.

Grandam, a superior milker.

Bred to Clovis No. 13, August 5th.

No. 338. **VASSAR.** No. 920.

(H. H B. Vol. 8, No. 6,957.) Calved May 2d, 1883. Imported by us in May, 1884. Three-fourths black, star, snip, white strip over shoulders to belly on right side, white spot over hips.

Sire, Rienk's fine black and white bull. His dam is an extra fine cow.

Dam, Anna, has a three-year-old record of 59½ lbs. in one day.

Bred to Robertus, No. 17, Aug. 11th.

No. 339.   **TRINTASIA.**   No. 921.

(H. H. B. Vol. 8, No. 6,958.) Calved April 15th, 1883. Imported by us in May, 1884. Two-thirds black, strip in face, irregular white over hips to belly, left side.

Sire, Rienk's bull. See No. 338.

Dam, Trijntje, has a two-year-old record of 41 1-6 lbs. in one day, and is straight, square, fine hair, good hide, fine bone, milk veins good and escutcheon very superior.

Bred to Prince Imperial, No. 5, July 28th.

No. 340.   **TRYPHENE.**   No. 922.

(H. H. B. Vol, 8, No. 6,959.) Calved April 3d, 1883. Imported by us in May, 1884. Two-thirds black, star, white over shoulders and hips to flank and belly on right side.

Sire, Rienk's bull. See No. 338.

Dam, Tettje, has a three-year-old record of 68 2-5 lbs. in one day, and has a fine head and neck, fine hair, hide and bone, good milk veins and escutcheon.

Grandam, an equally good cow.

Bred to Clovis, No. 13, July 10th.

No. 341.   **THEODATE.**   No. 923.

(H. H. B. Vol. 8, No. 6,960.) Calved April 1st, 1883. Imported by us in May, 1884. Three-fourths black, large star, snip, white spots over shoulders and hips.

Sire, Rienk's bull. See No. 338.

Dam, Sieteske, has a three-year-old record of 54 6-7 lbs.

Bred to Clovis No. 13, August 2d.

No. 342.   **ROSALPHA.**   No. 924.

(H. H. B. Vol. 8, No. 6,961) Calved March 15th, 1883. Imported by us in May, 1884. Two-thirds white, strip in face large irregular black spot on each side.

Sire. David. Sold to go to Germany. His dam is a fine milker, and gave 64 lbs. in a day as a four-year-old.

Dam, Woudman, has a three-year-old record of 54 6-7 lbs., and is straight, square, fine head, horns and bone, good milk veins and extra escutcheon.

Grandam, sold to go to Germany, has a four-year-old record of 64 lbs.

Bred to Prince Imperial No. 5, July 28th.

No. 343.   **GUERNDALE.**   No. 925.

(H. H. B Vol. 8. No. 6,962.) Calved April 3d, 1883. Imported by us in May, 1884. Four-fifths, black, star, white spot over hips.

Sire, David. See No. 342.

Dam, Wytska, has a three-year-old record of 54 6-7 lbs.

Grandam, an extra good milker.

Bred to Prince Imperial No. 5, July 26th.

No. 344.   **SYLPHA.**   No. 927.

(H. H. B. Vol. 8, No. 6,964.) Calved May 2d, 1883. Imported by us in May, 1884. Two-thirds black, strip in face, broad white over hips to flanks both sides.

Sire, Boersma's bull a fine animal from one of his best cows, which gave as a four-year-old 64 lbs. in one day.

Dam, Bontje, has a two-year-old record of 41 1-6 lbs. and is a large square cow, mostly white, fine hair and hide, looks like a good milker.

Bred to Clovis No. 13, July 31st.

No. 345.   **JACOB WIT'S BLANQUETTE.**   No. 953.

(H. H. B. Vol. 8, No. 6.967.) Calved April 24th, 1883. Imported by us in May, 1884. Two-thirds black, strip in face, large irregular black saddle over back, sides spotted.

Sire, Jacob Wit, (2,662), Jacob 4th, (N. H. B. 210.) See Jacob Wit's Volunteer No. 22.

Dam, Meerhof, has a record of 64 lbs.

Bred to Prince Imperial No. 5, August 1st.

No. 346.   **JACOB WIT'S LEOLA.**   No. 954.

(H. H. B. Vol. 8, No. 6,968.) Calved March 17th, 1883. Imported by us in May, 1884. Three-fourths white, cheeks and sides of neck black, large and small spots on each side.

Sire, Jacob Wit, (2,662), Jacob 4th, (N. H. B. 210.) See Jacob Wit's Volunteer, No. 22.

Dam, Boeder, has a four-year-old record of 64 lbs.

No. 347.   **PURITANIA.**   No. 958.

(H. H. B. Vol. 8, No. 6,971.) Calved March 16th, 1883. Imported by us in May, 1884. One-half black, strip in face, two large irregular black spots on each side.

Sire, Schrooder's bull, is a fine black and white bull, strip in face, straight, square, with an extra escutcheon.

Dam, Aaltje, has a record of 68 lbs. She is very straight

and square, fine bone, good mellow hide, good milk veins and fair escutcheon.

Bred to Clovis No. 13, July 27th.

No. 348.   **LADY ANSTYS.**   No. 959.

(H. H. B. Vol. 8, No. 6,972.) Calved April 5th, 1883. Imported by us in May, 1884. Two-thirds black star, snip, broad irregular white over shoulders to belly on right side, white spot over hips.

Sire, Schrooder's bull. See No. 347.

Dam, Betje, has a record of 68 2-5 lbs., and is one of the handsomest cows we saw in Holland; straight and square, very fine, mostly white, very fine horns, fine mellow hide, splendid milk veins and escutcheon. Her sire was the District bull.

Grandam also has a record of 68 2-5 lbs.

Bred to Robertus No. 17, July 23d.

No. 349.   **MISS SMYLIE.**   No. 965.

(H. H. B. Vol. 8, No. 6,973.) Calved Feb. 19th, 1883. Imported by us in May, 1884. Two-thirds black, large star, snip, large white spot on right shoulder, white over hips to flanks both sides.

Sire, District bull of Hoogwoud.

Dam, Geertje, gave as a five year-old 57 1-5 lbs. in one day.

Bred to Sir Henry 2d of Aaggie No. 4, Sept. 2d.

No. 350.   **SAXAFRAGIA.**   No. 967.

(H. H. B. Vol. 8, No. 6,974.) Calved March 14th, 1883. Imported by us in May, 1884. Two-thirds black, strip in face, irregular white over shoulders to belly right side, white over hips to flanks both sides.

Sire, District bull of Hoogcarspel.

Dam, Roosje, has a record of 64 lbs. in one day.

She is a very fine, handsome cow, straight, square, fine head and horns, good milk veins and escutcheon.

No. 351. **MOUSIE.** No. 968.

(H. H. B. Vol. 8, No. 6,975.) Calved March 7, 1883. Imported by us in May, 1884. Three-fourths black, large star, snip, irregular white spot over shoulders and one over hips.

Sire, District bull of Hoogcarspel. See No. 350.

Dam, Roosje 2d, has a two-year-old record of 54 6-7 lbs. in one day.

Bred to Clovis, No. 13, June 26th.

No. 352. **SUNNY SIDE.** No. 969.

(H. H. B. Vol. 8, No. 6,976.) Calved April 15th, 1883. Imported by us in May, 1884. Two-thirds white, strip in face, large irregular black spots on each side.

Sire, District bull of Hoogcarspel. See No. 350.

Dam, Roosje 3d, has a five-year-old record of 77 4-5 lbs in one day.

She is very handsome, straight and square, with fine horns, good head and neck, good milk veins and udder, and extra escutcheon.

Bred to Sir Henry Henry 2d of Aaggie, No. 4, Sept. 13th.

No 353.   **TRUE FAVOR.**   No. 970.

(H. H. B. Vol. 8, No. 6,977.) Calved March 1st, 1884. Imported by us in May, 1884. Three-fourths white, strip in face, three black spots on each side.

Sire, District bull of Hoogcarspel. See No. 350.

Dam, Jantje, has a five-year-old record of 91 3-5 lbs. She is a large, straight and square cow, with large udder and fine escutcheon, fine bone, long fine tail, good head and neck.

Bred to Prince Imperial No. 5, August 4th.

No. 353½.   **LAURENTINE.**   No. 972.

(H. H. B. Vol. 8, No. 6,979.) Calved Feb. 15th, 1883. Imported by us in May, 1884. Three-fourths black, strip in face, white over hips to flanks both sides.

Sire, District bull of Hoogcarspel. See No. 350.

Dam, Kobbus, has a three-year-old record of 45 4-5 lbs. She is fine and handsome, with fine hair, good udder and veins.

Bred to Clovis No 13, June 19th.

No. 354.   **PARTELLA.**   No. 974.

(H. H. B. Vol. 8, No. 6,981.) Calved March 15th, 1883. Imported by us in May, 1884. Two-thirds black, strip in face, white over shoulders to belly right side, white over hips to flanks both sides.

Sire, District bull of Hoogcarspel. See No. 350.

Dam, De Hart, has a four-year-old record of 73 1-5 lbs. She is a very large and very straight and square cow, with fine bone, good head and horns, long fine tail, and good udder and milk veins.

No. 355.   **TESTIMONY.**   No. 972.

(H. H. B. Vol. 8, No. 6,982.) Calved March 16th, 1883. Imported by us in May, 1884. Three-fourths white, black cheeks, sides spotted.

Sire, District bull of Hoogcarspel. See No. 350.

Dam, deWit, has a six-year-old record of 77 4-5 lbs. She is white and black, with fine horns, long fine tail, fine hair and hide, straight and square.

No. 356.   **EDWINA.**   No. 978.

(H. H. B. Vol. 8, No. 6,983.) Calved March 16th, 1883. Imported by us in May, 1884. Two-thirds white, large star, snip, large black spot on each side.

Sire, District bull of Hoogcarspel. See No. 350.

Dam, Torrel, has a three-year-old record of 54 6-7 lbs.

Grandam, a fine black and white cow, has a record of 68 2-5 lbs.

Torrel is a handsome heifer, square and fine, with good head, horns and escutcheon.

No. 357.   **LYBIA.**   No. 981.

(H. H. B. Vol. 8, No 6,984.) Calved May 1st, 1883. Imported by is in May, 1884. Three-fourths white, strip in face, sides spotted.

Sire, District bull of Beemster. (Lof's).

Dam, Grootmoeder, has a record as a five-year-old of 73 1-5 lbs. in one day.

She is white and black, straight and square, with fine bone and horns, and an extra escutcheon.

No. 358. **MRS. PINKHAM.** No. 982.

(H. H. B. Vol. 8, No. 6,985.) Calved March 20th, 1883. Imported by us in May, 1884. Four-fifths white, cheeks and neck black, sides spotted.

Sire, District bull of Beemster. See No. 357.

Dam, Neeltje, (N. H. B.), has a six-year-old record of 77 4-5 lbs. in one day

She is white and black, very straight and square, with good bone, yellow skin and handsome udder.

No. 359. **HARVESTA.** No. 983.

(H. H. B. Vol. 8, No. 6,986.) Calved March 6th, 1883. Imported by us in May, 1884. Three-fourths black, large star, small white spots on shoulders and hips.

Sire, District bull of Beemster. See No. 357.

Dam, Bruidje, (N. H. B), has a two-year-old record of 41 1-6 lbs., and as a three-year-old she gave 59½ lbs in one day. She is a sister to Philopena (2,864), is straight and square, with fine bone, fine hair and hide and good escutcheon.

Grandam, Paet Vink gave as a six-year-old 70 8-9 lbs. in one day.

No. 360. **LEMABEL.** No. 988.

(H. H. B. Vol. 8, No. 6,987.) Calved April 15th, 1883. Imported by us in May, 1884. Three-fourths white, star, large irregular black spot on right, numerous small black spots on left side.

Sire, District bull of Wormermeer.

Dam, Christine, has a record of 68 2-5 lbs.

Bred to Clovis No. 13, August 12th.

No. 361.　　　　　　**LENELLA.**　　　　　　No. 989.

(H. H. B. Vol. 8, No. 6,988.) Calved April 8th, 1883. Imported by us in May, 1884. Three-fourths, black, star, white spot over shoulders and one over hips.

Sire, District bull of Wormermeer. See No. 360

Dam, Anna, has a record of 73 1-5 lbs.

Bred to Robertus No. 17, May 10th.

No. 362.　　　　　　**SOMNAMBULA.**　　　　　　No. 1,047.

(H. H. B. Vol. 6, No. 6,990.) Calved March 5th, 1883. Imported by us in May, 1884 Two-thirds black, star, white over shoulders to belly both sides, white over hips to flank on left side.

Sire, Alexander 2d (1,552), (N. H. B. 171), he by Alexander (N. H. B. 83). See No. 171.

Dam, Aaggie Cornelia 2d (4,341). See No. 115.

Bred to Prince Imperial No. 5, July 23d.

No. 363.　　　　　　**MIRTH.**　　　　　　No. 1,048.

(H. H. B. Vol. 8, No. 6,991.) Calved March 25th, 1883. Imported by us in May, 1884. Two-thirds black, large star, snip, broad strip over shoulders to belly left side, white over hips to flank on left side.

Sire, Alexander 2d (1,552), (N. H. B. 171), he by Alexander (N. H. B. 83). See No. 171.

Dam, Oude Bles, has a record of 57 1-5 lbs.

Bred to Prince Imperial No. 5, July 4th.

No. 364.   **MUSIQUE.**   No. 1,049.

(H. H. B. Vol. 8, No. 6,992.) Calved April 5th, 1883. Imported by us in May, 1884. Mostly black, star, white spot on hips.

Sire, Alexander 2d (1,552), (N. H. B. 171), he by Alexander (N. H. B. 83). See No. 171.

Dam, Zwijn, has a five-year-old record of 57 1-5 lbs.

Grandam, a fine cow.

Bred to Clovis No. 13, July 11th.

No. 365.   **MIRANDOLA.**   No. 1,050.

(H. H. B. Vol 8, No. 6,993.) Calved April 16th, 1883. Imported by us in May, 1884. Three-fourths white, strip in face, large black spots on each side.

Sire, Tromp (N. H. B. 188). See Aaggie Beatrice No. 183.

Dam, Jonges Bles, has a four-year-old record of 57 1-5 lbs.

Bred to Clovis No. 13, July 28th.

No. 366.   **FOOCHOW.**   No. 1,051.

(H. H. B. Vol. 8, No. 6,994.) Calved March 15th, 1883. Imported by us in May, 1884. Three-fourth black, star, white over hips to flanks both sides.

Sire, Alexander 2d (1,552), (N. H. B. 171), he by Alexander (N. H. B. 83). See No. 171.

Dam, Mooi Stippel, has a four-year-old record of 57 1-5 lbs.

Grandam, has a record of 68 2-5 lbs.

Bred to Sir Henry 2d of Aaggie No. 4, Sept. 15th.

Heifer Calves.

No. 367. **JACOB WIT'S ADNAH.** No. 778.

(H. H. B. Vol. 8, No. 6,856.) Calved March 6th, 1884. Imported by us in May, 1884. Three-fourths white, spotted, strip on face.

Sire, Jacob Wit (2,662), Jacob 4th (N. H. B. 210). See Jacob Wit's Volunteer No. 22.

Dam, de Ruiter's Beatus (6,888). See No. 201.

Grandam, Catharine.

No. 368. **MYLA.** No. 806.

(H. H. B. Vol. 8, No. 6,901.) Calved March 17th, 1884. Imported by us in May, 1884. Three-fourths white, strip in face, irregular black spot on each side.

Sire, Lincoln (N. H. B. 120). See Clovis No. 13.

Dam, Emma, has a record of 75½ tbs. This calf is sister to Clovis No. 13.

No. 369. **MARAPOSA.** No. 807.

(H. H. B. Vol. 8, No. 6,902.) Calved March 10th, 1884. Imported by us in May, 1884. Mostly black, small star, small white spot on right shoulder, white spot over hips.

Sire, Lincoln (N. H. B. 120). See Clovis No. 13.

Dam, Marguerite, has a six-year-old record of 68 2-5 lbs.

Grandam, an extra fine cow.

Marguerite is mostly black with star, very large and square, fine hair and hide, very long tail, and good escutcheon.

No. 370.   **JACOB WIT'S FRELIA.**   No. 810.

(H. H. B. Vol. 8, No. 6,903.)   Calved Feb. 24th, 1884. Imported by us in May, 1884. Three-fourths white, strip in face, several black spots on each side.

Sire, Jacob Wit (2,662), Jacob 4th, (N. H. B. 210). See Jacob Wit's Volunteer, No. 22.

Dam, Zadelmaker 1st, has a record of 57 1-5 lbs. in one day. She is a fine, large, old cow, mostly white, with fine, large udder and veins, good hide and hair.

No. 371.   **JACOB WIT'S PHENE.**   No. 812.

(H. H. B. Vol. 8, No. 7,787.) Calved March 17th, 1884. Imported by us in May, 1884. Two thirds black, strip in face, irregular white over shoulders and hips.

Sire, Jacob Wit, (2,662), Jacob 4th, (N. H. B. 210). See Jacob Wit's Volunteer, No. 22.

Dam, Trintje, has a two-year-old record of 29¾ lbs. in one day. She is a very handsome, straight and square heifer. Her sire was Alexander (N. H. B. 83.) See No. 171.

Grandam, Groote Zwart, has a record of 52 2-5 lbs. in one day as a five-year-old. She is black and white with star, straight and square, good head, horns, hair and hide, long tail and good milk veins.

No. 372.   **JACOB WIT'S EMILY.**   No. 818.

(H. H. B. Vol. 8, No. 6.868.) Calved Feb. 24th, 1884. Imported by us in May, 1884. Four-fifths white, strip in face, sides spotted.

Sire, Jacob Wit (2,662), Jacob 4th (N. H. B. 210). See Jacob Wit's Volunteer No. 22.

Dam, Geeske (N. H. B. 685), (F. H. B. 278), has a six-year-old record of 77 4-5 lbs. She won First Prize at Alkmaar, and Second at Alkmaar in 1884; and Prize at International Exposition at Amsterdam in 1884.

Jacob's Wit's Emily is sister to Aaggie Ada (4,329).

No. 373.   **JACOB WIT'S MAYLIE.**   No. 819.

(H. H. B. Vol. 8, No. 7,788.) Calved March 13th, 1884. Imported by us in May, 1884. Two-thirds black, star, snip, irregular white over hips and shoulders to flank and belly left side.

Sire, Jacob Wit (2.662), Jacob 4th (N. H. B. 210). See Jacob Wit's Volunteer No. 22.

Dam, Groote Wit (N. H. B. 2,545), (De Groot), has a record of 68 2-5 lbs. as a four-year-old.

Jacob Wit's Maylie is sister to Aaggie Sophie No. 218.

No. 374.   **JACOB WIT'S HELLA.**   No. 820.

(H. H. B. Vol. 8, No. 7,789.) Calved March 15th, 1884. Imported by us in May, 1884. Two-thirds black, star, snip, large black spot on each side.

Sire, Jacob Wit (2,662), Jacob 4th, (N. H. B. 210). See Jacob Wit's Volunteer, No. 22.

Dam, Mantel (N. H. B. 2,544), has a four-year-old record of 68 2-5 lbs.

Jacob Wit's Hella is sister to Aaggie Ruth (4,395.)

No. 375. **JACOB WIT'S BERNIE.** No. 823.

(H. H. B. Vol. 8, No. 7,790.) Calved Feb. 21st, 1884. Imported by us in May, 1884. Two-thirds black, large star, snip, white over shoulder and hips to belly right side.

Sire, Jacob Wit (2,662) Jacob 4th, (N. H. B. 210.) See Jacob Wit's Volunteer No. 22.

Dam, Schippertje, has a five-year-old record of 64 lbs. She is a fine cow, straight and square, with very long tail.

Jacob Wit's Bernie is sister to Aaggie Ophelia (4,439).

No. 376. **JACOB WIT'S WATTEAU.** No. 827.

(H. H. B. Vol. 8, No. 6,906.) Calved Feb. 4th, 1884. Imported by us in May, 1884. Two-thirds white, large star, snip, large black saddle over back.

Sire, Jacob Wit (2,662), Jacob 4th (N. H. B. 210). See Jacob Wit's Volunteer No. 22.

Dam, Jonge Dekker, has a three-year-old record of 64 lbs. She is a fine large heifer, straight and square, and is dam of Evaletta (4,550).

No. 377. **WINGONIA.** No. 828.

(H. H. B. Vol. 8, No. 6,907.) Calved Feb. 28th, 1884. Imported by us in May, 1884. Three-fourths white, strip in face, sides spotted.

Sire, Lord of Benningbroek (2,523), (N. H. B. 256), imported, he by Napoleon (N. H. B. 182).

Napoleon's dam, Violet (N. H. B. 631). She was a great milker, but is now dead.

Dam, Porcelein, has a record of 59½ lbs.

Grandam, an extra good cow.

No. 378.   **JACOB WIT'S MYTH.**   No. 834.

(H. H. B. Vol. 8, No. 6,909). Calved March 23d, 1884. Imported by us in May, 1884. Three-fourths black, star and snip, white over shoulders and hips.

Sire, Jacob Wit (2,662), Jacob 4th, (N. H. B. 210.) See Jacob Wit's Volunteer, No. 22.

Dam, Trijntje, (N. H. B. 602), a very fine cow, with elegant escutcheon, good udder and milk veins. She has a milk record of 68 2-5 lbs. in one day. See Happy Thought, No. 238.

No. 380.   **JACOB WIT'S BELVA.**   No. 840.

(H. H. B. Vol. 8, No. 7,791.) Calved Feb. 18th, 1884. Imported by us in May, 1884. Three-fourths white, strip in face, large irregular black saddle over back.

Sire, Jacob Wit, (2,662), Jacob 4th, (N. H. B. 210). See Jacob Wit's Volunteer, No. 22.

Dam, Breggar, (N. H. B. 1,738.) She is white and black, straight, square and very handsome, fair hide, good escutcheon and yellow skin.

Jacob Wit's Belva is sister to Good Cheer, (4,423).

No. 381.   **JACOB WIT'S BERYLLA.**   No. 841.

(H. H. B. Vol. 8, No. 7,792) Calved Feb. 6th, 1884. Imported by us in May, 1884. One-half black, strip in face, irregular white over hips and back.

Sire, Jacob Wit (2,662), Jacob 4th (N. H. B. 210). See Jacob Wit's Volunteer No. 22.

Dam, Alkmaaria (N. H. B. 1,525), has a three-year-old record of 54 6-7 ℔s. She is straight and square, well marked, fine and handsome.

No. 382.   **JACOB WIT'S CLEORINE.**   No. 842.

(H. H. B Vol. 8, No. 7,793.) Calved March 17th, 1884. Imported by us in May, 1884. Mostly black, strip in face, white spot on shoulders, broad white over hips to flank left side.

Sire, Jacob Wit (2,662), Jacob 4th (N. H. B. 210). See Jacob Wit's Volunteer No. 22.

Dam, Groote, has a three-year-old record of 54 6-7 ℔s. She is descended on sires side from Alexander (N. H. B. 83).

No. 383.   **JACOB WIT'S CYRILLA.**   No. 843.

(H. H. B. Vol. 8, No. 7,794.) Calved March 23d, 1884. Imported by us in May, 1884. Three-fourths white, cheeks black, sides spotted.

Sire, Jacob Wit, (2,662), Jacob 4th, (N. H. B. 210) See Jacob Wit's Volunteer, No. 22.

Dam, de Schot, (N. H. B. 1,088), has a six-year-old record of 82½ lbs. She is a long, low, fine and handsome cow, straight and square, with elegant escutcheon, head and horns. One of the best cows we ever saw.

Jacob Wit's Cyrilla is sister to Glen Ella, (4,424).

No. 384.   **JACOB WIT'S CRANELLI.**   No. 844.

(H. H. B. Vol. 8, No. 7,795.) Calved March 24th, 1884. Imported by us in May, 1884. Three-fourths white, black spot around each eye, black over neck, black spots on sides.

Sire, Jacob Wit (2,662) Jacob 4th (N. H. B. 210). See Jacob Wit's Volunteer No. 22.

Dam, Groenvelde, has a two-year-old record of 45 4-5 lbs. in one day. She is a straight, square heifer and fine, with good hide and horns.

Grandam, owned by K. Slot of St. Martins, is a wonderful milker.

No. 385.   MIRACLE.   No. 847.

(H. H. B. Vol. 8, No 6,910.) Calved Feb. 25th, 1884. Imported by us in May, 1884. Three-fourths black, large star, snip, white over hips and shoulder.

Sire, Lincoln (N. H. B. 120). See Clovis No. 13.

Dam, Jantje, has a record of 68 2-5 lb. She is a large, low, fine and handsome cow, straight and square, with good udder and milk veins.

No. 386.   ARTIS' PRIDE.   No. 848.

(H. H. B. Vol. 8, No. 6 872.) Calved March 10th, 1884. Imported by us in May, 1884. Mostly black, star, white spot on shoulders and hips.

Sire, Artis, (N. H. B. 127), a large, straight, square, well marked bull, with good escutcheon. See Prince of Artis, No. 8.

Dam, Trijntje, (N. H. B. 1,541), has a four-year-old record of 73 1-5 lbs. in one day.

She is large, with fine horns, good hair and hide, good udder and splendid escutcheon.

No. 387.   ARTIS' CONSCIENCE.   No. 849.

(H. H. B. Vol. 8, No. 6,911.) Calved March 18th, 1884. Imported by us in May, 1884. One-half black, large star, snip, large black spot on left side.

Sire, Artis, (N. H. B. 127). See No. 8.

Dam, Geesje, has a five-year-old record of 77 4-5 lbs. in one day.

She is a very fine, large cow, about three-fourths black, with star, extra milk veins and escutcheon, long horns and fine bone.

No. 388.   ARTIS' COMPLIMENT.   No. 850.

(H. H. B. Vol. 8, No. 7,796.) Calved March 2d, 1884. Imported by us in May, 1884. Three-fourths black, star, white spot on hip and shoulders.

Sire, Artis (N. H. B. 127). See No. 8.

Dam, Hendrika (N. H. B. 1,539), has a five-year-old record of 68 2-5 lbs. She is a large, handsome, straight and square cow, with good head and horns, fine bone and splendid milk veins.

Na. 389.   ARTIS' CAMBRASIA.   No. 851.

(H. H. B. Vol. 8, No. 7,797.) Calved March 16th, 1884. Imported by us in May, 1884. Three-fourths black, large star and snip, irregular white over shoulders.

Sire, Artis (N. H. B. 127). See No. 8.

Dam, Edelje (N. H. B. 1,540), has a four-year-old record of 68 2-5 lbs. She is three-fourths black, with star, straight and square, of good size, good milk veins, fine long tail and an extra escutcheon.

No. 390.　　　　ARTIS' CARISA.　　　No. 854.

(H. H. B. Vol. 8, No. 7,798.) Calved March 26th, 1884. Immediately by us in May, 1884. Three-fourths black, star, snip, white from shoulder to belly right side.

Sire, Artis (N. H. B 127). See No. 8.

Dam, Nannie has a record of 73 1-5 lbs. See No. 9.

No. 391.　　　　ARTIS' ADIANTUM.　　　No. 856.

(H. H. B. Vol. 8, No. 6,912.) Calved Feb. 25th, 1884 Imported by us in May, 1884. Four-fifths white, strip in face, black over neck, several black spots on each side.

Sire, Artis (N. H. B. 127)). See No. 8.

Dam, Aafje 2d, has a three-year-old record of 64 lbs. She is a straight and square, fine heifer, of good size and fine milk signs.

Grandam, Neeltje (N. H. B.), has a record of 82⅓ lbs. She is a grand old cow, straight, square and fine, and with a mass of milk veins, and is dam of Statesman No. 20

No. 394.　　　　RIDING HOOD.　　　No. 865.

(H. H. B. Vol. 8, No. 6,915.) Calved March 22d, 1884. Imported by us in May, 1884. Three-fourths black, large star, snip, small white spot over shoulders, broad white over hips to right flank.

Sire, Wonder's bull, one year old. Sold to District of Sutgebroek. His dam is Teuntje, a handsome cow, straight and square, good head and horns, fine bone, very fine hair and hide, and very extra escutcheon.

Dam, Bowman 1st, has a record of 77 4-5 lbs. She is grandam of Wide Awake No. 309.

No. 395.   **LADY PATRIOT.**   No. 866.

(H. H. B. Vol. 8, No. 6,877)   Calved March 18th, 1884. Imported by us in May, 1884. Three-fourths white, large star, irregular white over shoulders and hips.

Sire, Pieter (N. H. B. 209). See No. 20.

Dam, Bowman 2d (N. H. B. 1,077), has a three-year-old record of 57 1-5 lbs. See Wide Awake No. 309.

No. 396.   **JACOB WITS' MIMMA.**   No. 872.

(H. H. B. Vol. 8, No. 6,917.) Calved Feb. 24th, 1884. Imported by us in May, 1884. Two-thirds black, strip in face, white over shoulders and hips to flank and belly on right side.

Sire, Jacob Wit's (2,662), Jacob 4th (N. H. B. 210). See Jacob Wit's Volunteer No 22.

Dam, Aaltje, has a record of 77 4-5 lbs. She by Rooker, the sire of Aaggie (901). See No. 98.

Grandam, Rondril, of a family owned by same breeder for fifteen years.

Aaltje is black and white with long star, very fine horns, elegant escutcheon, good udder and veins, and rich yellow skin. She is dam of Auggie of Chester (4,486).

No. 397.   **JACOB WIT'S BARBARINA.**   No. 873.

(H. H. B. Vol. 8, No. 6,918.) Calved Feb. 21st, 1884. Imported by us in May, 1884. Three-fourths white, black cheeks, numerous black spots on both sides.

Sire, Jacob Wit (2,662), Jacob 4th, (N. H. B. 210). See Jacob Wit's Volunteer, No. 22.

Dam, Pleuster 2d, has a two year old record of 41 1-6 lbs. in one day. She is a very straight and square, handsome heifer, white and black.

G-dam, Lady Griswold, (6,878). See No. 127.

G-g-dam, Pleuster, a splendid milker.

No. 398.   **JACOB WIT'S GODIVA.**   No. 874.

(H. H. B. Vol. 8, No. 6,919.) Calved Feb. 25th, 1884. Imported by us in May, 1884. Three-fourths black, strip in face, large irregular white over hips and shoulders.

Sire, Jacob Wit, (2,662), Jacob 4th, (N. H. B. 210). See Jacob Wit's Volunteer, No. 22.

Dam, Fredrika, has a three-year old record of $59\frac{1}{2}$ lbs. in one day.

No. 399.   **DUESSA.**   No. 891.

(H. H. B. Vol. 8, No. 7,800.) Calved March 20th, 1884. Imported by us in May, 1884. Three-fourths black, star, and snip, white spot on shoulders, white over hips to flanks on right side.

Sire, Willem 3d (N. H. B. 190). See No. 320.

Dam, Antje (N. H. H. B. 107), has a six-year-old record of 77 4-5 lbs. See No. 320.

No. 400.   **DURESSA.**   No. 892.

(H. H. B. Vol. 8, No. 7,801.) Calved March 24th, 1884. Imported by us in May, 1884. Three-fourths black, star and snip, white spot over shoulders and one over hips.

Sire, Willem 3d (N. H. B. 190). See No. 320.

Dam, Aagje (N. H. H. B. 106), has a four-year-old record of 64 lbs. in a day. She is a fine straight and square cow, with large milk veins.

Grandam has a record of 68 2-5 lbs. in a day.

Duressa is sister to La Capetaine (6,934).

No. 400½.   ST. PERPETUA.   No. 897.

(H. H. B. Vol. 8, No. 6,939.) Calved March 15th, 1884. Imported by us in May, 1884. Mostly black, star, long white spot on left shoulder, white spot on hips.

Sire, Willem 3d (N. H. B. 190). See No. 320.

Dam, Schuit (N. H. H. B). See No. 322. She has a record of 68 2-5 lbs. of milk in one day as a four-year-old, and is a large, straight, fine cow.

Grandam, a good milker.

No. 401.   JACOB WIT'S DRUSIE.   No. 903.

(H. H. B. Vol. 8, No. 7,802.) Calved March 1st, 1884. Imported by us in May, 1884. Two-thirds white, broad strip in face, two large irregular spots on left side and one on right side.

Sire, Jacob Wit (2,662), Jacob 4th (N. H. B. 210). See Jacob Wit's Volunteer No. 22.

Dam, Lady de Ruiter. See No. 177.

G-dam has given 64 lbs. of milk in one day.

G-g-dam has given 68 2-5 lbs. of milk in one day.

No. 402.   JACOB WIT'S DELNORA.   No. 1,052.

(H. H. B. Vol. 8, No. 7,803.) Calved March 30th, 1884. Imported by us in May, 1884. Three-fourths white, strip in face, large black spots on each side.

Sire, Jacob Wit (2,662), Jacob 4th (N. H. B. 210). See Jacob Wit's Volunteer No. 22.

Dam, Aaltje, has a four-year-old record of 52 2-5 lbs., and is a superior cow, splendid escutcheon, and very fine bone.

No. 403. **EGYPTA.** No. 1,057.

(H. H. B. Vol. 8, No. 6,999.) Calved March 20th, 1884. Imported by us in May, 1884. Three-fourths black, strip in face, white over hips to flank, left side.

Stre, K. Wit's bull.

Dam, Porcelein, (N. H. B. 1,739), has a two-year-old record of 45 4-5 lbs. in one day, and is a very handsome, straight, square heifer, splendid escutcheon, fine bone, head and neck.

No. 404. **ARTIS' ROLLORA.** No. 1,067.

(H. H. B. Vol. 8, No. 7.000.) Calved March 18th, 1884. Imported by us in May, 1884. Mostly white, black spot around each eye, black spots on neck and shoulders.

Sire, Artis, (N. H. B. 127). See Prince of Artis, No. 8.

Dam, Groote Wit, has a five-year-old record of 73 1-5 lbs. in one day, and is a fine white and black cow, with a fine escutcheon.

Grandam, has a record of 80 1-6 lbs. in one day.

No. 405. **ARTIS' QUEEN.** No. 1,068.

(H. H. B. Vol. 8, No. 7,001.) Calved March 10th, 1884. Imported by us in May, 1884. Three-fourths white, strip in face, spots on sides, black at rump.

Sire, Artis, (N. H. B. 127). See Prince of Artis, No. 8.

Dam, Groote Zwart, has a record of 73 1-5 lbs. in one day, and is a straight, square cow, with a fine escutcheon.

Grandam, Zwart, has a record of 82½ lbs. in one day.

No. 406. **ARTIS' ELFREDA.** No. 1,069.

(H. H. B. Vol. 8, No. 7,002.) Calved Feb. 21st, 1884. Imported by us in May, 1884. Three-fourths white, strip in face, black on neck, black spots on sides and black at rump.

Sire, Artis (N. H. B. 127). See Prince of Artis, No. 8,

Dam, Hanna (N. H. B. 720), has a four-year-old record of 73 1-5 lbs.

Grandam, Hendrika (N. H. H. 1,063), has a record of 75½ lbs. She is dam of Duke of Artis No. 12.

No. 407. **ARTIS' DORLISCA.** No. 1,070.

(H. H. B. Vol. 8, No. 7,804.) Calved Feb. 29th, 1884. Imported by us in May, 1884. Four-fifths black, star, white spot on hips.

Sire, Artis (N. H. B. 127). See Prince of Artis, No. 8.

Dam, Haarlemmermeer (N. H. B 1,020), has a three-year record of 57 1-5 lbs. She is dam of Cora Artis No. 223.

No. 408. **ARTIS' EDMONIA.** No. 1,071.

(H. H. B. Vol. 8, No. 7,805.) Calved March 5th, 1884. Imported by us in May, 1884. Three-fourths black, star, snip white spots on shoulders and hips.

Sire, Artis (N. H. B. 127). Prince of Artis, No. 8.

Dam, Zwaantje 2d, has only three teats but is a choice cow and a good milker.

Grandam, Zwaantje (3,743), (N. H. B. 599), imported, has a record of 77 4-5 lbs. in one day.

Zwaantje 2d's sire, Tromp, won First Prize at Mydrecht, and was sold to go to Africa.

Zwaantje 2d is the dam of Bessie Artis. See No. 224.

Zwaantje (3,743), (N. H. B. 599), is the dam of Elsie Artis. See No. 220.

No. 409.   ARTIS' JACQUETTA.   No. 1,072.

(H. H. B. Vol. 8, No. 7,003.) Calved March 1st, 1884. Imported by us in May, 1884. Three-fourths black, large star, and snip, white spots on shoulders and one over hips.

Sire, Artis, (N. H. B. 127). See Prince of Artis, No. 8.

Dam, Trijnte, has a record of 68 2-5 lbs. She is black and white and has a fine escutcheon.

No. 410.   NETHERLAND COUNTESS 3d.   No. 492.

(H. H. B. Vol. 8, No. 6,068.) Calved Jan. 22d, 1884. Three-fourths black, sides of face black, black on each side of muzzle, white spot on each shoulder, small white over hips.

Sire, Netherland Prince (716). See No. 2.

Dam, Netherland Countess (2,634). See No. 133.

No. 411.   MILLICENT 2d.   No. 496.

(H. H. B. Vol. 8, No. 6,064.) Calved Feb. 11th 1884. Three-fourths black, large star, snip, white over shoulders and over hips.

Sire, Netherland Prince (716). See No. 2.

Dam, Millicent (2,825). See No. 163.

No. 412.   **AAGGIE LEILA** 2d.   No 497.

(H. H. B. Vol. 8, No. 6,067.) Calved Jan. 30th, 1884. Four-fifths white, black cheeks, black spots on neck, body and legs.

Sire, Sir William of Aaggie (1,455), (imported by us), he by de Ruiter (N. H. B. 89). See Sir Henry 2d of Aaggie No. 4, and milk records of the Aaggie family, page 22.

Sir William of Aaggie's dam, Cornelia, gave 77$\frac{3}{4}$ lbs. of milk in one day.

Dam, Aaggie Leila. See No. 164.

No. 413.   **NETHERLAND BARONESS** 2d's   No. 01.
PRINCESS.

(H. H. B. Vol. 8, No. 6,466.) Calved Feb. 24th, 1884. Three-fourths white, ears, spot over neck and large spot on each side black, several other black spots on each side.

Sire, Netherland Prince, (716). See No. 2.

Dam, Netherland Baroness 2d, (2,636). See No. 141.

No. 414.   **NETHERLAND JEWEL** 3d.   No. 02.

(H. H. B. Vol. 8, No. 6,066.) Calved Feb. 7th, 1884. One-half black, black spot around left eye and back of right eye, large irregular black spot over back to belly both sides, other black spots scattered over body.

Sire, Prince Imperial, (1,164). See No. 5.

Dam, Netherland Jewel, (2,642). See No. 160.

No. 414.   **AAGGIE IDALINE** 3d's **RUTH.**   No. 03.

(H. H. B. Vol. 8, No. 6,415.) Imported by us in dam in August, 1883. Calved Feb. 15th, 1884. Mostly white, tips of ears black, numerous small black spots scattered over the body.

Sire, Stippeltje, a large, fine, spotted bull, District bull of Oostwoud in 1883.

Dam, Aaggie Idaline 3d, (4,364). See No. 128.

No. 416. **BEAUTY OF NINON 2d.** No. 08.

(H. H. B. Vol. 8, No. 6,065.) Imported by us in dam in June, 1883. Calved Feb. 11th, 1884. Two-thirds white, black cheeks, long black spot over shoulder, large black spot on each side, black spots near rump.

Sire, Lincoln, (N. H. B. 120). For extension, see Clovis, No. 13.

Dam, Beauty of Ninon, (4,541). See No. 207.

No. 418. **PRINCESS ROSAMOND 3d.** No. 010.

(H. H. B. Vol. 8, No. 6,060.) Calved March 3d, 1884. Three-fourths black, star, narrow strip over shoulders, white over hips and back.

Sire, Neptune, (711). See No. 1.

Dam, Princess Rosamond, (2,868), by Velzeboer's bull.

G-dam, Wittwenter, gave 64 lbs. of milk in one day as a three-year old.

G-g-dam, a great milker.

Princess Rosamond gave as a two-year-old, the first season after importation, 6,501 lbs. of milk in eleven months and nineteen days.

No. 419. **SILENE 2d.** No 028.

(H. H. B. Vol. 8, No. 6,054.) Calved April 5th, 1884. Two-thirds white, strip in face, white over shoulders to belly left side, white over hips and rump to flanks and belly both sides.

Sire, Prince Imperial, (1,164). See No. 5.

Dam, Silene, (2,890). See No. 161.

Grandam, Kossen, winner of First Prize at Schagen for most and best milk. She has a record of 82½ lbs. in one day.

No. 420.   **MOTTLED BEAUTY 3d.**   No. 029.

(H. H. B. Vol. 8, No. 6,055.) Calved April 1st, 1884. One-half black, large star and snip, white over shoulders nearly to belly both sides, white over hips and rump to belly both sides.

Sire, Prince Imperial (1,164). See No. 5.

Dam, Mottled Beauty (2,828). See No. 146.

No. 421.   **NETHERLAND PEERESS 2d.**   No 033.

(H. H. B. Vol. 8, No. 6,059.) Calved March 6th, 1884. Three-fourths black, large star, snip, white spots on neck, white over back and hips extending to root of tail.

Sire, Prince Imperial (1,164). See No. 5

Dam, Netherland Peeress (2,640). See No. 116.

No. 422.   **AAGGIE BONNIE 2d.**   No. 038.

(H. H. B. Vol. 8, No. 6,053.) Calved April 11, 1884. Three-fourths white, black on cheeks and over neck extending to left foreleg, numerous black spots scattered over body.

Sire, Sir Henry 2d of Aaggie (1,451). See No. 4.

Dam, Aaggie Bonnie (2,608). See No. 137.

No. 423.   CROWN JEWEL 2d's PRINCESS.   No. 039.

(H. H. B. Vol. 8, No. 6,402.) Calved April 5th, 1884. Two-thirds black, white in face, white over shoulders nearly connected with large spot over hips and rump.

Sire, Netherland Prince (716).   See No. 2.

Dam, Crown Jewel 2d (2,697).   See No. 206

No. 424.   LIGHTSOME 2d.   No. 040.

(H. H. B. Vol. 8, No. 6,057.) Calved March 27th, 1884. Three-fourths black, star, white strip from left shoulder to belly, and one from right hip over back and down to left flank.

Sire, Prince Imperial (1,164).   See No. 5.

Dam, Lightsome (2,784).   See No. 158.

No. 425.   BETSY TROTWOOD 2d.   No. 041.

(H. H. B. Vol. 8, No. 6,058.) Imported by us in dam in June, 1883. Calved March 16th, 1884. Three-fourths black, star, white spot over shoulders, and large irregular spot over hips and rump.

Sire, Netherland Marquis (2,484.) See Bonanza King No. 60.

Dam, Betsy Trotwood (4,418).   See No. 199.

No. 426.   AAGGIE CORNELIA 6th.   No. 047.

(H. H. B. Vol. 8, No. 6,734.) Imported by us in dam in June, 1883. Calved Feb. 28th, 1884. Three-fourths black, strip in face, narrow white strip over shoulder left side, large white over hips and rump, small white spot on right shoulder.

Sire, Jacob Wit (2,662), Jacob 4th (N. H. B. 210), he by Jacob 2d (N. H. B. 56), (See cut.) See chart, and milk records of the Aaggie family.

Jacob 4th's dam, Heiltje (N. H. B. 1,006.)

Dam, Aaggie Cornelia (4,310). See No. 102.

No. 428. **SUSIE LEE 2d.** No. 053.

(H. H. B Vol. 8, No. 6,468.) Calved May 15th, 1884. Three-fourths white, strip in face, large black spot on each side containing small white spots, numerous small black spots on each side.

Sire, Neptune (711). See No. 1.

Dam, Susie Lee (2,900). See No. 155.

No. 429. **CAMEO 3d.** No. 054.

(H. H. B. Vol. 8, No. 6,469.) Calved May 16th, 1884. Mostly white, ears and spots under eyes black, small black spots scattered over body.

Sire, Netherland Prince (716). See No. 2.

Dam, Cameo (1,267). See No. 120.

No. 430. **NETHERLAND DOWAGER 2d's** No. 055.
PRINCESS.

(H. H. B. Vol. 8, No. 6,404.) Calved April 18th, 1884. Three-fourths black, muzzle and lower jaws white, small white spot on left shoulder, large white over hips and rump.

Sire, Netherland Prince (716). See No. 2.

Dam, Netherland Dowager 2d (2,633). See No. 153.

No. 431. **MEADOW LILY 4th.** No. 057.

(H. H. B. Vol. 8, No. 6,472.) Calved June 10th, 1884. Three-fourths white, small black spot on forehead, ears and spot around each eye black, black over neck to left fore leg, large black spot on right side, containing three small white spots, small black spot on right fore leg and one forward of left fore leg.

Sire, Netherland Prince (716).   See No. 2.

Dam, Meadow Lily (863).   See dam of No. 69.

Grandam, Dirk Jonges.

Meadow Lily 4th, is twin sister to Meadow Lily's Prince No. 69.

No. 432. **AAGGIE CORNELIA 3d's NEPTUNIA.** No. 058.

(H. H. B. Vol. 8, No. 6,473). Calved June 21st, 1884. Two-thirds black, star, white over shoulders to belly right side, broad white over hips to flank and belly left side, small white spot on right shoulder, black to left gambrel, black on right fore leg to knee back side.

Sire, Neptune (711). See No. 1.

Dam, Aaggie Cornelia 3d (4,342). See No. 132.

No. 433.   **BELLE ALEXANDER 2d.**   No. 059.

(H. H. B. Vol. 8, No. 6,470.) Calved May 18, 1884. Five-sixths black, star, white spot over hips, fore legs black to ankles, hind legs black to below gambrels, small black spot on each hind leg front side, switch white.

Sire, Netherland Marquis, (2 484). See No. 70.

Dam, Belle Alexander, (4,408). See No. 179.

No. 434.   **NETHERLAND QUEEN 4th's**   No. 062.
                        PRINCESS.

(H. H. B. Vol. 8, No. 6,403.) Calved April 10, 1884. Three-fourths white, ears black, black spot under left eye, around right eye extending to lower jaw, large black spot over neck, spot at right shoulder, large black spot on left side.

Sire, Netherland Prince, (716). See No. 2.

Dam, Netherland Queen 4th, (2,105). See No. 211.

No. 435.   **VALLEY BEAUTY 2d's**   No. 063.
MARCHIONESS.

(H. H. B. Vol. 8, No. 6,474.) Calved June 21st, 1884. Two-thirds black, strip in face, wide strip of white over shoulders to belly left side, white over hips and rump to flank and belly right side, two small white spots on left side.

Sire, Netherland Marquis (2,484). See No. 70.

Dam, Valley Beauty 2d (4,532). See No. 203.

No. 436.   **MOTTLED BEAUTY 2d's PRIDE.**   No. 064.

(H. H. B. Vol. 8, No. 6,467.) Calved May 4th, 1884. Three-fourths white, strip in face, large black spot on each side, and other small black spots on both sides.

Sire, Prince Imperial (1,164). See No. 5.

Dam, Mottled Beauty 2d (2,829). See No. 205.

No. 437.   **AAGGIE AURELIA 2d.**   No. 065.

(H. H. B. Vol 8, No. 6,471.) Calved May 29th, 1884. Black predominating, very small star, spot on shoulders and one on hips, narrow strip on belly and spots on hind legs below gambrels white, part of switch white.

Sire, Prince Imperial (1,164). See No. 5.

Dam, Aaggie Aurelia (2,630). See No. 208.

No. 438.   AAGGIE ROSA 3d's DIORA.   No. 076.

(H. H. B. Vol. 8, No. ——.) Calved August 23d, 1884.

Sire, Netherland Prince (716). See No. 2.

Dam, Aaggie Rosa 3d (2,611) See No. 197.

No. 439.   NETHERLAND PRINCESS 4th.   No. 080

(H. H. B. Vol. 8, No. 6,475). Calved June 28th, 1884. Three-quarters black, star, irregular white spot on right shoulder, white over hips to flanks both sides, large black spot on right flank, right fore leg black to ankle.

Sire, Netherland Prince (716). See No. 2.

Dam, Netherland Princess (862). See No. 123.

No. 441.   DAME TROT 3d.   No. 090.

(H. H. B. Vol. 8, No. 7,271.) Calved June 2d, 1884. Three-fourths black, star, small snip. large white spot over shoulders and one over hips, small white spot below right shoulder, two on left hind leg, black on outside right fore leg to below knee.

Sire, Kenmore (1,174). See No. 57.

Dam, Dame Trot (2,698), imported by us. She by Van Kampen's bull. She was sold before she calved and her present owner has kept no record of her milk.

Grandam, Kaatje gave as a four-year-old 59¼ lbs. in one day.

No. 442.   MISS FRISBIE 2d.   No. 091.

(H. H. B. Vol. 8, No. 7,272.) Calved June 22, 1884. Four-fifths black, star, narrow white spot on right shoulder and one over back at roots of tail, small white spot on left fore leg, fore legs black to knees, two-thirds tail white.

Sire, Kenmore (1,174). See No. 57.

Dam, Miss Frisbie (2,734), imported by us. She by the District bull of Hauwert.

She was sold before she calved and was a fine promising heifer, but her present owner keeps no record of her milk.

Grandam, Jaantje, gave as a three-year-old 59½ lbs. in one day.

No. 443 **VALLEY BEAUTY 4th.**

(H. H. B. Vol. 8, No. 6,477.) Calved July 15th, 1884. Three-fourths white, small black spot between horns, ears and small spot back of each eye black, large black spot over back containing small white spot on left side, large black spot near left hip.

Sire, Netherland Prince (716). See No. 2.

Dam, Valley Beauty (4,562). See No. 106.

No. 444. **NETHERLAND QUEEN 2d's HEIRESS.**

(H. H. B. Vol. 8, No. 6,478.) Calved July 21st, 1884. Three-fourths black, large star, snip, white on throat and under side of neck, white over shoulders and from hips to right flank, black spot on right flank, one on left fore leg and two just forward of left fore leg.

Sire, Netherland Prince (716). See No. 2.

Dam, Netherland Queen 2d (560). See No. 126.

No. 445. **CLOTHILDE 5th.**

(H. H. B. Vol. 8, No. ——.) Calved Aug. 31st, 1884.

Sire, Netherland Prince (716). See No. 2.

Dam, Clothilde (1,308). See No. 118.

No. 446.   **FANNY FERN 4th.**

(H. H. B. Vol. 8, No. ——.) Calved June 22d, 1884. Three-fourths black, star, snip.

Sire, Prince Bismark (780), he by Corujum (424), imported.

Prince Bismarck's dam Vlaaske (655), imported.

Prince Bismark won Second Prize three years in succession at the New York State Fair.

Vlaaske has no record, but her daughter, Dagmar (659), half sister to Prince Bismark, gave 61 lbs. 2 oz. in one day as a four-year-old. She won Second Prize as a two-year-old; First as a three-year-old, and Second as a four-year-old at the New York State Fair.

Dam, Fanny Fern (1,289), imported by us; she by the District bull of Opmeer.

Fanny Fern has a record of 65 lbs. in one day.

Grandam, Van, gave 68 2-5 lbs. in one day.

No. 447.   **ELLIE LEE 2d.**

(H. H. B. Vol. 8, No. ——.) Calved July 20th, 1884.
Sire, Netherland Marquis (2,484). See No. 70.

Dam, Ellie Lee (4,414), imported by us, she by the District bull of Beemster (Lof's).

Grandam, Immetje, gave as a four-year-old 73 1-5 lbs. in one day.

Ellie Lee was sold before she calved, and we cannot give her record.

No. 448.   **ADDIE 2d.**   No. 070.

(H. H. B. Vol. 8, No. ——.)   Calved Oct. 10th, 1884.
Sire, Netherland Princess (716).   See No. 2.
Dam, Addie (873).   See No. 122.

No. 449.   **MIGNONETTE 4th.**

(H. H. B. Vol. 8, No. ——.)   Calved Oct. 16th, 1884.
Sire, Netherland Prince (716).   See No. 2.
Dam, Mignonette (2,826).   See No. 165.

ERRATA.

Sir Henry 2d of Aaggie (1,451), page 35, is not Ruiter N. H. B. 89.

Robertus (3,306), page 47, was calved June 17th, 1883, and not January 17th.

Verona, page 91, was calved July 5th, 1884, and is not recorded in Vol. 5, 1884.

Aaggie Idaline 4th's Rowland (3,122), page 53, should be Aaggie Idaline 4th's Roland.

The names of the following animals have been changed since the catalogue was printed, the former names having already been used in the Herd Book:

Jacob Wit's Dexter, page 52, to Jacob Wit's Dittmar (3,455).

Jacob Wit's Judson, page 53, to Jacob Wit's Bardolph (3,454).

Jacob Wit's Frank, page 57, to Jacob Wit's Mercutio (3,459).

Jacob Wit's Michael, page 59, to Jacob Wit's Plumed Knight (3,458).

Jacob Wit's Philip, page 59, to Jacob Wit's Conesus (3,457).

The following named animals have been recorded since catalogue was printed, and assigned the numbers set opposite their names:

Jacob Wit's Mirick, page 54, Vol. 8, No. 3,456.

Jacob Wit's Anthony, page 55, Vol. 8, No. 3,460.

ERRATA.

Jacob Wit's Cornelius, page 58, Vol. 8, No. 3, 462.
Jacob Wit's Samuel, page 58, Vol. 8, No. 3, 461.
Edwin S., page 88, Vol. 8, No. 3, 422.
Eldred S., page 89, Vol. 8, No. 3, 421.
Nourmahal, page 171, Vol. 8, No. 7, 784.
Jacob Wit's Minella, page 173, Vol. 8, No. 7, 785.
Appoline, page 188, Vol. 8, No. 7, 786.

INDEX.

BULLS.

A
	Page.
Aaggie Cora's Wilfred	68
Aaggie Constance's Sir Henry	74
Aaggie Cornelia 4th's Clinton	51
Aaggie Hannah's Prince	83
Aaggie Eva's Rufus	51
Aaggie Idaline 2d's Albert	50
Aaggie Idaline 4th's Rowland	53
Aaggie Josie's Marquis	79
Aaggie Kathleen's Marquis	62
Aaggie May's Horace	67
Aaggie Pauline's Prince	72
Aaggie Rosa's Prince	81
Aaggie Rosa 2d's Emperor	78
Alfric	63
Ambassador	52
Artis' Tomah	42

B
Basil	73
Bonanza King	71
Bruyn	91

C
Captain Artis	64
Captola	80
Czarowitz	71
Chesterfield	38
Chilperic	49
Clovis	42
Concord	64

D
	Page.
Demetrius S	85
Dermot S	84
De Ruiter's Lad	56
Donatus S	85
Domingo S	87
Dugald S	86
Dunstan S	87
Duke of Artis	42
Duke of Medina	59

E
Edgar S	87
Edward S	88
Eldred S	89
Ensign	72
Edwin S	88
Edmund S	88

I
Ira	92
Ibis	70

J
Jacob Wit's Anthony	55
" Cornelius	58
" Dexter	52
" Frank	57
" Judson	55
" Michael	59
" Mirick	54
" Philip	59
" Samuel	58
" Volunteer	50

L

	PAGE.
Lad of Palmyra	43
Lee Morgan	46
Lola's Gift	92
Lyra's Prince	68

M

Mackenzie	40
Meadow Lily's Prince	79

N

Nantasket	75
Naomi	91
Naugatuck	82
Neptune	31
Netty's Armand	90
Netherland Carl	83
" Chancellor	73
" Conqueror	48
" Deputy	81
" King	44
" Leo	66
" Prince	32
" Statesman	84

O

Otselic	62
Ogontz	54

P

	PAGE.
Prince of Artis	39
Prince Imperial	37
Pionis	40
Philosopher	69
Pompino	64

R

Randall	56
Robertus	47
Rossmore	57
Rothesay	66
Rugby Prince	65

S

Saratoga	61
Statesman	49
Strathmore	34
Seymour	77
Sir Donald of Aaggie	38
Sir Henry 2d of Aaggie	35
Sir William of Aaggie's Warren	90

T

Tioga	65
Tom Artis	58

V

Verona	91

Y

Young Apollo	48

COWS.

A

AAGGIE	95
" Anna	124
" Anna 2d	179
" Aurelia	153
" Aurelia 2d	242
" Alice	168
" Beauty	106
" Beauty 2d	127
" " 3d	178
" " 4th	179
AAGGIE,—Beatrice	142
" " 2d	163
" Belle	109
" Bonnie	118
" " 2d	238
" Camille	173
" Careno	173
" Cleora	147
" Cornelia	97
" " 2d	105
" " 3d	115

INDEX.

	PAGE.
AAGGIE,—Cornelia 3d's Lass	175
"Cornelia 3d's Neptunia	241
" " 4th	137
" " 5th	175
" " 6th	239
" Cora	118
" Constance	141
" Eva	145
" Ethel	157
" Fidelia	169
" Hannah	114
" Idaline	100
" " 2d	105
" " 3d	113
" " 3d's Ruth	236
" " 4th	145
" " 6th	164
" Isadora	115
" Isadora 3d	174
" Juliet	172
" Kathleen	103
" Kate	140
" Lee	136
" " 2d	166
" Leila	132
" " 2d	236
" Lotta	164
" Lucille	166
" May	125
" " 2d	177
" Merrel	139
" Pauline	142
" Peeress	167
" Rachel	171
" Rosa	101
" " 2d	120
" " 3d	148
" " 3d's Diora	243
" " 4th	181
" Roxana	168
" Sarah	116
" " 2d	176
" Sadie	138

	PAGE.
AAGGIE,—Sophie	159
Abdaletta	188
Almartha	189
Agnace	190
Aspasia	191
Alhambra	198
Ægis	93
" 2d	104
" 4th	121
" 6th	134
" 9th	156
Alexander's Queen	137
Alexia of Lakeside	189
Addie	109
Addie 2d	246
Albino	131
Albino 2d	178
Aldine	135
African Maid	199
Artis' Adiantum	229
" Cambrasia	228
" Carisa	229
" Compliment	228
" Conscience	228
" Dorlisca	234
" Elfreda	234
" Edmonia	234
" Jacquetta	235
" Pride	227
" Queen	233
" Rollora	233
Ambronetta	190
Appoline	188
Antique	155
Aquila	205
Azuleah	190

B

Black Queen	192
Beatrix	195
Beauty of Ninon	153
Beauty of Ninon 2d	237
Beauty of Waltham	141
Bella Artis	161

	PAGE.		PAGE.
Berthalda	195	Duessa	231
Belle Alexander	140	Duressa	231
Belle Alexander 2d	241		
Bessie Artis	162	**E**	
Betsy Trotwood	149	Easter Maid	144
Betsy Trotwood 2d	239	Embassadress	197
Benola Fletcher	194	Executrix	148
Bonanza Maid	144	Esther Alexander	142
Bomba	165	Egberta	196
Boston Queen	207	Edwina	217
		Ellie Lee 2d	245
C		Elsie Artis	160
Cameo	108	Eula Lee	120
Cameo 3d	240	Eula Lee 2d	186
Careno	123	Egypta	233
Carrie Fair	147		
Carlotta	108	**F**	
Calistra	200	Fanny Fern 4th	245
Charlene	187	Fatinitza 2d	150
Clara Hamilton	163	Fleecy Cloud	198
Cely	193	Fontana	192
Chelsea Maid	197	Foochow	220
Colianthus	207		
Comedia	137	**G**	
Clothilde	107	Gabuna	194
Clothilde 2d	123	Glad Tidings	200
Clothilde 2d's Duchess	187	Golden Era	157
Clothilde 3d	149	Guerndale	212
Clothilde 4th	184		
Clothilde 5th	244	**H**	
Clovette	209	Happy Thought	169
Cora Artis	162	Harvesta	218
Crown Jewel 2d	152	Highland Ida	165
Crown Jewel 2d's Princess	239		
		I	
D		Idol 2d	185
Dame Durden	199	Imogenia 2d	182
Dame Trot 3d	243		
Daziel	201	**J**	
Dream of Holland	96	Jacob Wit's Adnah	221
De Ruiter's Beatus	150	" Barbarina	230
De Ruiter's Bona	150	" Blanquette	213
Divinia	138	" Belva	225
Dorrice	197	" Bernie	224

	PAGE.
Jacob Wit's Berylla	225
" Cranelli	226
" Cleorine	226
" Cyrilla	226
" Delnora	232
" Drusie	232
" Emily	223
" Frelia	222
" Godiva	231
" Hella	223
" Leola	213
" Maylie	223
" Mimma	230
" Minella	173
" Myth	225
" Phene	222
" Solace	201
" Watteau	224
Josie Lyle	170

K.

Kappijne	114
Katie Lander	170

L

Lady Anstys	214
" Artis	146
" of Castlewood	196
" De Ruiter	139
" Emma	158
" Elmwood	158
" Fay	111
" Gladstone	159
" Griswold	113
" Netherland	96
" Patriot	230
La Capetaine	205
Lambertina	97
Lass of Winsum	210
Laurentine	216
Lemabel	218
Lenella	219
Leonne	204
Lilla	126

	PAGE.
Lightsome	129
Lightsome 2d	239
Little Wonder	122
Lybia	217
Lyra	129

M

Madame Stapel	204
Mala	193
Mantissa	204
Maraposa	221
Maxima	202
Meadow Lily	111
Meadow Lily 4th	240
Meadow Maid 2d	184
Mercedes 3d	180
Mignonette	133
Mignonette 3d	
Millicent	132
Millicent 2d	235
Miracle	217
Mirandola	220
Mirth	219
Mrs. Pinkham	218
Miss Frisbie 2d	243
" Lincoln	191
" Nanna	130
" Smylie	214
Mottled Beauty	123
" 2d	152
" 2d's Pride	
" 3d	238
Mousie	215
Musique	220
Mycale	198
Myla	221

N

Netherland Aaggie	185
" Baroness	98
" Baroness 2d	121
" Baroness 2d's Princess	236
" Baroness 4th	143
" Baroness 5th	182

INDEX.

	PAGE.
Netherland Belle	119
" Chaperone	102
" Consort	117
" Countess	116
" Countess 3d	235
" Dorinda	102
" Dowager	94
" Dowager 2d	126
" Dowager 3d's Princess	240
" Duchess	103
" Gem 2d	124
" Jewel	130
" Jewel 2d	181
" Jewel 3d	236
" Lass	175
" Maid	177
" Oconto	176
" Pamela	102
" Peeress	106
" Peeress 2d	238
" Pride	143
" Princess	110
" Princess 3d	182
" Princss 4th	243
" Queen	99
" Queen 2d	112
" Queen 2d's Heiress	244
" Queen 3d	134
" Queen 4th	156
" Queen 4th's Princess	241
" Waupaca	177
" Waukesha	119
Noontide	125
Nourmahal	171

O

Orange Bud	203
Orphan Queen	192

P

Partella	216
Pansyne	202

	PAGE.
Princess Rosamond 3d	237
Polianthus	202
Postmistress	208
Prunella	128
Puritania	213

Q

Quenith	203
Queen of Kennet	203

R

Riding Hood	229
Ruth Artis	159
Rosalpha	212
Rozalia Somers	206

S

Saxafragia	214
St. Catharine	138
St. Perpetua	232
Stelleta	205
Stella Artis	161
Signet	122
Silene	131
Silene 2d	237
Simplicity	147
Sincerity	151
Spinaway	208
Sir Henry of Aaggie's Cressa	206
Sir Henry of Aaggie's Elland	196
Sir Henry of Aaggie's Luzelle	193
Sir Henry of Aaggie's Phlox	206
Sir Henry of Aaggie's Uintah	172
Soldene	135
Somnambula	219
Susie Lee	128
Susie Lee 2d	240
Sunny Side	215
Sylpha	212

T

Tweedledum	208
Theodate	211

	PAGE.
Testimony	217
Trintasia	211
Topaz 2d	154
Topaz 4th	184
True Favor	216
Tryphene	211

V

Valley Beauty	100
Valley Beauty 2d	151
Valley Beauty 2d's Marchioness	242
Valley Beauty 3d	163
Valley Beauty 4th	244
Vassar	210
Village Lass	207
Viroqua	170

W

Warwick Maid	209
Wide awake	200
Wikolis	210
Wingonia	224

www.ingramcontent.com/pod-product-compliance
Lightning Source LLC
Chambersburg PA
CBHW032103230426
43672CB00009B/1624